CLINICAL
SUPERVISION

To Bruce
With whom
I work and play

CLINICAL
SUPERVISION
A SYSTEMS APPROACH

Elizabeth L. Holloway

SAGE Publications
International Educational and Professional Publisher
Thousand Oaks   London   New Delhi

For information address:

SAGE Publications, Inc.
2455 Teller Road
Thousand Oaks, California 91320
E-mail: order@sagepub.com

SAGE Publications Ltd.
6 Bonhill Street
London EC2A 4PU
United Kingdom

SAGE Publications India Pvt. Ltd.
M-32 Market
Greater Kailash I
New Delhi 110 048 India

Printed in the United States of America

Library of Congress Cataloging-in-Publication Data

Holloway, Elizabeth L.
    Clinical supervision: a systems approach / Elizabeth L. Holloway.
      p.   cm.
    Includes bibliographical references and indexes.
    ISBN 0-8039-4223-0.—ISBN 0-8039-4224-9 (pbk.)
    1. Psychotherapists—Supervision of. 2. Counselors—Supervision
of. I. Title.
RC459.H65 1995
616.89'14'0711—dc20   95-7711

This book is printed on acid-free paper.

98 99 00 01 02 10 9 8 7 6 5 4 3

Sage Production Editor: Diana E. Axelsen
Sage Typesetter: Andrea D. Swanson

Contents

List of Tables

List of Figures

List of Research Boxes

List of Transcripts

Preface:
A Scientist-Practitioner's Journey

 Recently, my colleague, who has long taught and practiced supervision and is a well-respected process researcher, reflected on an esteemed counseling psychologist's comment to her: "Research in supervision is the biggest joke in our profession. There is no distinct body of knowledge to uncover."

It must be admitted that supervision, in the broader domain of professional psychology, has largely been devalued or unnoticed. The supervisory enterprise has not been much more than a footnote of professional psychology, undoubtedly because of its connection to practice (Holloway & Wolleat, 1994).

In fact, supervision was not recognized as a unique practice until the 1980s. Educators have often assumed that the act of teaching counseling is not much different from the act of doing counseling—that counselors become supervisors because they are counselors.

That supervision has a distinct knowledge base was established at last by using empirical research to develop models of practice. This is true even though supervision is ironically based on "practice" and "the teaching of practice." Furthermore, the knowledge generated by practitioners has not been integrated with empirical knowledge or recognized in the professional research literature. Yet the learning of practice, the application of principles of practice in a systematic and deliberate way, is critical to the teaching of supervision. Students of professions want to know "what and how to do." They also need to discover what is "effective doing." Unfortunately, the work of research to date is not often relevant to the scientist-practitioner of supervision.

My struggle to uncover the tacit knowledge of practitioners of supervision has been shaped by the people with whom I have worked over the last 19 years in research, practice, and teaching. The weaving together of the insights gained from my experiences is the mission of this book. I have tried to bring forth the relevant and critical questions that go beyond the scattered musings of my own reflections. I must admit that I have never written this way about supervision before—I have only talked this way. Although I have studied supervision empirically for many years and led workshops on the practice of supervision, I myself began to bridge the knowledge of the working supervisor and the knowledge of science only with my goal clearly in mind.

My process of asking different questions is intrinsically woven into the substance of this book. I have not written a typical training manual, listing techniques in one, two, three fashion. Instead, the chapters challenge practitioners and educators to reflect on *what they* do in supervision, examine the *meaning* of their work, uncover their own *intuition*, and *articulate* to others what they know.

In attempting to synthesize the research and practice knowledge of supervision, I have looked for examples and models that are immediately practical and relevant to the reflective questioner. These examples offer but a glimpse of all that can happen in the multilayered relationships we create in supervision. By working through the examples, one can reveal a way to apply a framework, the Systems Approach to Supervision (SAS) to the real work of supervision. The framework both comes from the work and simultaneously gives back to the work a specific way to talk about it. It is a model that leads to a critical analysis of what we do and, in turn, how supervisees and clients are affected. From the mindful regard of the relational contexts comes the possibility of the articulation of our efforts. In the end, I have discovered, we collectively benefit by a more grounded and considered approach to supervision.

I remember the story a colleague told me about her teaching. She asked graduate students to join her on a guided fantasy in which they were to imagine themselves as researchers. The pictures they drew were of people alone, alienated from friends, white-coated, hair-bunned, and in a sterile environment. As she told this story, I was struck with what the students were conveying. To be a researcher was to be involved in a solitary, individual process in a pictureless world. To them, the research world was totally separate from where most of these students imagined themselves—the practice world filled with colorful stories and felt experiences.

The picture of researchers the students made is remarkably different from my own experience and has far-reaching adverse consequences for the development of a practitioner-relevant body of conceptual and empirical knowledge in supervision. For this reason, I include here two stories in which I articulate my process of bridging my practice and science selves. Besides describing and acknowledging events and people along the way, stories are intrinsically a part of the process as well. The following story (see Holloway, 1992a) provides an example of how each intentional expression of the learner's experience can lead to the next building block of understanding.

The Grievance

I returned recently to the University of Wisconsin, the bed of my beginning. I've had many flashbacks. The same halls that I walk now I walked 15 years ago to prepare for a future life. I've looked from a distance at my old office, the one that used its window to look inward. There, I began my work in supervision, for one of my jobs was to supervise master's students' work in counseling. One experience supersedes the view of all others.

I became his supervisor in his last term of practice. It never felt to me that he was present. His clients begged for his attention even though he often spoke to them. Watching his work, his separateness from self struck me full force. I consulted. I documented. I worked to help him learn. With my adviser's support, I told him that I could not pass him on.

He asked to record our sessions so he could expand his skills, to keep working at it. I said of course. Later, I received notice. I was to meet with the collegewide grievance board.

I walked into the room, and facing me were five very full professors. On the expansive wood table in front of them stood a small, black tape recorder. I knew it held my conversations in supervision. I sat down, looked across at them, and began responding to their queries regarding work with my student. I was clear and articulate, calmly referring to my notes of dates and clients and evaluative criteria . . .

I was screaming on the inside—"They've heard my words. Do I know anything about supervision? About him? Will my words betray me?"

It was time. They pushed it on. I heard my voice. I heard his voice. I heard our conversation, disjointed and forced. They looked at me disapprovingly. Could I make sense of this jumbled talk? Didn't they see that was just it? I struggled to explain the meaning of the interactional process. What they heard would be just what they would hear with his clients, too. Is this someone they would go to for help? He dropped out. He's not to be a counselor. I made a dissertation of supervision.

I learned in the moment of defending my act of supervision that it is not sufficient to just "do." I must also reflect on my own process of doing in a manner that makes it accessible to others. As a teacher, my goal became to connect science and practice, the true nature of supervision.

Discover With Science

I came to Santa Barbara to work at the university. I bought a wardrobe and unpacked my data. I stayed fascinated with the talk of supervision. In a year's time I had collected more boxes of audiotapes. I did supervision, I taught it, and I did research on it. These acts were never consciously hooked. I remember the moments with my collaborator in the computer room on campus. He, copying the last of the printouts. I, nattering on about statistical methods of interrater reliability and sequential analysis with the master. "But, instead, why couldn't we do it this way? Why won't it work? Why isn't there another way? There is a question."

Looking up from his swirling numbers, his face very still, his eyes with an edge of amusement, he said, "I think that you are onto something." I thrilled. I laughed. I danced across the room. I gloated.

We wrote a paper together. We began a life together. We collaborated. We populated.

To me, the great potential before us as supervisors is to explicitly live out the connections between science knowledge and practice knowledge. The result will be a scientific practice that encompasses not just knowledge gained from traditional research but also knowledge transferred from critical inquiry methods into our practice. Most of all, it is the articulation of our findings—what knowledge we use, how we are uncovering that knowledge, and how it is relevant to the immediacy of the client or supervisee dilemma—that is the heart of a systematic and deliberate supervisory process.

We each find our own way of discovering, organizing, and understanding the supervisory process. For many of us, there is a history of being supervised, supervising, and being trained to supervise. Through thinking, through talking, through writing, we can share with excitement and humility our discoveries, learn each other's languages of knowing, and open ourselves to all aspects of our work. My hope is that this book will contribute to a language of supervision, a way to ask questions, and a way to express knowledge that will result in a more meaningful empiricism.

Acknowledgments

☙ This book had its origins in my work with Martin Acker at the University of Oregon. The many hours that we spent talking about supervision practice and teaching led to our first joint workshop at the Oregon Association for Counselor Education and Supervision in 1988. A matrix for analyzing task and function in supervision was the focus of our approach—Engagement and Power in Clinical Supervision (EP-ICS). Chapter 2 was developed from this initial conceptualization. From this approach, we developed a series of vignettes depicting supervisory dilemmas. The transcripts of some of these vignettes appear in this book. Later, we developed the reflected interview that makes up Chapter 5 of this book. Marty's contribution to supervision is apparent in his reflections as the supervisor in this interview. Our collaboration during my years at Oregon encouraged and taught me how to integrate the science and practice knowledge of work in supervision. Marty's complexity of thinking and grace of being have greatly enriched my work and my life.

1

The Essence of Supervision

Describing Supervision

-℧ To supervise is to "oversee," to view another's work with the eyes of the experienced clinician, the sensitive teacher, the discriminating professional. Supervision provides an opportunity for a student to capture the essence of the psychotherapeutic process as articulated and modeled by the supervisor and, subsequently, to recreate this process in an actual counseling relationship.

Ideally, the supervisee does not indiscriminately adopt the supervisor's methods and views. What takes place, rather, is at best a unique improvisation of the principles and means inherent in the professional knowledge provided by the supervisor. A supervisee is called on to reconstruct each session in a way that is appropriate for a particular client at a specific point in the counseling process.

By exploring the supervisory relationship, this book emphasizes the supervisor's challenge to create a learning context that will enhance the supervisee's skill in constructing relevant frames of reference from which to devise effective strategies in working with clients. Although the supervisee will operate primarily from research-based techniques and principles, there remains the untold area of "artistry" in practice. By encouraging this latter kind of knowledge, "artistry as an exercise of intelligence" (Schon, 1983, p. 12), supervisors play a most critical role.

1

> Learning all forms of professional artistry depends, at least in part, on . . . freedom to learn by doing in a setting relatively low in risk, with access to coaches who initiate students into the "traditions of the calling" and help them, by "the right kind of telling" to see on their own behalf and in their own way what they need most to see. (Schon, 1983, p. 17)

The highest calling for teachers of supervision is to articulate the components of instruction. In the helping professions, a number of approaches have been used to unravel the complexity of supervisory instructional methodology. Psychology, psychiatry, social work, and education have all made substantial contributions to this task.

Furthermore, Schon's (1983) concepts of the "reflective practitioner" describe supervisory or apprenticeship processes in several fields of professional education, including architecture, music, and business. The analogy to the master craftsperson-apprenticeship model common to education, however, does not capture the elements of the supervisory process in fields of applied science where the delivery of effective service is the goal. When there is a service demand, human interaction consequently becomes the dominant construct of educating.

The act of applying knowledge requires certain elements that are unknown until a service need is apparent. During supervision, the professional must be taught to treat each case uniquely, to understand and conceptualize the situation, and then selectively adapt known methods. The professional must be capable of strategically adapting to the unfolding needs of the client, delivering interventions through discourse on a moment-to-moment basis. Most important, as the supervisor identifies and describes the covert processes of this dynamic context, the learner is also assisted in the articulation of his or her own process.

Articulating the layers of thinking, understanding, conceptualizing, and applying is the task of the supervisor; the supervisor is the translator of theory and research to practice. Holloway and Wolleat (1994) maintain that

> because the goal of clinical supervision is to connect science and practice, supervision is among the most complex of all activities associated with the practice of psychology. The competent clinical supervisor must embrace not only the domain of psychological science, but also the domains of client service and trainee development. The competent supervisor must not only comprehend how these various knowledge bases are connected, but also apply them to the individual case." (p. 30)

In understanding the purpose and structure of supervision, it must first be asked whether the primary context of a supervisory situation is administrative or clinical. Administrative or managerial supervisors have the task of overseeing, directing, and evaluating the work of clinicians, students, and staff members in a bureaucratic organization. Their objective is to assist the organization in running smoothly and effectively. Clearly defined responsibilities of administrative supervisors might include recruiting, delegating, and monitoring work; being a managerial buffer; and acting as a change agent within the organization (Kadushin, 1985).

In contrast, clinical supervisors focus on the professional development of the supervisee's skills within the organization. Clinical supervision emphasizes the educational and supportive functions of the supervisory role.

It is the primary purpose of the supervising role that differentiates these two approaches. Is it the organization that must first be served or the professional development of the supervisee? The supervisor who understands his or her priorities can then devise a suitable structure in which supervision is to take place.

Administrative supervision often takes place on an as-needed basis or as a result of a pressing need, change in policy, or scheduled evaluation period (Kadushin, 1985). In both social work and education, the administrative supervisor is not expected to form ongoing, collaborative relationships. The hierarchical structure of the organization and the organizational role of the supervisor dictate the transitory nature of the supervisory relationship.

Professional psychology has focused almost entirely on clinical supervision. Because of the emphasis on supervision as an instructional method in the early training of psychologists (for example, interviewing, practica, and internship), the educative and supportive functions of supervision have been researched extensively (Holloway, 1992b; Holloway & Poulin, in press; Russell, Crimmings, & Lent, 1984). The role of evaluation is closely tied to this study. Although early on it was felt that the function of evaluation and education should be separated, contemporary theorists have been clear that evaluation is an important component of the educational function (Bernard & Goodyear, 1992). Clinical supervisors are in the best position to evaluate the performance of the supervisee because they have direct knowledge of work performance and professional competence. In fact, the supervisor is continually evaluating the supervisee as a function of the instructional role (Mueller & Kell, 1972); thus, evaluation is one of the most critical issues in establishing the supervisory relationship.

In this book, the term *supervision* refers to clinical supervision. Clinical supervision takes place between two individuals, one of them designated as the supervisor and the other as the supervisee or trainee. During supervision, the two individuals meet on a regular basis and discuss clinical and professional issues as they relate to the professional growth of the supervisee. Although the organizational context and administrative policies of every work site will affect the supervisory relationship, it is not the utmost purpose of clinical supervision to carry out managerial or administrative functions.

Models in Supervision

Supervision has been the focus of considerable speculation in the helping professions since the 1950s. Ekstein and Wallerstein (1958) distinguished between the *practice* of psychotherapy and the problem of *teaching* and *learning* psychotherapy. In their seminal text, they focused on "how to transmit these skills (of psychotherapy) to another, how to supervise rather than how to do psychotherapy" (p. xii). At first, supervision models mirrored theories of counseling. Not surprisingly, the names of these models imitate counseling theories, for example, client-centered supervision (Patterson, 1983), social learning approach to supervision (Hosford & Barmann, 1983), and supervision in rational-emotive therapy (Wessler & Ellis, 1983). Although models are intended to aid in interpreting complex phenomena and help in learning complex skills, the "counseling-bound" models of supervision provided few directions for either research or practice (Russell et al., 1984). Because of this parochialism, important knowledge from relevant disciplines, such as developmental, educational, and social psychology, has been precluded. Research on the process of supervision has revealed that supervisors do not practice supervision and counseling alike; a supervision interview has features different from the counseling interview (Russell et al., 1984). Thus challenged, the counseling-bound models are being replaced by others that incorporate knowledge from related psychological subdisciplines and that provide frameworks for empirical inquiry. Recognition that the teaching of psychotherapy is different from doing supervision is reflected in cross-theoretical models of supervision that incorporate aspects of individual difference, social role theory, and instructional psychology. Two major cross-theoretical approaches have appeared since 1979—developmental models and social role models.

Developmental models draw from developmental psychology, including theories of Loevinger (1976), Perry (1970), Chickering (1969), and Hunt and Sullivan's (1974) person-environment matching model in education. Although approximately 18 different developmental models have been described, the ones receiving the majority of research attention (Worthington, 1987) are Stoltenberg (1981) and Loganbill, Hardy, and Delworth (1982) and, more recently, Stoltenberg and Delworth (1988). Reviews of developmental models appeared in Holloway (1987, 1988), Stoltenberg and Delworth (1988), Worthington (1987), and Bernard and Goodyear (1992). Basically, these models advocate that supervisors match the structure and style of supervision to the trainee's level of development as a counselor.

A similar approach advocating person-environment matching is Abbey, Hunt, and Weiser's (1985) experiential learning model. They relied on Kolb's (1984) learning styles theory but did not include a developmental perspective in their model. They did, however, refer to individual differences in trainees' cognitive or learning styles as a basis for structuring supervisory environments (Sugarman, 1985).

Social role models have been described by Boyd (1978); Bernard (1979); Hess (1980); Littrell, Lee-Borden, and Lorenz (1979); and Bartlett (1983). In these models, the position of supervisor includes a set of roles that, when performed, establish certain expectations, beliefs, and attitudes. As a result, the supervisor, engaging in this set of recurring actions consistent with the expected role, promotes an experience of behavioral consistency and certainty for the trainee. Although role model approaches have focused almost exclusively on the supervisor as role sender, the trainee is also expected to play certain roles (Holloway, 1984). Typically, counseling psychologists familiar with the roles prescribed for the supervisor use these models as a heuristic tool in guiding practice (Hess, 1980). There is little research, however, that directly tests social role models (Holloway, 1992b). Nonetheless, cross-theoretical and empirical investigations of supervision have established the groundwork for translating theory and research into practice. The Systems Approach to Supervision (SAS), a theory of practice modeled in the following chapters, has been built on this beginning.

Theory and Research Into Practice

Sergiovanni (1983) states that a theory of practice should be concerned with four questions:

1. What is reality in a given context?
2. What ought to be reality?
3. What do events that constitute this reality mean to individuals and groups?
4. Given these three dimensions, what should supervisors do? (p. 177)

Educators and practitioners of supervision thus need four components of support: (a) a descriptive base, (b) guidelines stating common goals and imperatives, (c) a way to discover meaning as it relates to participants and the profession, and (d) a systematic mode of inquiry to determine objectives and strategies for interaction during supervision.

The purpose of this book is to provide a model that meets these four needs. Herein is a systems approach to understanding supervision that comes from a synthesis of the existing conceptual and empirical literature

in combination with the professional reflective knowledge of my colleagues, my students, and myself through years of teaching and practicing supervision. I have designed a heuristic tool to incorporate three
sources of knowledge—theory, research, and practice. These bases of
knowledge are presented in different forms, including text, transcripts,
and graphics. The format of the book attempts to weave the different
sources together while keeping their specific identities intact.

Principles of a Systems Approach

To access differing knowledge bases, experience has shown the
value of a systems approach grounded in principles that emphasize a
learning alliance between the supervisor and supervisee based on
multiple interlinking factors in the relationship of supervision. The
goal of supervision is the enhancement of the student's effective professional functioning, and the interpersonal nature of supervision provides an opportunity for the supervisee to be fully involved toward
that end. In this way, the supervisee is empowered in the process of
acquiring attitudes, skills, and knowledge for independent, effective
professional practice. Being aware of "the big picture," the supervisor
is able to access strategies and attitudes during supervision that will
enhance the learning environment for a particular supervisee. With
knowledge of the whole system, deliberate choices can be made by
both supervisor and supervisee within the context of specific relevant
supervisory factors.

The assumptions of empowerment and relationship are related to
the SAS:

- The goal of supervision is to provide an opportunity for the
  supervisee *to learn* a broad spectrum of professional attitudes,
  skills, and knowledge, in an effective and supportive manner.
- Successful supervision occurs within the context of a complex
  professional relationship that is ongoing and mutually involving.
- The supervisory relationship is the primary context for facilitat-
  ing the *involvement of the learner* in reaching the goals of supervision. The essential nature of this interpersonal process bestows
  power to both members as they form the relationship.
- For the supervisor, both the *content and process* of supervision
  become integral parts of the design of instructional approaches
  within the relationship.
- As the supervisor teaches, the trainee is further empowered by
  (a) acquiring the skills and knowledge of the professional work
  and (b) gaining knowledge through experiencing and articulating interpersonal situations.

Therefore, the primary goal of supervision is the establishment of an ongoing relationship in which the supervisor designs specific learning tasks and teaching strategies related to the supervisee's development as a professional. In addition, the supervisor empowers the supervisee to enter the profession by understanding the attitudes, skills, and knowledge demanded of the professional and by guiding the relationship strategically to facilitate the trainee's achievement of a professional standard.

Clinical supervision is the training of a professional and thus adheres to a model that supports the use of professional knowledge and skills. This model, however, does not entertain the notion that individuals are dependent and reliant on experts as a source of power and self-learning. Supervision provides an opportunity for the recognition of a professional's own resources in combination with the information and skills available. If the learner remains dependent solely on the supervisor, then successful supervision has not taken place. Clearly, the development of such independence is a process of learning about oneself, the consumer one serves, and the profession. As Rappaport (1986) defines empowerment, it is a sense of autonomy that comes from feeling capable of making a difference in one's world and the world of others. This sense comes through the acquisition of knowledge and skills that contribute to helping oneself and others to gain personal control over their lives. Supervisors are well-advised therefore to allow the supervisee's unique improvisation, adaptation, and creation of methods and approaches in practice. A supervisee cannot be expected to adhere to the supervisor's ways of doing. The provision of an opportunity for empowerment is a difficult and challenging task for supervisors, not only because they must confront their own narcissistic needs and issues of self-aggrandizement, but they also must distinguish between the supervisor's responsibility to maximize the trainee's unique professional resources on one hand and the demands of the profession to evaluate the supervisee's competence on the other.

A Systems Approach Model

Seven dimensions have emerged from the empirical, conceptual, and practice knowledge bases of supervision. These dimensions have been integrated conceptually into the SAS as seven factors of the overall model. In Figure 1.1 the seven factors are represented as six wings connected to the body of supervision—that is, the relationship. Task and function are represented in the foreground of the interaction with the more covert influences of supervisor, trainee, client, and institution in the background. The relationship is the core factor and contains the process of the supervision interaction. This depiction is the foundation of the SAS. As a system, this model has been designed

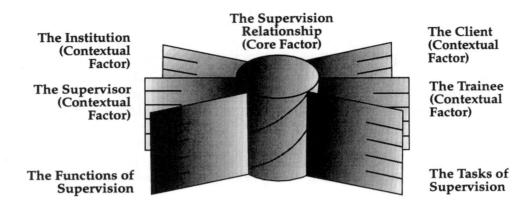

The Institution
(Contextual
Factor)

The Supervisor
(Contextual
Factor)

The Functions of
Supervision

The Supervision
Relationship
(Core Factor)

The Client
(Contextual
Factor)

The Trainee
(Contextual
Factor)

The Tasks of
Supervision

Figure 1.1. A Systems Approach to Supervision: Seven Dimensions

to suggest that each wing can be examined independently from the others and then also examined in the context of a particular item, all items, or both. It is understood that the components of the model are also part of a dynamic process in that they mutually influence one another and are highly interrelated. The process is influenced by each of the factors, and reciprocally, the process itself influences the factors (see Chapter 4, Figure 4.1 for completed model).

Imagine this picture spinning in light, creating shadows on a screen. The projected images would reflect the idiosyncratic patterns of task, function, and the contextual factors as specifically relevant to the moment-to-moment interactions of the supervisor and trainee. A detailed examination of the screen would provide up-to-date information about (a) the nature of the task, (b) what function the supervisor was carrying out, (c) the character of the relationship, and (d) what contextual factors were relevant to the process. The graphic model is used to identify anchor points in this complex process and to encourage supervisors to discover and name the most salient factors in a particular piece of work.

This book is meant to raise questions about what each of us does as a supervisor rather than to tell a supervisor what to think and what to do. The systems model provides a common language of supervision that is relevant to supervisors and educators of different theoretical points of view. It is an effort to create a meaningful approach to understanding and practicing supervision. In spite of such efforts to capture the essence of the phenomenon itself, the artistry of supervision remains elusive. The very act of asking questions, I suggest, ultimately uncovers meaning and is critical in developing an epistemology of practice.

To illustrate the variety of sources inherent in the supervisory experience, the chapters that follow offer examples of the multiplicity and interrelatedness of ways of learning. The different formats include (a) tables for transcripts and reflections on their meaning, (b) graphics with labels that reflect the research in the area, (c) boxes that summarize the empirical work relevant to particular claims in the model, and (d) plain text to connect these various sources of information into the structure of the model of supervision.

Chapter 2 begins with the presentation of the primary factors describing the act of supervision—tasks and functions. Chapter 3 discusses the relationship of supervision. Chapter 4 uncovers the contextual factors of supervision—relationship, supervisor, trainee, client, and institution. Chapter 5 contains an entire supervision interview with the accompanying reflective comments of the participants and an analysis using the SAS model. Chapter 6 demonstrates the use of the model to supervisory cases in the context of a consultation group on supervision. Throughout the book, dialogue and examples of actual supervisory interactions define and illustrate the key constructs of the model. In several instances, I have presented these examples of practice without further explanation so that the reader may create his or her own meaning by drawing on past experiences and practical knowledge of counseling and supervision.

2

Tasks and Functions of Supervision

-⊘ Essentially, the goal of supervision is the establishment of an ongoing relationship that has specific tasks related to the supervisee's development as a professional. In the Systems Approach to Supervision (SAS), the teaching tasks and supervisory function are used to describe the action of the supervision process. This chapter discusses the characteristics of task and function as they are defined in both the empirical and practice literatures and provides examples from process transcripts of supervision.

Identifying Tasks and Functions in Practice

To illustrate all the tasks and functions of supervision, unedited excerpts from supervision interviews are presented as Transcripts 2.1 through 2.5. Because the focus of supervision often shifts quickly, the accompanying text explains each characteristic separately in order not to risk losing the context of the interview. The text also refers back to examples from the transcripts as a whole. The left column reflects the supervisory interaction, the middle column the supervision tasks, and the right column the supervisory function. Tasks and functions are in boldface type for easy identification. In addition, general comments to help the reader keep track of my own understanding of the session are included in the middle column.

The reader is encouraged to use the transcripts by referring to them as they are introduced in the accompanying text. Thus, in reading through the text definitions of supervision *tasks*, refer to the left and middle columns of the transcripts. When reading the definitions of supervisor *functions*, refer to the left and far right columns.

In addition to the transcripts and explanatory text, this chapter provides information in the form of a research box containing a summary of empirical work relevant to the characteristics of task and function of supervision. Each reader will likely choose when and how often to access this supplementary material.

The Tasks of Supervision

A task is defined as "a definite piece of work assigned or expected of a person" (Stein, 1975). The tasks of supervision are defined by a body of professional knowledge requisite of the counselor role. This base of professional knowledge can be referred to as "domain specific," the definition of which is not straightforward and has been the object of considerable debate in education. Alexander and Judy (1988), after an extensive review of the literature in teacher education and instructional psychology, concluded that domain-specific knowledge in any particular field encompasses three types of knowledge—declarative, procedural, and conditional. Each, although not mutually exclusive, can be defined as follows:

> *Declarative knowledge* refers to factual information (knowing what). *Procedural knowledge* is the compilation of declarative knowledge into functional units that incorporate domain-specific strategies (knowing how). *Conditional knowledge* entails the understanding of when and where to access certain facts or employ particular procedures [italics added]. (Alexander & Judy, 1988, p. 376)

Although these areas of knowledge are related to one another, there is very little research telling how they interact during learning. There are, however, two undisputed findings. First, individuals who already know about a subject area are better able to understand and remember new information (e.g., Chi, 1985; Glaser, 1984). Second, individuals who monitor and regulate how they are learning while engaged in a task perform better than those individuals who do not (e.g., Flavell, 1981; Garner, 1987).

These definitions of knowledge seem very relevant to teaching traditions in counseling. Knowing what to do with a client's problem, knowing how to intervene or articulating the procedure of intervention, and knowing when to intervene in the problem are often referred to in counseling procedure texts (Cormier & Hackney, 1993; Egan, 1982; Ivey, 1993). Conditional knowledge is similar to the concept of "timing and judgment" in counseling.

Although there remains considerable ambiguity in the characterization of critical factors of psychotherapy (Bergin & Garfield, 1986;

Greenberg & Pinsof, 1986), a supervisor has a set of general expectations regarding the skills necessary to become a professional counselor—that is, domain-specific tasks in counseling. From this larger pool of knowledge, the supervisor and student will choose those specific learning goals that match the individual needs of the trainee. Such goals may involve declarative knowledge, procedural knowledge, conditional knowledge, or all three. Although progress in characterizing critical process variables of psychotherapy has been made in the last 10 years there is still considerable ambiguity in the definition of effective practice. The supervisors make judgments regarding a supervisee's performance on explicit behavioral criteria and on tacit knowledge (Polanyi, 1967) of what is "right" or "wrong" in practice. Unquestionably, tacit knowledge is not only difficult to quantify but difficult to hold one accountable for; nonetheless it is a part of professional judgment that each supervisor knowingly or unknowingly exercises. Thus, the supervisor is faced with the task of articulating in an understandable and relevant way the use of these knowledge bases to model for the trainee the use of higher-order skills. In many instances, supervisors may find themselves unable to identify the cognitive processes they engaged in to arrive at a particular conceptualization or choice of intervention. Because the literature tells us very little beyond general areas of inquiry, it is incumbent on supervisors to actively reflect on their own use of knowledge as a part of devising and implementing domain-specific goals (see Research Box 2.1 for a summary of expert-novice and counselor competencies research).

Operationalizing the Tasks

The numerous characteristics and skills identified in the literature can be grouped into five broad areas. Categories of teaching objectives include counseling skills, case conceptualization, professional role, intra- and interpersonal emotional awareness, and self-evaluation (Holloway & Acker, 1988) (see Figure 2.1).

Counseling Skills

Supervision counseling skills might include the following: communication patterns; empathy; personalization; techniques of counseling, such as symptom prescription, desensitization, reinforcement; or any of the specific skills that the supervisor identifies as both fundamental to counseling knowledge and specifically relevant to a particular trainee. The task of counseling skills focuses on what action to take with the client (see Transcript 2.1, Excerpt 2, col. 2, pp. 18-20). Notice that although the trainee describes his emotional response in relation to the client and the supervisor in turn acknowledges that concern, the supervisor chooses to focus on teaching an intervention strategy rather than on pursuing the meaning of the trainee's feelings.

Research Box 2.1

Research on Counselor Competencies

There is little research in this area, and the focus has been primarily on the counselor role. Early in the history of our profession, numerous authors spoke to the question "What does a counselor need to know?" (for reviews, see Altucher, 1967; Chenault, 1968; Wolleat, 1974). Many of these statements reflected the concern with the counselor as a person, a holistic view of the individual's character and the manner in which certain personal qualities would be necessary and of benefit in the counselor role. The interest in personal analysis for the trainee was an important component of these early training programs, because it was within the context of psychotherapy that such qualities could be recognized and enhanced.

Another approach to domain-specific expectations for the counselor was the development of behaviorally oriented lists of competencies (e.g., Friedlander, Ward, & Ferrin, 1984; Hector, 1977; Jabukowski-Spector, Dustin, & George, 1971). These statements defined more precisely what was expected of the successful counselor trainee and served as guides for the evaluation of performance in the counselor role. Menne (1975) asked 75 experienced counselors from a variety of work settings to indicate those competencies they believed necessary for effective counseling. From a list of 132 competencies, 12 factors were identified. These included professional ethics, self-awareness, personal characteristics, listening and communicating, testing skills, counseling comprehension, behavioral science, societal awareness, tutoring techniques, professional credentials, counselor training, and vo-

cational guidance. The importance of these dimensions varied depending on the respondent's work setting, professional affiliation, theoretical background, and experience.

In addition to the counselor role, both supervisor and supervisee begin supervision with expectations regarding the appropriate behavior for the roles in the supervisory relationship. Although new supervisees have only a vague understanding of the supervisory relationship, supervisors usually have clear role prescriptions both for their own behavior and that of the supervisee. Hess and Hess (1987) and Holloway (1984) have remarked that supervisors make judgments regarding supervisee's competence and interpersonal skill based on their performance as a supervisee. However, there was only one study found, a thesis referred to in Hess and Hess (1987) that prescribes role behavior for the supervisee. Swain (1981) identified the following dimensions as critical supervisee behaviors from the perspective of supervisors: interest in the client and client welfare; preparation for supervision; theoretical knowledge; self-exploration, disclosure, self-esteem, and self-awareness; openness to suggestions; expertise, clinical skills, and interpersonal skills; boundary management, and decision-making abilities.

Drawing from the expert/novice literature in teacher education and psychology, researchers in counseling have hypothesized that experts would process information about a client differently. Studies using greater experience as a definition of "more expert" found

Research Box 2.1

Continued

that more experienced counselors made more accurate diagnoses (Lambert & Werthemier, 1988); confronted more, responded less verbosely, met fewer client demands, used immediacy, and showed greater flexibility in using confrontative responses (Tracey, Hays, Malone, & Herman, 1988); used more interpretative and confrontative responses, conceptualized client dynamics more effectively, considered issues of timing and appropriateness of therapeutic interventions and specific techniques (Hill, Charles, & Reed, 1981; Hirsch & Stone, 1983); and showed more convergence in asking questions related to their conceptualizations (Hirsch & Stone, 1983). Thus, case conceptualization or the representation of the problem by more experienced counselors included the use of higher-order skills, such as monitoring, listening, and integrating verbal and nonverbal data; generating and testing hypotheses; and accessing and activating relevant schemata and semantic networks.

A small group of researchers have investigated differences in identified novice and expert counselors rather than just relying on experience level as an indicator of expertise. Martin and his associates have engaged in a systematic program of research that has investigated differences between experts and novices in case conceptualization tasks. In one study, Martin, Slemon, Hiebert, Hallberg, and Cummings (1989) found that although expert and novice counselors did not differ in general counseling conceptualization, there was a reliable difference between counselors of different experience when conceptual-

izing a specific case problem. Novices added more client-specific information than experts. They did not find differences on measures of integration, hierarchical organization, and higher-order concepts. In the next study by Cummings, Hallberg, Martin, Slemon, and Hiebert (1989), a qualitative analysis of four counselor conceptualizations was done. They confirmed that experienced counselors used certain concepts across all sampling periods when conceptualizing a client's problem. These included family background, interpersonal relationships, self-esteem, and self-image. Experts used more declarative than procedural knowledge compared to novices.

Burns (1994) summarized the findings on expert and novice conceptualization of client problems. She concluded that as experience increased, clinicians produced more features and agreed more among themselves concerning clinical features of salience (Murphy & Wright, 1984). However, the differentiation or distinction of features that were used was less with experts. Furthermore, experts felt more knowledgeable about cases and gained more information from case materials than did novices (Hillerbrand & Clairborn, 1990). Experts used a single conceptualization of change in counseling based on counseling principles for both general and specific cases. Their conceptualizations were concise and parsimonious, whereas novices conceptualized general change processes similarly but added more detail (Martin et al., 1989). Finally, experts used declarative concepts more extensively and more consistently than novices (Cummings et al., 1989).

The Tasks of
Supervision

| Counseling Skill |
| Case Conceptualization |
| Professional Role |
| Emotional Awareness |
| Self-Evaluation |

Figure 2.1. The Tasks of Supervision

Case Conceptualization

Case conceptualization involves the supervisor and supervisee in understanding the client's psychosocial history and presenting problem. The development of a conceptual framework that is applicable across many different types of clients and that is simultaneously congruent with the therapist's beliefs of human development and change is critical in training. Frequently, conceptualizing the case is the focus of teaching because the supervisor strives to have the trainee understand the client's behavior and then connect it to theoretical bases of knowledge. In most supervisory sessions, there is discussion of the client's situation, the counseling relationship, and the course of the therapeutic process, usually leading to the formulation of a diagnosis and treatment plan.

Reflecting on and "figuring out" the meaning of a client's behaviors are relevant to the formulation of strategic interventions. At the same time, in the development of conceptualization, the bases of the participants' theoretical orientation to counseling become evident as, for example, the supervisor uncovers his or her own declarative, procedural, and conditional knowledge of practice.

Excerpt 1 of Transcript 2.1 (pp. 17-18) illustrates a strong emphasis on case conceptualization. The supervisor focuses on understanding the dynamic between the trainee and the client. He formulates both a strategy for intervening with the client's storytelling and, later, a supervisory

TRANSCRIPT **2.1**

Supervision Tasks and Functions

Excerpt 1

Supervision Interview	*Supervision Tasks*	*Supervision Function*
Trainee Ah, well, then I probably will ask . . . I might ask him a question or something and then he'll kind of, a lot of time he'll say something back in a brief phrase and then kind of pick up on the story again, so it's like, you know, it's like I get attention for a minute, but it's sort of like, he just sort of brushes me away and goes back into his story.	The trainee presents his perception of the dynamics of the interaction of the counseling session and provides the information for **case conceptualization.**	
Supervisor OK, so you're getting caught by him telling stories to you. . .	The supervisor begins to **conceptualize** what is happening in the interaction.	The supervisor **advises** trainee of his opinion about what the dynamic is in the counseling relationship.
Trainee Umm, uh, . . .		
Supervisor You feel like he's, he's taking the direction away from the purpose that you have in mind or what you seem to be wanting to explore. And you feel that he is using storytelling as an avoidance technique then.	The supervisor elaborates on the **case conceptualization** by labeling the trainee's interpretation of why the client is storytelling.	The supervisor **advises** the trainee of his opinion.
Trainee Yeah, I guess . . . I'm not completely sure what all the reasons are, why he uses stories. But that's . . .	The trainee questions whether the supervisor's interpretation is accurate.	
Supervisor That's the way it feels . . .	The supervisor extends trainee's **emotional awareness of self** (i.e., trainee).	The supervisor **supports** trainee's paying attention to feelings.
Trainee Yeah, it feels like it's his way of feeling comfortable maybe, and umm, maybe relating to me. Maybe he gets a lot of positive feedback from people just saying, he's a	The trainee starts to **conceptualize** the case dynamics by interpreting the counseling behavior as indicative of more generalized patterns of behavior in the client's life.	

(continued)

TRANSCRIPT 2.1   **Continued**

Supervision Interview	Supervision Tasks	Supervision Function
good storyteller, so probably a lot of people will just go "umm, that's a real interesting story, Hank" or something like that.		
Supervisor OK. There are a couple of possibilities. One is maybe his stories have something to do with what he is asking. Have you looked at that? Are they some way peripherally related as a way that he is trying to tell you something about the questions that you have asked?	The supervisor encourages the trainee to continue his **case conceptualization.**	The supervisor advises the trainee of various hypotheses that might relate to the client's behavior and **consults** with the trainee to gain more specific information.

Excerpt 2

Supervisor I think that was in the right direction, but I think you need to apply your intervention there. One, the point you are making is that "Hey, you are using up airtime with storytelling that doesn't seem to be to the point of what our goals are here." I think you can even be more direct in the sense that you can talk to him about storytelling. Because you are having feelings about the way, about his storytelling. You don't have negative feelings about other interventions or other things that he says to you or other ways that he interacts with you.	The supervisor focuses conversation on **counseling skills** that might be used to intervene in the client's storytelling.

Although the supervisor remarks on the trainee's feelings they are not the main focus. | The supervisor first **supports** the trainee, then models an intervention, and then **advises** the trainee on how to intervene. |
| I think that you are getting into a position where you can be more direct with him. About what | **Counseling skills** focus continued. | |

(continued)

TRANSCRIPT 2.1 **Continued**

Supervision Interview	*Supervision Tasks*	*Supervision Function*
you are perceiving him to be doing with the session. As opposed to what you perceive him doing outside of the session in his life and the stories that he tells you.		
Trainee OK.		
Supervisor There are important questions for him to look at. Particularly, it seems like questions that have to do with feelings. Basically, it is a way of avoiding talking about the feeling. It may be a way that he talks about feelings.	The supervisor returns to **conceptualize the case** and offer hypothesis regarding the client's motivation.	The supervisor **advises** the trainee of his opinion.
But I think one of the things that you may want to teach him is that there are other ways to talk about feelings than telling stories. So given those few points, how might you restructure your intervention?	The supervisor finishes by asking the trainee to reflect on **counseling skills** that might have been used with the client.	The **advising** function continues, but the supervisor switches to giving a suggestion to the trainee on how to intervene with the client.
Trainee Well, I do have . . . I should tell you that I guess I have a worry about doing this also, and as you were describing this, I began to remember, I guess it's a feeling like if . . . I mean, what is it, five sessions now we're talking about?	The trainee returns to immediate interpersonal **emotional** state in the supervision session.	
Supervisor Umm, hmm.		
Trainee Since that is his main way of relating to me, I'm a little bit nervous that if all of a sudden I say "Hey, wait a minute, we're going to change the rules here." I mean, I know you have been, you know. . . It's like, I feel like maybe I will harm		

(continued)

TRANSCRIPT 2.1 Continued

Supervision Interview	Supervision Tasks	Supervision Function
our relationship if I come on too strong and confront him with this. Is this . . . is this . . . can I do this without really harming the relationship?		
Supervisor Well, I think you can, but I think you have a reasonable fear. You don't want to alienate him, and storytelling is a major tool for him. I think we could, ya know, role-play this; maybe would be a nice way for us to try and work on it. OK?	The supervisor acknowledges **emotional awareness** again in service of attending to the development of the trainee's **counseling skills.**	The supervisor supports the trainee's fear but returns to **advising** him on what to do and suggests a technique to work on the intervention he (the supervisor) has suggested.
Trainee Umm . . . Umm.		
Supervisor I don't think you need to alienate him, I think it's a way of perhaps drawing him into a closer relationship. You see, confrontation doesn't push people away. It can really be a binding thing if you can work through it. OK? So there's an opportunity for you to make this intervention and maybe make your relationship with him stronger. But it's how you are going to do it that counts.	The supervisor adds to **case conceptualization** by discussing effects of intervention, then focuses on the **counseling skill** of confrontation.	The supervisor directly **advises** by providing information about the effects of the technique of confrontation and its particular potential in this counseling relationship.
Trainee Yeah, yeah, I want to be careful about how I did it, you know.	Counseling skill remains the focus of the teaching.	The supervisor counsels by asking the trainee's opinion about how to go about his learning the technique (**consulting**).
Supervisor We can role-play if you want me to be the client and run through it. Or do you want to try being the client, and I'll run through being the counselor?		

(continued)

TRANSCRIPT 2.1 **Continued**

Supervision Interview	Supervision Tasks	Supervision Function
Trainee I think if I were Hank, I'd get a better feel for what it felt like to receive the intervention.	The trainee **self-evaluates** by making a judgment as to how he (the trainee) will learn best.	
Supervisor Good idea. OK, let's go with that.		The supervisor **supports** the trainee's decision on how to arrange the role-play.
(Supervisor and trainee proceed to role-play the counseling intervention.)	As the counselor, the supervisor will demonstrate the counseling skill of confrontation.	Although this transcript stops just before the role-playing, because the supervisor is the counselor, he **models** how to do the intervention.

This transcript is taken from the videotape series *Engagement and Power in Clinical Supervision* by Martin Acker and Elizabeth Holloway, University of Oregon, Eugene, OR, 1988. Used by permission of Martin Acker and Elizabeth Holloway. (Videotapes not available for distribution.)

technique (role-playing) to demonstrate how to accomplish this goal. As one will notice from the transcripts, case conceptualization is almost always present in the supervision interview as the basis of formulating the counselor's plan for intervention with the client.

Professional Role

Professional role relates to how the trainee will (a) use appropriate external resources for the client; (b) apply principles of professional and ethical practice; (c) learn tasks of record keeping, procedure, and appropriate interprofessional relationships; and (d) participate in the supervisory relationship. The management of a supervisory relationship is critical to professional development because forming this relationship is a part of the counselor's contractual agreement to engage in the learning process. As described in Chapter 1, this relationship allows trainees to gain awareness of their own interpersonal style while learning to articulate and translate their knowledge to the counseling role. Participants' attention to both the boundaries and responsibilities of their respective roles is vital to an ethical and effective learning environment. In Transcript 2.2 (col. 2, pp. 22-24), the director maintains boundaries between his various roles of supervisor, trainee, and the director of training. Notice that the director focuses attention almost

TRANSCRIPT **2.2**

Supervision Tasks and Functions

Supervision Interview	Supervision Tasks	Supervision Function
Director Laura, how are you?		
Trainee I'm a little . . . umm . . . miffed I guess with a client that I have and that's why I wanted to come and talk to you about it. Because it's kind of gotten me very discouraged and frustrated at the same time. And I guess the reason I'm seeking you out is, umm, I've talked to many people, and I kind of wanted to get an idea . . . umm, some other input, as to what I might be able to do if anything.	The trainee begins by stating the purpose of her visit. Her comments establish that she has consulted with a number of people before coming to the director of training for assistance. Also she expresses her **feelings about the awareness of counseling relationship.**	
Director Now as I understand it you are being supervised by Doug, is that right?	The director immediately addresses the issue by clarifying the **supervisory relationship.**	The director **monitors** the status of the trainee's supervisory arrangement.
Trainee . . . umm uh umm uh		
Director And have you had a chance to talk with him, about this client?	The director determines whether she has used supervision to discuss the client.	**Monitoring** continues as he attempts to establish the events that have preceded the trainee coming to him for help.
Trainee Oh, yea, yea we've been going around with this client for a while, you know, back and forth. What can I do? I'm still feeling quite frustrated with it.	The trainee addresses briefly the **professional role** task but reiterates her lack of satisfaction with the process by returning to her **intrapersonal awareness (emotional awareness).**	
Director You also mentioned that you were talking with some other counselor about this client.	The director requests additional information about the trainee's consultative actions.	The director **monitors** the situation by clarifying the trainee's actions around consulting.

(continued)

TRANSCRIPT 2.2 **Continued**

Supervision Interview	*Supervision Tasks*	*Supervision Function*
Trainee Yeah, well, you know, you kind of talk to your peers in passing; you know, you mention also in group supervision what . . . you know, who you are working with and what's going on. So I've brought that client out just 'cause I'm feeling so frustrated, you know, what do I do with this person. Umm, so yeah, I have spoken with some people and asked, you know, "What would you do?" with this kind of situation?	Again the trainee passes over the issue of **professional management** and returns to her dissatisfaction with the help that she is receiving in doing her clinical work.	
Director And is the feedback you're getting from them any different than what you got from Doug?	The director addresses the **professional management** of her relationship with her supervisor.	The director is primarily **consulting** here; however, he may also be monitoring supervision efficacy because the director is responsible for the supervisor's performance.
Trainee Umm, yeah. The feedback is different, but it still is not real satisfying for me. I'm, you know, I'm taking that information and using it in the session, but I'm just not sure . . . I don't feel like the client is making any moves.	The trainee responds briefly to her supervision experience and then back to her **emotional awareness** of dissatisfaction with both the supervisory and counseling relationship.	
Director Umm, uh.		
Trainee I feel I have a pretty resistant client, and umm, the more resistive he becomes, the more frustrated I become in the session.		
Director I can appreciate, you know, that frustration that you are having; umm, my concern is		

(continued)

TRANSCRIPT 2.2 **Continued**

Supervision Interview	Supervision Tasks	Supervision Function
here not to, I guess, step into what Doug's been doing with his work with you. I wouldn't want him to feel as if I were going over his head and working with one of his trainees. You know, I'd very much like doing supervision and helping out where I can be of help. It's important for me and I think also for your relationship with Doug that if we come up with an idea that you might want to try with this client that you inform Doug first.	The director acknowledges the trainee's feelings but then addresses the issue of working outside the supervisory relationship and his concerns of how that might be interpreted by her assigned supervisor. He begins to clarify his **professional role as director of training** and the extent of his willingness to help.	The director **supports** her but is clear that he is more concerned with the boundary issues in supervision and advises her of his rationale in this regard. He **shares** his feelings about participating in a supervisory relationship but **advises** her clearly of his professional responsibilities to her supervisor.
And I guess my next question is, was he aware that you were going to meet with me and discuss this client?	The director establishes boundaries for supervision and models **management** of boundaries in professional relationships.	The director returns to **monitoring** the trainee's previous actions with her own supervisor.

This transcript is taken from the videotape series *Engagement and Power in Clinical Supervision*, by Martin Acker and Elizabeth Holloway, University of Oregon, Eugene, OR, 1988. Used by permission of Martin Acker and Elizabeth Holloway. (Videotapes not available for distribution.)

entirely on the context of the trainee's supervisory situation. In spite of the trainee's emotional appeal for help, the director is not sidetracked into a discussion of the client.

Emotional Awareness: Intra- and Interpersonal

Emotional awareness refers to the trainee's self-awareness of feelings, thoughts, and actions that result from working with the client and with the supervisor. Both intra- and interpersonal awareness are relevant to counseling and supervision. Many theories of counseling stress the importance of understanding one's own emotional material both historically as well as immediately with the client. The participants' emotional responses in the relationship of supervision may also be an important subject for their work with the client. Oftentimes, the supervisor may draw awareness to the supervisee's emotional reaction to something said in supervision or perhaps to the reenactment of the emotional dynamic of the supervisory relationship. This latter process, usually considered a task of emotional awareness, is often referred to as *parallel process*. The context for the development of parallel processes is discussed in more detail in Chapter 4 under Client Factors. In Transcript 2.3 (pp. 26-28), issues of emotional awareness affecting the supervisee-client relationship are the primary task of supervision.

Self-Evaluation

Self-evaluation is a task necessary for all counselors as they work with clients. The willingness and skill to recognize limits of competence, effectiveness, and client progress in counseling are an ethical responsibility and critical for the counselor's continued professional growth. Learning the limits of one's competence and effectiveness is particularly important in a field where much of the work is done confidentially with only the client and counselor as witness. Even if the counselor is being supervised, the supervisor still often depends on the supervisee to contribute what needs to be worked on in supervision. The supervisor is constantly modeling aspects of self-evaluation; however, there are times when the self-evaluation task must be more explicitly focused. Transcript 2.4 (col. 2, pp. 29-31) exemplifies a supervisor promoting the trainee's self-evaluative process. Notice how the supervisor encourages the trainee to focus on what happened in the counseling interview and to assess what effect it had on the client. He consistently highlights a self-evaluating process rather than making a judgment himself about the supervisee's behavior.

Functions of Supervision

A function is "the kind of action or activity proper to a person or thing; the purpose for which something is designed or exists; to perform a specialized action or activity" (Stein, 1975). Role labels (see Chapter 1) have been useful in providing a common language for describing functions in educational and mental health supervision. Supervisory behaviors have been attributed to the roles of teacher, counselor, and consultant (Ellis & Dell, 1986; Ellis, Dell, & Good, 1988), and findings from process research corroborate the power structure of common roles in supervision (Holloway & Poulin, 1995). Notice that here these roles have been transformed (from a noun to a verb) and simplified to emphasize their dynamic nature as well as to suggest a more cohesive approach to the role of supervisor.

The five primary functions that the supervisor engages in while interacting with the supervisee are (a) monitoring and evaluating, (b) instructing and advising, (c) modeling, (d) consulting, and (e) supporting

TRANSCRIPT **2.3**

Supervision Tasks and Functions

Supervision Interview	Supervision Tasks	Supervision Function
Supervisor Hi, Anne, what did you want to talk about today?		The supervisor **consults** by asking the trainee to identify the issues to discuss in the supervision interview.
Trainee I guess I want to talk about my last client I've been seeing . . . It's kind of an interesting situation; I don't know, I'm a little jarred by it. I guess I've just been noticing . . . I've been noticing some nonverbal stuff and also some verbal stuff with the sort of nonverbal stuff that I'm kind of wondering what some of the issues are. I guess one of the things I've been noticing . . . the client has been moving closer to me, actually physically closer. We'll have our chairs arranged in a certain way, and I notice that we are closer together than we were before.	The trainee introduces client's dynamic behavior and her emotional response to it, **conceptualizing** the case and revealing her **emotional awareness** of the counseling relationship.	
Supervisor What client is that?		The supervisor **consults** by asking for clarification.
Trainee This is Jill.		
Supervisor OK . . . So she seems to be scooting up closer to you.	The supervisor focuses on client information to establish a base for **case conceptualization.**	The supervisor continues **consultative** process to gain information about the case.
Trainee Yeah, it's been interesting. I know we've been seeing each other for quite a while, but it seems that there's more actual touching on her part.	The trainee continues with client focus and counseling interaction to further the **case conceptualization** process.	
Supervisor How does that feel for you?	The supervisor shifts to trainee's **emotional awareness** in reaction to the client's behavior.	The supervisor **consults** regarding the trainee's feeling state.

(continued)

TRANSCRIPT **2.3** **Continued**

Supervision Interview	*Supervision Tasks*	*Supervision Function*
Trainee Umm . . [long pause]. Well, I've been noticing it for a while, and I think that, before, touch hasn't been much of an issue. I think it's been pretty appropriate, I think, on both of our parts to emphasize a point or something like that. However, this time I think it's coupled with more of, it does feel more inappropriate to me. It seems like it's not there for emphasis, it's just more, umm, a longer lingering touch, and I think that it's also coupled with, on her part, what I see is more of a willingness to agree with everything that I have to say.	The trainee does not respond to the request for emotional awareness but continues to discuss client and counseling relationship through **case conceptualization.**	
Supervisor What do you make of that?	The supervisor returns to **case conceptualization** by asking the trainee to think through the implications of the client's behavior.	The supervisor **consults** regarding the trainee's opinions.
Trainee Umm [pause] it seems that she's really wanting to please me, that it seems that I've become very important to her, and this is something that we've talked about too in the relationship and how it is when you have to come [to therapy]. She's related before that she finds it a very positive thing and she finds it a very helpful thing in the relationship that we have cultivated. [pause]	The trainee continues process of **case conceptualization.**	
Supervisor I'm wondering if you are aware of any feelings on your part? Any reactions to her pleasing behavior towards you. What you call	The supervisor returns to task of **emotional awareness** of the trainee.	The supervisor provides **support** for the trainee's emotional self-reflection.

(continued)

TRANSCRIPT 2.3 **Continued**

Supervision Interview	*Supervision Tasks*	*Supervision Function*
inappropriate touching. Emotions . . . what kinds of feelings are you having?		
Trainee . . . Well, I think basically there are warning bells going off on this because I'm not quite figuring out exactly what is going on in the context of this relationship; I mean what the issues are. Also there is this certain amount of flattery on my part too. In some ways talking and giving some ideas or suggestions or interpretations that quite obviously show interest in another person could be flattery. Although I am really anxious about that because I'm not quite sure, I mean I don't think flattery is what I want to be feeling in this.	The trainee responds with her concerns with the situation rather than feelings. Finally, she adds feeling flattered and begins to address her **emotions.**	
Supervisor What about anxiousness?	The supervisor follows up with attention to the trainee's interpersonal **emotional awareness** as it relates to the **counseling relationship.**	Supervisor **consults, seeking information about trainee.** The supervisor also **supports** trainee's exploration of her feelings about **counseling relationship.**
Trainee Well I think that [pause] well I think first of all I don't want to cultivate that feeling within myself of wanting to be flattered . . . you know, of wanting to act out my part in maybe closer courtship almost. Would that prohibit me from trying to confront on certain issues or maybe being more directive?	The trainee moves back to issues of the case by discussing issues of **counseling skill.**	

This transcript is taken from the videotape series *Engagement and Power in Clinical Supervision*, by Martin Acker and Elizabeth Holloway, University of Oregon, Eugene, OR, 1988. Used by permission of Martin Acker and Elizabeth Holloway. (Videotapes not available for distribution.)

TRANSCRIPT **2.4**

Supervision Tasks and Functions

Supervision Interview	*Supervision Tasks*	*Supervision Function*
Trainee I found myself kind of . . . saying things like "It will be OK," things that I knew were not good counseling. I found myself slipping out of being a counselor and being a nurturer. So I got real conflicted in what happened and real confused. I haven't seen the tape yet and I am sort of anxious to go back and look at the tape, and I wanted to . . . maybe that's one of the things we can do later in the session is just look at that portion of the tape and get an idea of what went on.	The trainee comments on his own perception of **professional role** in the counseling relationship. Then he begins to describe his **intrapersonal emotional awareness.**	
Supervisor I'd like to do that. What happens when you get confused in general; when you feel confused what happens for you?	The supervisor follows up on the trainee's **intrapersonal emotional awareness.**	The supervisor **supports** the trainee in examining his feelings.
Trainee I don't know what to say next. I start getting kind of jammed up, you know, my words started getting jammed up.	The trainee discusses his general **intrapersonal emotional response** to similar situations outside of counseling.	
Supervisor Did you find that happening when you were with your client?	The supervisor focuses on trainee's **counseling response** (i.e., **skills**).	The supervisor **consults** by asking for the trainee's perception of events that occurred in the counseling session.
Trainee Yeah, I found out it was my issues that I was looking at, not his. It was my feelings that came out.	The trainee comments on his **awareness** of his own **emotional** process in the counseling relationship.	
Supervisor Were you able to continue processing the other side of what was going on, the interaction?	The supervisor asks trainee to reflect on what **counseling skill** he was able to maintain in session.	The supervisor continues to **consult** regarding the trainee's observations of the counseling session.
Trainee I think that is a good question because I tried to do that. Umm,	The trainee begins to **self-evaluate** his counseling behavior.	

(continued)

TRANSCRIPT 2.4 **Continued**

Supervision Interview	*Supervision Tasks*	*Supervision Function*
I tried to look at what I had done in order to deal with that in the past. 'Cause I thought I knew the result. I thought I had resolved that by acknowledging that my father was inappropriate. That my father was a destructive parent. But I guess I hadn't worked on the anger, you know.		
What happens to me when I start feeling the anger, and that's what I was feeling . . . that's when I really start to shut down, and I felt like I was really shutting down . . . and then I really wanted to get out of the counseling situation.	The trainee continues to connect his **intrapersonal emotional awareness** with being in the counseling relationship.	
Supervisor But you didn't. You stayed in the counseling session.	The supervisor refocuses on the trainee's **self-evaluation** of counseling skills.	The supervisor reinforces and **supports** trainee's behavior in session.
Trainee Yeah, I know. I wonder what that means?	The trainee is wondering about the meaning of his performance, unable here to self-evaluate more fully his behavior.	
Supervisor You stuck with it. What was it that pulled you out of that and let you continue with the session? Can you recall the process that you went through from having him spark off something in you and then the feeling of anger and confusion that came up? What was it that led you out of that and back into the counseling situation?	The supervisor continues to focus on **self-evaluation** of counseling behaviors, particularly interpersonal emotions.	The supervisor again **supports** trainee's behavior and then **consults** with him to help him determine what he did and why.
Trainee Well I tried to get back into the present. I tried to pull it back into the present . . . and I said, "You just gave, you just disclosed something that	The trainee begins to analyze through **self-evaluation** his counselor behavior in the session. He reflects on the **counseling skills** he used in the session.	

(continued)

TRANSCRIPT 2.4 **Continued**

Supervision Interview	Supervision Tasks	Supervision Function
was difficult for me. Can you tell me how that felt?" And so we got right into the present with it, and that seemed to make a difference, for me anyway.		
Supervisor So you're bringing it back to the present by literally getting into talking.	The supervisor focuses on the **counseling skills** the trainee used.	The supervisor **supports** the trainee by pointing out what he did correctly.
Trainee And another thing that happened too was that I acknowledged my anger. "Because I'm feeling some anger right now you know . . . I'm feeling some anger right now because of what it is that you had to go through." I said, "Look at you here . . ."	The trainee goes further in his description of his **counseling skills.**	
I don't know if this was appropriate or not. I really don't know. I said, "You're a good-looking attractive person who's got a lot of talent and capabilities." And I said, "And you don't feel very good about yourself because of this crap that your father dumped on you a long time ago and the way he treated you." And I said, "I'm angry about that." And . . . that, I don't know if it's appropriate.	In this aside the trainee is asking if his intervention was appropriate, asking for help in the **self-evaluation** process.	
Supervisor How could you decide that? How would you go about making a decision about whether it was appropriate based on what happened with the client?	Here, the supervisor asks directly for the trainee to determine how he would **self-evaluate.**	He **consults** by asking the trainee to problem solve his dilemma.
Trainee I guess I'd have to look at his response.		

This transcript is taken from the videotape series *Engagement and Power in Clinical Supervision*, by Martin Acker and Elizabeth Holloway, University of Oregon, Eugene, OR, 1988. Used by permission of Martin Acker and Elizabeth Holloway. (Videotapes not available for distribution.)

Table 2.1

Types of Power

Reward power	The perception that the other person has the ability and resources to mediate reward
Coercive power	The perception that the other person has the ability and resources to mediate punishment
Legitimate power	A person's perceived trustworthiness as a professional, socially sanctioned provider of services
Expert power	Attributed to a person because of his or her mastery of knowledge and skills
Referent power	Derived from a person's interpersonal attraction

and sharing (Holloway & Acker, 1988). Each of these functions can be characterized by behaviors typical of their respective social role and the form of relational power governing that function.

The conceptual connections between role, function, and power bridge two streams of research in supervision—social role research and supervision process research (see Research Box 3.2). French and Raven's 1960 classification of power has been used to characterize supervisory behavior (see Research Box 4.5) according to five different types of power (see Table 2.1).

Types of power inherent in the role of the supervisor are evaluative (i.e., reward and coercive), expert, and legitimate power. Referent power results from the personal and interpersonal attributes of the supervisor. Referent power can emerge only as a relationship develops. The participants in an ongoing relationship as involved as supervision come to know each other's values, attitudes, beliefs, and action. The interpersonal attributes of the supervisor may encourage the offering of referent power from the trainee to the supervisor. On the other hand, the trainee may find the supervisor to be very unattractive interpersonally and not attribute referent power to the supervisor. Both participants will influence the process of learning and teaching; however, in the SAS model, it is the supervisor's responsibility to create an effective learning environment for the trainee. The trainee is in a position of seeking skills or expertise and holding no current legitimacy in the profession except as one-in-training. Therefore, the SAS model focuses on the supervisor's use of power. This focus on the supervisor is not meant to suggest that the trainee does not also hold power as a part of the relational nature of supervision but, rather, that the trainee does not have the same responsibilities for formal evaluation and teaching.

The exercise of function (i.e., power) shifts in any particular conversation and across the course of a relationship. Relationships, therefore, need to remain flexible enough to accommodate various functions (i.e., distribution of power), consistent with immediate supervisory objectives. For example, although the supervisor has legitimate and

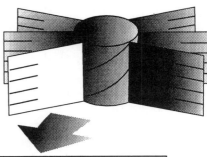

The Functions of Supervision

Monitoring / Evaluating
Instructing / Advising
Modeling
Consulting
Supporting / Sharing

Figure 2.2. The Functions of Supervision

evaluative (i.e., reward and coercive) power, the trainee's developing expertise, personal needs, and self-presentational style influence the supervisor's effectiveness when using expert and referent power. In conclusion, the French and Raven (1960) conceptualization of power provides a useful heuristic in describing types of power inherent in the supervisory role and will be used in the SAS model to help define the functions of supervision.

Operationalizing the Functions

Each of the functions of supervision interaction is defined in this section by using dimensions of the supervision social role and process research (see Figure 2.2). The functions are depicted by identifying the communication pattern monologic (primarily one person speaking) or dialogic (primarily two-way communication) according to the supervisor's use of interpersonal power, as described by the French and Raven (1960) classification scheme.

Monitoring and Evaluating

The professional responsibility of the supervisor is to oversee the supervisee's work and provide a formative and summative evaluation.

In training situations, the evaluation may be a formal and standardized procedure, whereas supervision that takes place between peers or in posttraining is often less explicit. In any case, the supervisor's opinion and judgment, implicit or explicit, are important.

In the SAS model, the supervisor's act of monitoring and evaluating performance is a function of supervision and distinguished from the criteria for evaluation. Criteria for evaluation are specifically defined tasks or skills required by the profession, the training program, the supervisor, and the trainee's specific learning needs (see Chapter 4 under Institutional Factors, Supervisor Factors, and Trainee Factors). Responsible supervisors are in a position to use both reward and coercive power as defined by French and Raven (1960). They are, in a sense, always monitoring because they are responsible both pedagogically and ethically for the trainee's practice.

Poulin (1994; see Research Box 4.1) found that the foundational element of supervision is evaluation. In her study, supervisors monitored trainees in their roles as counselor, student, and supervisee as well as in the relationship of trainee roles to their personal characteristics. Supervisors consistently thought about and acted on the obligation of the monitoring function as they engaged with the supervisee on a variety of supervisory tasks.

In the SAS model, the monitoring and evaluative function is restricted to instances in which the supervisor communicates judgments and evaluation of the trainee's behavior as it relates to his or her professional role. In these instances, because the reward and coercive power of the supervisor is being exercised, the hierarchy of the relationship is accentuated, and communication is largely controlled by the supervisor (i.e., unidirectional). In Transcript 2.5 (col. 3, p. 35), the supervisor communicates directly to the supervisee his judgment of the supervisee's work with the client. He is evaluating that work first somewhat positively and then negatively. The overall sense from this evaluation is that the judgment is negative, particularly because the supervisor proceeds to advise the trainee on an alternative approach.

Instructing and Advising

The instructing and advising function consists of the supervisor's providing information, opinions, and suggestions based on professional knowledge and skill. Expert and legitimate power (French & Raven, 1960) is exercised in the advising function. According to process research in supervision, this dominant pattern of interaction is an instructing and advising behavior by the supervisor followed by the trainee's agreement with or encouragement of the supervisor who is giving advice (Holloway, 1992b). Holloway and Poulin (1995) have characterized this as a "teacher-student" function.

TRANSCRIPT 2.5

Supervision Tasks and Functions

Supervision Interview	*Supervision Tasks*	*Supervision Function*
Trainee Right. Right. Now, I have some, uh, concerns that could take a while with her to, to get that across to her because . . .	The trainee expresses his concerns in his **counseling skills.**	
Supervisor That's right.		
Trainee . . . in some ways she's resistant to me.	The trainee begins to **conceptualize** the client's behavior.	
Supervisor Right. But we would say that unless you take the risk, you're wasting your time		The supervisor **advises** by giving his opinion on the trainee's conceptualization of resistance.
Trainee OK. I'm, I'm trying to get . . .		
Supervisor If you were helping her, and what you did, incidentally, was very good from one framework of therapy; that she's going to like you, and trust you, et cetera; and I say it's almost a complete waste of time; she'll get sick of it.	The supervisor focuses on **counseling skill.**	The supervisor first **supports** the trainee's counseling performance but then infers that his behavior is not right from another frame of reference. He is engaged in **monitoring** the trainee's behavior through **evaluation.**
Trainee OK.		
Supervisor You see, because you haven't really changed—help change her basic philosophy. And she can take her philosophy with dire need for love and use it toward you, Sigmund Freud, or anybody. But . . . so . . . we would want you to try to see what her basic assumptions are, and, uh . . .	The supervisor focuses on **case conceptualization** and **counseling skill.**	The supervisor **advises** the trainee on intervention with client.

This transcript is taken from the videotape series *Psychotherapy Supervision by Major Theorists,* by R. K. Goodyear. (1982). [Videotape series.] Manhattan: Kansas State University, Instructional Media Center.

Communication largely controlled by the supervisor (i.e., unidirectional) emphasizes the hierarchy of the relationship and is marked by considerable interpersonal distance. When participants are more equally matched in perceived expert power, a decreased amount of advising might result. Advising is frequently noted in the transcripts. For example, in Transcript 2.5 (col. 3, p. 35) the supervisor is giving his opinion of how the case should be conducted, and in Transcript 2.1 (p. 17) the supervisor explains to the trainee his thinking about the client's behavior and the dynamics between the client and the counselor.

Modeling

The supervisor acts as a model of professional behavior and practice, both implicitly in the supervisory relationship and explicitly by role-playing for the supervisee or client. The use of expert and referent power is relevant to this function. Expert power is based on the supervisor's demonstrating skill or knowledge for the benefit of the trainee. As a mentor, a more implicit process, the supervisor becomes a role model of professional practice and conduct. When supervisees see the supervisor as having values and attitudes similar to their own or as having the professional skills and knowledge to which they aspire, the referent power of the supervisor is significant. Communication here is largely bidirectional: interpersonal distance is reduced because the exercise of power is a collaborative process. In Transcript 2.1 (Excerpt 2, col. 3, p. 18), the modeling function is illustrated when the supervisor role-plays the counselor for the trainee. Transcript 2.2 (col. 3, pp. 22-24) is an example of the Director of Training's modeling the exercise of professional boundaries.

Consulting

The supervisor facilitates problem solving of clinical and professional situations by seeking information and opinions from the supervisee. Again the use of expert and referent power is most relevant. For effective consultation to take place, the trainee must trust and respect the supervisor enough to engage in a collaborative rather than an adversarial relationship. Communication is bidirectional and interactive as the participants collaborate on fact finding and problem solving. Often, at the beginning of each interview, the supervisor consults with the trainee about recent developments with the client's or trainee's specific agenda items for the supervision session. Transcript 2.4 (col. pp. 29-31) is an example in which the supervisor consults with the trainee about his behavior in the counseling interview as the primary function in the interview. The consulting process seems particularly appropriate because the supervisor is encouraging the trainee to self-evaluate his counseling behavior rather than making a judgment of the trainee's behavior. Consulting equalizes the power between the participants. It offers the trainee an opportunity to learn skills of self-evaluation and engages him or her in an interpersonal process that places value on judgment and intuitive expertise.

Supporting and Sharing

The supervisor supports the supervisee through empathic attention, encouragement, and constructive confrontation. Supervisors often support trainees at a deep interpersonal level by sharing their own perceptions of trainees' actions, emotions, and attitudes. This direct communication may include confrontation, which can increase the affiliation of the participants if done constructively and appropriately. Referent power is involved in exercising this function because to attribute importance to the supervisor's views on issues of a personal and interpersonal nature, the trainee must experience the supervisor as significant, respected, and trustworthy. Communication is bidirectional and interactive, and the participants are highly engaged with little interpersonal distance. Refer to Transcript 2.4 (col. 3, p. 29) and 2.3 (col. 3, pp. 27-28) for examples of the supervisor's using a supporting function to gather and clarify information about the counseling case.

Task + Function = Process

In this chapter, I have focused on two aspects of the supervisory activity—task and function—and described broad categories within each. The interrelatedness of identifying *what* is the teaching task with deciding *how* one will function to accomplish that task is known as the process of supervision. This pragmatic, heuristic approach is characterized by the presence of task and function in the ongoing interchange between supervisor and trainee (Holloway & Acker, 1988).

Other factors also influence the understanding of the supervisor's effectiveness in choosing a particular task and function. These *contextual* factors will be discussed in Chapter 4. For now, it is important to focus only on a task and function analysis of the supervision process as depicted in the process matrix of Figure 2.3.

Supervisor tasks and functions are the combination of the supervisor and trainee working together on a particular type of problem with a particular approach; in other words, what the objectives are and what subsequent teaching and learning strategies are adopted. In the transcripts in this chapter, it is possible to identify the factors of task and function and then use this information to chart them in transcripts as a graphic matrix. Hypothetically, a supervisor may engage in any of the teaching objectives with any of the functions or strategies. Realistically, there are

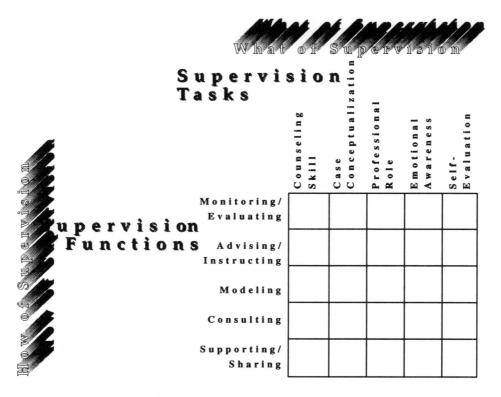

Figure 2.3. A Matrix of Supervision Process

probably some task and function matches that are more likely to occur in supervision—for example, the use of a supporting function when working with interpersonal emotional awareness or an advising function when focusing on counseling skills.

Although the deliberate choice of such matches will be influenced by certain factors, such as the trainee's experience, the client's situation, and the relationship structure between supervisor and trainee, nonetheless, the task and function can be identified in the process of the interview. Using this method of matching task and function, supervisors can analyze the effectiveness of a prior session and plan supervisory focus and strategies for subsequent sessions. The efficacy of matches between task and function in the interview can be examined because the analysis includes the trainee's immediate response to the supervisor's interventions as well as more long-term indices of trainee learning, placing the immediate discourse within the context of the ongoing teaching goals.

A few examples of using the matrix will help to demonstrate how the process of supervision can be analyzed using this heuristic tool. In Transcript 2.1 (see Figure 2.4), the cell Case Conceptualization × Advising is used by the supervisor to teach the trainee how to think about

Supervision Interview	Supervision Tasks	Supervision Function
[Trainee] Ah, well then I probably will ask...I might ask him a question or something and then he'll be kind of, a lot of time he'll say something back in a brief phrase and then kind of pick up on the story again, so it's like, you know, it's like I get attention for a minute, but it's sort like, he just sort of brushes me away and goes back into his story.	Supervisee is presenting his perception of the dynamics of the interaction of the counseling session and providing the information for case conceptualization.	
[Supervisor] OK, so you're getting caught by him telling stories to you... [Trainee] Ummm huh.	The supervisor begins to conceptualize what is happening in the interaction.	The supervisor advises the trainee of his opinion about what the dynamic is in the counseling relationship.
[Supervisor] You feel like he's, he's taking the direction away from the purpose that you have in mind or what you seem to be wanting to explore. And you feel that he is using storytelling as an avoidance technique then.	He elaborates on the case conceptualization by labeling the supervisee's interpretation of why the client is storytelling.	The supervisor advises the trainee of his opinion.
[Trainee] Yeah, I guess...I'm not completely sure what all the reasons are, why he uses stories, but that's...	The trainee is questioning whether the supervisor's interpretation is accurate.	
[Supervisor] That's the way it feels...	Supervisor extends the trainee's emotional awareness of self (i.e. trainee).	The supervisor supports the trainee's paying attention to feelings.

Figure 2.4. Process Analysis: Example 1

the client's storytelling behavior in the counseling session. Notice in this interview that the supervisor provides some support for the trainee's emotional expression (Emotional Awareness × Support). He acknowledges it and then moves on to advising the trainee how to handle the current counseling dilemma.

Read through the transcripts again, noticing this time the relationship between task and function. Then create an icon to represent the intersecting task and function as per the preceding examples. This method of analysis can be used to analyze one or several interviews with the same or different trainees. The supervisor's identification of tendencies for using certain functions or tasks, or using them in particular combinations, can be informative with respect to the supervisor's style of supervision. Specific knowledge about supervisory actions can encourage the supervisor to question or reflect on past behavior. Are the choices of task and function primarily a reflection of the supervisor's comfort with a particular style of presentation? Are some choices most frequent with a particular trainee or at a particular phase of the supervisory relationship? Do the choices of task and function facilitate the empowerment of the trainee?

Questions can be generated from the simple identification of task and function and can encourage further exploration of factors influencing the supervisor's actions. As depicted in the SAS model, numerous factors might influence supervisors' choice of learning objective and their approach to working with a supervisee. Although sometimes these factors are apparent, just as often they may be evident only at a latent, rather than manifest, level of the interaction. In the next chapter, these factors are discussed as part of the dynamic element of supervision, that of the *relationship* of supervision.

3

The Relationship of Supervision

⤴ Relationship is the dynamic element of supervision. The structure and character of the relationship embody all other factors and in turn all other factors are influenced by the relationship. The process of supervision—with *process*, defined as a "systematic series of actions directed to some end" (Stein, 1975)—is enacted within the relationship. Understanding the relationship is understanding the process because there is

> a symbiotic relationship between communication and relational development. Communication influences relational development, and in turn (or simultaneously), relational development influences the nature of the communication between parties to the relationship. (Miller, 1976, p. 15)

Each supervisor and supervisee brings to the relationship of supervision his or her own expectations of how the process will unfold. Some of these expectations will be the result of experience in being in supervision. Expectations will also come from other formal and informal relational experiences, and some will come from knowledge of supervision gained through anecdotal materials and literature. These past experiences will shape the process just as the process will contribute to the development of a relationship structure that will in turn influence uniquely the participants' engagement in the process.

In the systems approach to supervision (SAS), relationship is the container of dynamic process in which the supervisor and supervisee negotiate a personal way of using a structure of power and involvement

41

that accommodates the trainee's progression of learning. This structure becomes the basis for the process by which the trainee will acquire knowledge and skills—the empowerment of the trainee. Chapter 3 demonstrates how both the supervisor and the supervisee are responsible for establishing a relational structure that is flexible enough to accommodate the trainee's particular professional needs in an intense, collaborative learning alliance. The supervisor, however, exercises the guiding function (i.e., how the supervisor is different from the trainee) of evaluation and support within the structure of this professional relationship. In addition to being defined in the text, the relationship factors are illustrated both by transcripts of supervision interviews and by "reflected," or recall interviews of supervision. The reflected interview captures the meaning the supervisor and supervisee attribute to the supervision interaction. Participants were asked to listen to the recording of one of their supervision interviews and to comment on what was perceived as their experience or thinking at that moment in the supervision session. Both supervisors and trainees, independently and without knowledge of their partners' comments, completed the recall interview of the same session. Transcripts of both the supervision interview and the related recall interviews are presented. Column 1 contains the transcript of the supervision interview; Column 2, the supervisor and or trainee's remarks; and Column 3, the SAS analysis of the contextual factors.

There has been considerable research on the relationship and process of supervision (for reviews, see Holloway, 1992b; Russell et al., 1984). From the empirical base and practice knowledge, I have identified three essential elements:

1. interpersonal structure of the relationship—the dimensions of power and involvement;
2. phases of the relationship—relational development specific to the participants; and
3. supervisory contract—the establishment of a set of expectations for tasks and functions of supervision.

The relationship is the core of the SAS model as depicted in Figure 3.1. The moving spiral in the center of the model suggests the interrelatedness and nonhierarchical nature of the three factors: structure, phase, and contract. Next is a description of the three elements of the relationship of supervision.

Interpersonal Structure

Power and involvement are helpful constructs in understanding the nature of the supervisory relationship. Supervision is a formal

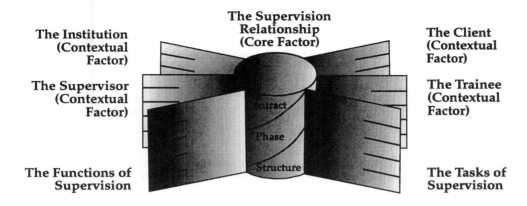

The Institution (Contextual Factor)

The Supervision Relationship (Core Factor)

The Client (Contextual Factor)

The Supervisor (Contextual Factor)

The Trainee (Contextual Factor)

The Functions of Supervision

The Tasks of Supervision

Contract

Phase

Structure

Figure 3.1. The Supervision Relationship

relationship in which the supervisor's task includes imparting expert knowledge, making judgments of trainees' performance, and acting as a gatekeeper to the profession. Formal power, or power attributed to the position, rests with the supervisor, and in this regard, the supervisory relationship is a hierarchical one. The exercise of power cannot be accomplished independently, however. The mutually influential process of relationship and the ongoing interaction between individuals allow for a shared influence to emerge. Hinde (1979) comments,

> Power is in fact rarely absolute. In the first place, it is inevitably limited by the capacities of both individuals. Second, it usually involves at most an influence by one partner on the relative probabilities of actions by the other. Third, the exercise of power is usually limited by the controlled party: the worker can strike, or seek employment elsewhere. Fourth, in many relationships one partner has power in some contexts and not in others, the power distribution being the result of negotiation between them. These two latter points indicate that power is a property of the relationship and not of one or other individual. (pp. 256-257)

It appears from Hinde's definition that power may take very different forms, depending on the personal and institutional resources available and the type of involvement of the individuals, a point of view not always given consideration.

From a Eurocentric perspective, a worldview that has dominated Western institutional structures, power has been viewed as a vehicle of control and dominance. To be powerful is to wield influence and control resources and information. In the helping professions, power has often been viewed pejoratively because the concept of control and dominance has seemingly been antithetical to the tenets of mutuality and unconditional positive regard. This interpretation limits the ability of power in constructing a mutually empowering relationship.

Dunlap and Goldman (1991), in a review of the historical roots of power in educational settings, concluded that, essentially, power has been regarded as "power over" or domination. Early work of Follett (1924/ 1951), however, introduced the idea of "power with," a concept that was pluralistic and representative of an ever-evolving process of human interaction. Her conception of power offers an alternative based on involvement and mutual influence. This basis for power is more consistent with psychotherapy and supervision, where the intent is not to control but, rather, to empower individuals to exercise self-control and determination.

Three preferred methods have been used in supervision research to describe the power of the supervisor: French and Raven's (1960) sociological typology; Strong, Hill, and Nelson's (1988) circumplex model; and Penman's (1980) communication matrix (see Research Box 3.1). French and Raven's conceptualization of power (see Chapter 2) does not fully operationalize the involvement of the participants, whereas the other schemes include power and involvement as equally important in the relational structure.

Leary's (1957) circumplex model, on which both the Strong et al. (1988) and Penman (1980) classification systems are based, provides a framework to place power in a relational system that includes an involvement or affiliation dimension that, in his view, every relationship has by definition. Involvement might also be referred to as intimacy that includes "attachments," the degree to which each person uses the other as a source of self-confirmation (Miller & Rogers, 1987). Affiliation influences the exercise and effect of power in the dyadic relationship and is crucial in creating more individualized versus more role-bound relationships. Both participants determine the distribution of power or the degree of attachment to one another. "Mutual perception and acceptance of the degree and distribution of influence potential in the relationship represents a major dynamic determining the nature of the relationship" (Morton, Alexander, & Altman, 1976, p. 119).

The degree of relational influence potential will determine the degree of social bonding and thus the persuasiveness of the relationship. As the relationship develops, the participants will use more personally relevant interpersonal, psychological, and differentiated information to make predictions of each others' behavior and thus reduce interpersonal uncertainty. The basis of mutuality adjusts to these new levels of personal knowledge.

> Where mutuality is defined as a consensus about the definition of that relationship between the participants and that mutuality is a generic characteristic of the interpersonal relationship itself . . . relationships develop as they redefine the basis of the mutuality. These are called relationship crises that might entail periods of non-mutuality as the relationship is being redefined. If a new definition of mutuality cannot be attained then the relationship may terminate. (Morton et al., 1976, p. 105)

Research Box 3.1

Power and Involvement in Supervision Relationships

A comprehensive review of the observation methods and analyses of microanalytic studies in supervision appears in Holloway and Poulin (1995).

In the first microanalytic studies, researchers were interested in discovering if supervision was a process distinct from counseling. They used content analysis schemes drawn from classroom interaction and therapeutic process studies to determine whether supervisors used different types of messages or different proportions of the same messages in counseling and supervision interactions (Holloway & Wolleat, 1981; Lambert, 1974; Rickards, 1984; Wedeking & Scott, 1976). Lambert (1974) and Wedeking and Scott (1976) directly examined this question by comparing supervisors' behaviors in counseling and supervision interviews. Rickards (1984) and Holloway and Wolleat (1981) described supervisors' and trainees' verbal behaviors in supervision interviews. The results of all four of these studies indicated that the supervisor spends more time providing information, opinions, and suggestions, that is, task-oriented behavior, than giving emotional support or attending to the trainee's emotional life. These results contrasted with findings in counseling interviews where social-emotional behaviors were more prevalent. Investigators concluded that supervision was a process distinct from counseling.

Studies have examined patterns of verbal behavior across the life span of the supervision relationship. Wedeking and Scott (1976) found that supervisor messages changed from the beginning to the final stages of the relationship. Supervisors spent more time with informative verbal behaviors in the beginning session than in the final sessions. Supervisors used rapport-building strategies and structured the interview more

in the initial part of beginning interviews, whereas these strategies were more prevalent in the middle of the interviews in final sessions of the relationship. The association of relationship phase with supervisory behaviors has been investigated in case study designs using microanalytic techniques (Friedlander, Siegel, & Brenock, 1989; Martin, Goodyear, & Newton, 1987; Strozier, Kivlighan, & Thoresen, 1993). Martin et al. (1987) used an intensive, longitudinal case study approach to examine participants' judgments of supervisory events and the characteristics of the discourse in supervision. The microanalytic data indicated that the supervisee decreased her proportional use of deferential messages across the relationship.

The introduction of the Penman (1980) classification scheme to supervision research heralded the use of a content analysis system that could be understood from the larger perspective of relational qualities. The Penman scheme is based on the interpersonal theory of personality (Leary, 1957), and categories are arranged to provide information about the dimensions of power and involvement in a relationship. Three studies in supervision have used this classification scheme (Holloway, Freund, Gardner, Nelson, & Walker, 1989; Martin et al., 1987; Nelson & Holloway, 1990). In an effort to delineate the predominant verbal patterns of supervision, Martin et al. (1987) also found that the process of supervision largely involved the supervisor's provision of advice, information, opinions, and suggestions, with few supportive or social-emotional statements. These base rate values and high proportion of transitions from supervisor advice giving to trainee's conceding messages confirmed findings from other content analyses of

Research Box 3.1

Continued

supervision (Holloway et al., 1989; Holloway & Wampold, 1983; Nelson & Holloway, 1990). Holloway et al. (1989) used a sequential analysis technique in a multiple-case-study format. This study introduced the concept of examining larger systems of interactions by statistically defining patterns, circuits, and systems of interaction between supervisor and trainee. Findings confirmed existing evidence that supervisors and trainees predominantly engage in a complementary teacher-learner interactional pattern, specifically that the significant pattern across supervisors of differing theoretical orientations was the supervisor's giving advice and the trainee's agreeing or encouraging the supervisor in this activity. Although supervisors differed even with the same trainee in the type of involvement they sought in supervision, they consistently demonstrated use of high-power messages of varying types. The supervisor was again in the superordinate position and the trainee, the subordinate. Friedlander et al.'s (1989) study of parallel process in supervision also revealed that there was little competitive symmetry or struggle for control in supervisory process, and the primary verbal patterns were complementary in that the supervisor tended to use one-up communications with the trainee more often than one-down. Strozier et al. (1993), although finding greater instances of support and affectively oriented material than previous studies, confirmed the findings that the supervisor holds the "relational control" in the interaction.

In a field study, Nelson and Holloway (1990) used a group design to examine the relationship of gender and role to patterns of interaction between the supervisor and trainee. Message categories in this study were combined to reflect the power structure of the interaction. Thus, deferential and ascending patterns were examined both from supervisor to trainee and vice versa. These high-power/low-power patterns were predominantly supervisor-advising messages followed by trainee agreement. The prevalence of this pattern confirms previous evidence of a teacher-to-student role in supervision. Gender of the student, however, appears to influence the supervisor's interactional behavior, and female students are not encouraged to break out of this deferential, subordinate role as male trainees appear to be.

Summary of Immediate Outcomes. What have microanalytic studies contributed to our pragmatic knowledge of supervision? Studies of interactional processes in supervision have contributed to our understanding of the sequence of events in supervision and the characteristics of the relationship as described by the verbal messages of the participants. The primary conclusions that can be drawn from the content analysis research are that (a) supervision and counseling processes are distinct; (b) there are significant changes in discourse across the relationship; (c) there is a predominant pattern of verbal behaviors that is analogous to teacher-student interactions; and (d) the relationship structure of supervision has hierarchical characteristics (Holloway & Poulin, 1995).

Content analysis of supervision has revealed that supervisors and trainees primarily enact through conversation the formal, hierarchical structure of a teacher-student relationship. Deviations from the standard superordinate-to-subordinate relational patterns appeared to be related to trainee experience level, supervisor orientation, gender, and the phase of the supervisory relationship.

Research Box 3.1

Continued

It must be noted that with the exception of Holloway et al. (1989) these micro-analytic studies have studied therapists-in-training rather than experienced professionals. Nonetheless, within the context of graduate training, these findings have informed us of the immediate effects of the supervisor's efforts at influencing or aiding the trainee to learn the skills of the profession, along with the trainee's immediate responses to these verbal strategies. In other words, these outcomes provide information about the immediate efficacy of specific verbal interventions by the supervisor.

Microanalytic techniques, however, have assessed conversational strategies primarily through the structural analysis of discourse. This approach has limited our knowledge of the supervision process to (a) the structural and topical message characteristics of the coding scheme and (b) the immediacy of act-by-act analysis. Consequently, the implication for strategy in supervision is, in the first case, restricted to what kinds of messages supervisors and trainees use and, in the second case, the relationship of a message to the immediately preceding message. The restriction of the contextual information to antecedent and subsequent acts prevents understanding of the development of strategies over the interview or relationship. Clearly, both supervisors' and supervisee's choice of teaching and learning strategies are based on the cumulative information gained throughout the conversation. How earlier events in conversation influence the choice of a strategy remains largely unknown. These studies pave the way, however, for future studies of process and outcome in supervision in that final outcomes—for example, the performance of the trainee in therapy sessions—can be related to the supervisor-trainee interactions within supervision.

Leary's (1957) theory of interpersonal relations undergirds the SAS interpersonal structure of the supervision relationship (power through involvement). Although the relationship takes on a unique character that can be defined by power and involvement, the participants bring their own history of interpersonal style. These interpersonal histories influence how the supervisor and trainee ultimately present themselves in forming their new relationship. Self-presentation is an element of supervisor and trainee factors; however, at this point, the focus is the influence of relationship on the action and thinking of the participants during the supervisory process.

In Transcript 4.1 (col. 2, p. 67), the relationship between the supervisor and trainee has been strained during an earlier exchange, and there is considerable reflection on the trainee's part about the supervisor's power in the relationship. She refers to his use of expert power when he substantiates his claims of knowledge by referring to his amount of experience. Later in the interview (Transcript 4.1, col. 2, p. 69), she remarks that he is the "wise professor" and she is only the student.

TRANSCRIPT **3.1**

Relationship Factors

Supervision Interview

Supervisor Well, it might be good for you to listen to this or for us to listen to part of it together. That way . . . be- cause, ah, I could point out to you how it occurs and you might say, "That's fine" or you might say, "yeah," and I don't like it and want to change that way. It may coincide with periods when you think, "I wish to hell she'd [client] do something positive for a change."

Trainee [Laughter]

Supervisor So it might be worth our looking at this tape in that way be- cause there are those dis- tinct, you know, excessive periods where it alter- nates in that way. Would you like to do it?

Trainee Yeah, why don't we do that; that might be real interesting.

Supervisor We can't do it today.

Trainee No, we can't.

Supervisor But, ah, we could do it the next time.

Trainee OK.

Recall Interview

Supervisor I always take special care to test out if I am alienating the supervisee. I really didn't want the trainee to feel I'm putting her down for this but I also wanted her to recognize that it is a problem in her relation- ship with any client. But at the same time, I want to use whatever is good in our relationship to make it acceptable.

Trainee Umm, the last part, this little interaction part here, lays the scene for the whole of the next supervisory session that we had together and probably the subsequent sessions. At the time when my supervisor made those comments I didn't feel particularly . . . I felt a bit criticized, but it seemed real appro- priate because that made sense to me, what he de- scribed in my behavior.

Sas Analysis

The supervisor is very conscious of the trainee's **learning needs** as well as his possible personal reac- tion at being criticized. The supervisor depends on the character of the **su- pervisory relationship (structure)** to make his suggestion more palat- able. Nonetheless, he ne- gotiates with the trainee on taking this strategy for learning in the next ses- sion **(supervisory con- tract).**

The trainee recognizes on reflection the importance of this **contract** that they have made to examine a particular aspect of his be- havior. Also note that he did not respond defen- sively in spite of feeling somewhat criticized. He references the **phase of the relationship** as rele- vant to his emotional re- sponse to the supervisor.

Unpublished supervision interview. Based on an actual transcript altered to protect the confi- dentiality of the participants.

Here, the exercise of expert power, when it is perceived as being withheld by the supervisor, is a source of friction in the relationship. When he later responds by telling her directly his suggestion, she switches her view almost immediately and perceives the interaction as a powerful learning experience.

Phases of the Relationship

Although the process research in supervision describes the structural characteristics of discourse, it has not examined the underlying rules that evolve in the relationship and, for the most part, has not examined the evolution of the relationship across time (two exceptions are Friedlander et al., 1989, and Martin et al., 1987). The development of noninterpersonal to interpersonal relationships, however, has been of considerable interest in the social-psychological literature.

In the development of informal relationships, two factors have consistently been observed. First, as a relationship evolves, the participants rely less on general cultural and social information and more on idiosyncratic information of the participant. Predictions regarding the other persons' behaviors come from information that differentiates the person from other members of his or her corresponding social group. The other becomes unique in the eyes of the perceiver, and the relationship is said to have moved from a noninterpersonal to an interpersonal one (Miller, 1976).

As the relationship evolves to an interpersonal one, there is a process of reduced uncertainty. After initial interactions, participants come to know one another better and are thus more accurate in their predictions about the other person's reactions to their messages. With decreased uncertainty, they are better able to use control strategies and communicative modes that will reduce the level of conflict in the relationship. Participants also become increasingly more vulnerable and more willing to risk self-disclosure, whereas in the initial stages, genuine self-disclosure is seldom observed.

The following are three principles related to the progression toward a more intimate relationship (Morton et al., 1976):

1. change in the relationship occurs because of the need to increase or decrease the likelihood of attaining a reward;
2. the definition of relational change assumes a decision that change can be made by one or both persons in the relationship; and
3. changes in the relationship are caused by changes in the content of communications between relational partners. People can escalate

their relationship by providing information about themselves or seeking more information about the other.

These findings are interesting in light of Rabinowitz, Heppner, and Roehlke's (1986) supervision study. They found that whether advanced or beginning level, supervisees sought to reduce ambiguity and increase support and assurance from their supervisor at the beginning of the relationship. Advanced trainees, although still seeking initial support, more quickly desired experiences that included personal challenge and confrontation regarding their own interpersonal behaviors in counseling and supervision. Although some of these findings have been interpreted to reflect a developmental shift in the trainee, they might also be viewed as indicating a natural development in a relationship to attempt to reduce uncertainty as interactional patterns become established. Extrapolating from the friendship studies, it could be suggested that the advanced supervisees, having a blueprint for the relationship of supervision from previous experience, were able to truncate the discomfiture of uncertainty and resultant need for reassurance by relying on known general expectancies for supervisory roles. Thus, they could move more quickly to establish specific expectancies of an interpersonal (as opposed to noninterpersonal) relationship by self-disclosing personal aspects of self-relevancy to their counseling performance. On the other hand, the beginning-level trainee might still be discovering the role expectations of the supervisory relationship and must clarify these general cultural, social, and formal rules before moving to an interpersonal relationship.

The development of an interpersonal relationship promotes a focus on shared idiosyncratic rules created just for that particular relationship, even though supervision is a formal, professional relationship defined by certain relational rules and is more role bound than friendship relations. Initially, supervision provides a general expectancy base for certain interactive behaviors; as the relationship develops, however, it is individualized around the learning needs of the trainee and the teaching approaches of the supervisor. The participants will need to learn these idiosyncratic, reciprocal rules in the interactive process (Miller & Rogers, 1987). Rabinowitz's et al. (1986) findings that regardless of the trainee's level of experience, there was consistently a need for support at the beginning of a new supervisory relationship are consistent with the view that uncertainty about role expectations will be a part of the initial learning in a relationship.

In and of itself, phase does not determine the level of involvement in the relationship. Individual differences also play a part. Altman and Taylor (1973) have named the process of providing more personal information "social penetration," which is significantly affected by both phase of relationship and personal characteristics. Some individuals, because of their personal or cultural history, have a predisposition to

Table 3.1

Phases of the Relationship

Beginning phase
    Clarifying relationship with supervisor
    Establishing of supervision contract
    Supporting teaching interventions
    Developing competencies
    Developing treatment plans

Mature phase
    Increasing individual nature of relationship, becoming less role bound
    Increasing social bonding and influence potential
    Developing skills of case conceptualization
    Increasing self-confidence and self-efficacy in counseling
    Confronting personal issues as they relate to professional performance

Terminating phase
    Understanding connections between theory and practice in relation to particular
      clients
    Decreasing need for direction from supervisor

---

reveal themselves, whereas others are more reluctant. There is evidence that still other factors may influence the course of supervision. For example, Tracey, Ellickson, and Sherry's (1989) research demonstrated that both the individual presentational style of the trainee (defined as "reactance potential") and the urgency of the client's problem (whether a suicide threat or not) had a significant effect on the participants' need for a more structured and supportive approach. Ultimately, research studies demonstrate the absolute need to consider all of the contextual factors that influence supervisory behaviors in devising any strategy in supervision.

Notice in Transcript 4.1 (col. 2, p. 69) the trainee's reflection on the relationship with her supervisor. She puts her concern regarding the supervisor's feedback in the context of the phase of the relationship. She implies in her reflection that the relationship's not being new influenced her ability to understand the supervisor's intentions and thus decrease her feelings of defensiveness.

SAS has described the relationship phases of supervision in a way that reflects the convergence of findings in friendship research (Berger & Calabrese, 1975; Morton et al., 1976) and supervision relationships (Mueller & Kell, 1972; Rabinowitz et al., 1986). I have used Mueller and Kell's (1972) conceptualization of the beginning, mature, and termination phases of the supervisory relationship to provide a framework for the description (see Table 3.1).

The Supervisory Contract

Each supervisor and supervisee will have idiosyncratic expectations of roles and function in supervision. Some will be the result of experience in engaging in supervision, and others will be more directly related to the personal and cultural characteristics of both participants. As in any working relationship, the clarity of these expectations directly affects the relationship and the establishment of specific learning goals. Because the trainee is in a position of relatively lesser evaluative and expert power, the supervisor has a responsibility to ensure that the trainee is clearly informed of the evaluative structure of the relationship, the expectancies and goals for supervision, the criteria for evaluation, and the limits of confidentiality in supervision.

Research on the nature of the relationship expectancies and needs is considerable. Much of this research has used self-report, paper-and-pencil instruments to access participants' perceptions of the quality and purpose of the supervision. In practice settings, the Supervisory Styles Questionnaire (SSQ; Friedlander & Ward, 1984), the Learning Alliance Inventory (Efstation, Patton, & Kardash, 1990), and the Supervisor Reaction Personal Reaction Scale and the Trainee Personal Reaction Scale (Holloway & Wampold, 1983, 1986) can be useful to the supervisor in determining the expectancies of the trainee regarding focus on task, personal self-disclosure, degree of involvement, and level of trust (see Research Box 3.2).

Inskipp and Proctor (1989) have identified the contract as critical to establishing a way of being together in the supervisory relationship. Not only do the participants negotiate specific tasks, but they also define the parameters of the relationship. The negotiation of norms, rules, and commitments at the beginning of any relationship can reduce uncertainty and move the involvement to a level of trust that will promote the degree of vulnerability needed for the task to be done. This clarification sets up both content and relational characteristics to be expected in the relationship and establishes a trajectory for types of interactions in which the supervisor and supervisee will engage. The supervisor, by initiating the contract, is dealing directly with the inherent uncertainty of the system. By acting openly and purposefully, the supervisor increases the probability that both participants will behave congruently with established expectations (Miller & Rogers, 1987). More important, the supervisee will receive an opportunity to participate in the construction of the relationship.

The supervisor must be alert to the changing character of the relationship and thereafter initiate discussion on renewed goals and relational expectations. Not only will the trainee's learning needs change as experience increases or clients develop, but also his or her increasing skill and interpersonal confidence will influence issues of relational control. Ongoing negotiation of topics and processes is built

Research Box 3.2

Measuring the Supervision Relationship

There are very few instruments that have been developed specifically for the measurement of the supervisory relationship. The majority of instruments used to assess the quality of the supervisory relationship have been adopted from counseling research. For instance, prominent in the early literature were studies that used the facilitative conditions (Carkhuff & Berenson, 1967; Truax & Carkhuff, 1967), the Barrett-Lennard Relationship Inventory (BLRI; Barrett-Lennard, 1962), and the Counselor Rating Form (CRF; Barak & LaCrosse, 1975) to describe the relationship. The importance of having measurement devices that are specific to the supervisory context has been recognized in the ensuing years (for reviews, see Hansen, Robins, & Grimes, 1982; Holloway, 1984; Lambert 1980). Three instruments that measure supervisory relationship characteristics have been developed: the Supervisor Personal Reaction Scale (SPRS) and Trainee Personal Reaction Scale (TPRS; Holloway & Wampold, 1986); the Supervisory Styles Inventory (SSI; Friedlander & Ward, 1984); and the Supervisory Working Alliance Inventory (SWAI; Efstation et al., 1990).

The SPRS was originally developed by Sundland and Feinberg (1972) as an adaptation of Ashby, Ford, Guerney, and Guerney's (1957) Therapist and Client Personal Reaction Scales. Subsequently, Holloway and Wampold (1983, 1986) developed the TPRS and factor analyzed the SPRS and TPRS to yield a 12-item multifactor scale to measure (a) Judgment of Other, (b) Judgment of Self, and (c) Level of Comfort in the supervisory interaction. Confirmatory factor analysis with supervisory dyads of differing theoretical orientation and trainee experience levels are needed to improve the psychometric qualities of these scales.

The SSI has the most adequate reliability and validity characteristics. There are two versions of the scale—one to be completed by the trainee to describe supervisory characteristics and one to be completed by the supervisor to describe his or her own behavior in supervision. Friedlander and Ward (1984) conducted a series of studies that revealed three factors describing the perceptions of heterogeneous samples of trainees and supervisors: Attractiveness; Interpersonal Sensitivity; and Task Orientation. These scales have received considerable use in describing supervisory relationships since their appearance in the literature (for a review, see Worthington, 1987) and provide an excellent example of the construction of an instrument specific for supervision.

Efstation et al.'s (1990) development of an inventory to measure the relationship in supervision represents the latest effort in establishing a reliable and supervision-specific instrument. Influenced by the extensive work on the working alliance in counseling and the probable importance of the relationship in supervision process (Holloway, 1987, 1988), the authors constructed two parallel forms of a 30-item inventory that would reflect the supervisors' and supervisees' judgment of the supervisory relationship. There were three orthogonal factors for the supervisor version: Client Focus; Rapport; and Identification. Two factors emerged for the trainee version, Rapport and Client Focus. This instrument will be a valuable resource in uncovering the different emphases in the relationship across supervisors and trainees of varying experience levels and in different clinical contexts.

Perceptions of the Relationship and Outcome Measures. A number of studies have examined the relationship between characteristics of the supervisory relationship, participants' satisfaction, and supervisee learning. Examples of early work in this area are studies by Hansen and Barker (1964) and Hansen (1965).

Research Box 3.2

Continued

The first study's (Hansen & Barker, 1964) findings indicated that supervisees who rated the relationship high on the BLRI (Barrett-Lennard, 1962) had higher levels of experiencing in supervision as measured by Gendlin's Experiencing Scale (Gendlin, 1962). This finding was not consistent with the supervisors' perceptions, however, because in only one supervisor group was there a positive correlation between level of experiencing and the supervisor's rating of the relationship. The second study (Hansen, 1965) examined trainees' expectations of the supervisory relationship before and after their experience in supervision as measured by the BLRI. The trainees did not expect the degree of empathy, support, and congruency they experienced from their supervisors, because they had feared the evaluation component as an overriding supervisory purpose.

Recent studies have expanded the search for relationship characteristics that may be related to trainee and supervisor outcome variables. Friedlander, Keller, Peca-Baker, and Olk (1986), in an analogue study designed to investigate role demands in the supervisory relationship, examined the relationship of a disagreement on intervention strategy between supervisor and trainee to trainees' anxiety level, self-statements regarding experience of conflict, and plans for a counseling interview. Trainees' self-efficacy expectations were used as a covariate. They found that planning performance of beginning-level counselors did not appear to be affected when conflict situations were present. However, there was a significant inverse relationship between anxiety and performance, and anxiety and self-efficacy.

Kennard, Stewart, and Gluck (1987) were interested in what variables in the supervisory relationship might best predict congruence in the supervisors' and supervisees' perceptions of the quality of the relationship. The participants represented supervisory experiences at first practicum through internship training levels. The findings suggest that trainees who reported positive supervisory experiences were evaluated more highly by supervisors than trainees who reported negative supervisory experience on two dimensions: interest in the supervisor's feedback and the supervisor's suggestions for professional development. Trainees who reported a positive experience rated their supervisors significantly higher on supportiveness and on instructional and interpretative competence than did the negative-experience group. Supervisors' self-perceptions as confrontational and instructional in supervision were significant variables in the type of experience reported as well as match in theoretical orientation between supervisor and trainee.

In a recent study, Carey, Williams, and Wells (1988) examined the relevancy of Strong's (1968) social influence model to trainees' judgments of the supervisory relationship (as measured by the Supervisor Rating Form; Heppner & Handley, 1982) and trainees' performance (as measured by the Counselor Evaluation Rating Scale [CERS]; Myrick & Kelly, 1971). The investigators asked ongoing supervisory dyads to participate after they had completed at least six sessions. Trustworthiness of the supervisor proved to be related significantly to all CERS scales and accounted for larger proportions of variance in relationship judgments than did expertness and attractiveness. Furthermore, trustworthiness was related to trainee performance in counseling. The results supported previous research in this area by Dodenhoff (1981), Heppner and Handley (1982), and Friedlander and Snyder (1983). An important element of this study is the inclusion of trainee counseling performance as an outcome variable in supervision research.

Table 3.2

Dimensions of the Supervision Interview

Framing a context for the discussion of the supervisory material
Determining a focal point for the discussion
Identifying a teaching-learning goal within this context
Choosing a strategy appropriate for the teaching goal and the context in which
  supervisor and trainee are working
Evaluating the appropriateness of the goal and the effectiveness of the teaching
  and learning.

SOURCE: Poulin (1994).

on the initial contract for teaching and learning and the quality of relationship that the participants have built. Poulin's (1994; see Research Box 4.1) dimensional analysis identified five primary dimensions that supervisors attended to in their sessions (see Table 3.2).

Although Poulin's (1994) findings were based on individual interviews, these tasks are relevant to the overall context and goals of any particular supervisory relationship. The supervision session often begins with the supervisor's asking the trainee what he or she would like to discuss—a negotiation of the topic of conversation. Although there may be shifts in direction throughout the course of the interview, these are often points of subtle negotiation between the participants. In Transcript 3.1 (p. 48), the supervisor and trainee are discussing the way in which they will work together for the next session. Notice how the supervisor uses his understanding of the relationship to judge the trainee's response and openness to examining material that might be difficult.

The relationship contains the supervisory process. It can be described by the terms of contract, phase, and relationship. However, there are factors that have been related to the formation of relationship and the efficacy of supervision. These factors I have named *contextual factors*. They are described in Chapter 4 through an analysis of supervision interviews and, in some cases, of participants' comments on their supervisory behavior.

4

Contextual Factors of Supervision

℘ In Chapter 2, the fundamental elements of strategic supervision were described as task and function. They can be pictorially represented as two surfaces that cross to create a process matrix of supervision. In Chapter 3, the relationship was discussed as the "container" of the supervision process. In this chapter, I will describe contextual factors of supervision—conditions related empirically and practically to the supervisor's and supervisee's choice of task and function and the formation of the relationship (Holloway & Acker, 1988). These factors include the supervisor, the trainee, the client, and the institution. The description of these factors completes the Systems Approach to Supervision (SAS) model (see Figure 4.1).

Whereas task and function are inferred from the process of communication, contextual factors are sometimes not obviously differentiated from the actual interactional process. In addition to the intentions of their own messages, participants in an interaction perceive and understand their own and the other person's messages "inside their heads" as they engage in the conversation. Factors that might influence information processing and decision making in supervision must be inferred by the observer. Although such inferential information is useful, it is different from information that might be gained from asking supervisors or trainees to reflect on their own or the other's actions.

Schon's writings (1983) have focused attention on the value of the "thinking-in-action" of the expert practitioner. Because supervisors often make judgments based on *tacit knowledge* (Polanyi, 1967)—that

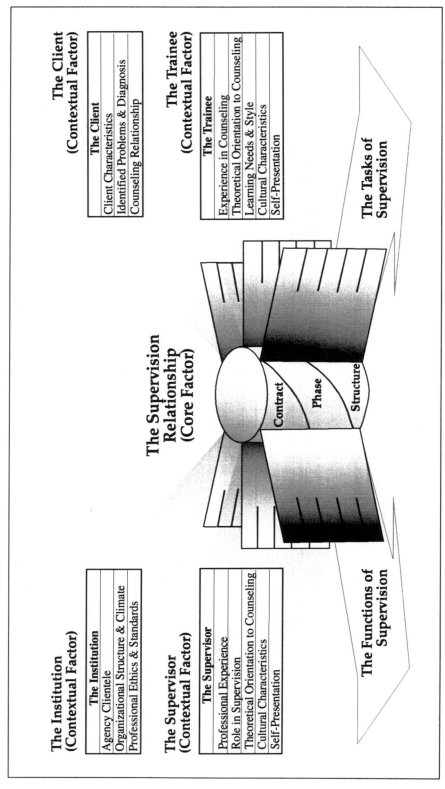

The Institution (Contextual Factor)

The Institution
Agency Clientele
Organizational Structure & Climate
Professional Ethics & Standards

The Supervisor (Contextual Factor)

The Supervisor
Professional Experience
Role in Supervision
Theoretical Orientation to Counseling
Cultural Characteristics
Self-Presentation

The Client (Contextual Factor)

The Client
Client Characteristics
Identified Problems & Diagnosis
Counseling Relationship

The Trainee (Contextual Factor)

The Trainee
Experience in Counseling
Theoretical Orientation to Counseling
Learning Needs & Style
Cultural Characteristics
Self-Presentation

The Supervision Relationship (Core Factor)

Contract

Phase

Structure

The Tasks of Supervision

The Functions of Supervision

Figure 4.1. The Systems Model of Supervision: Tasks, Functions, and Contextual Factors

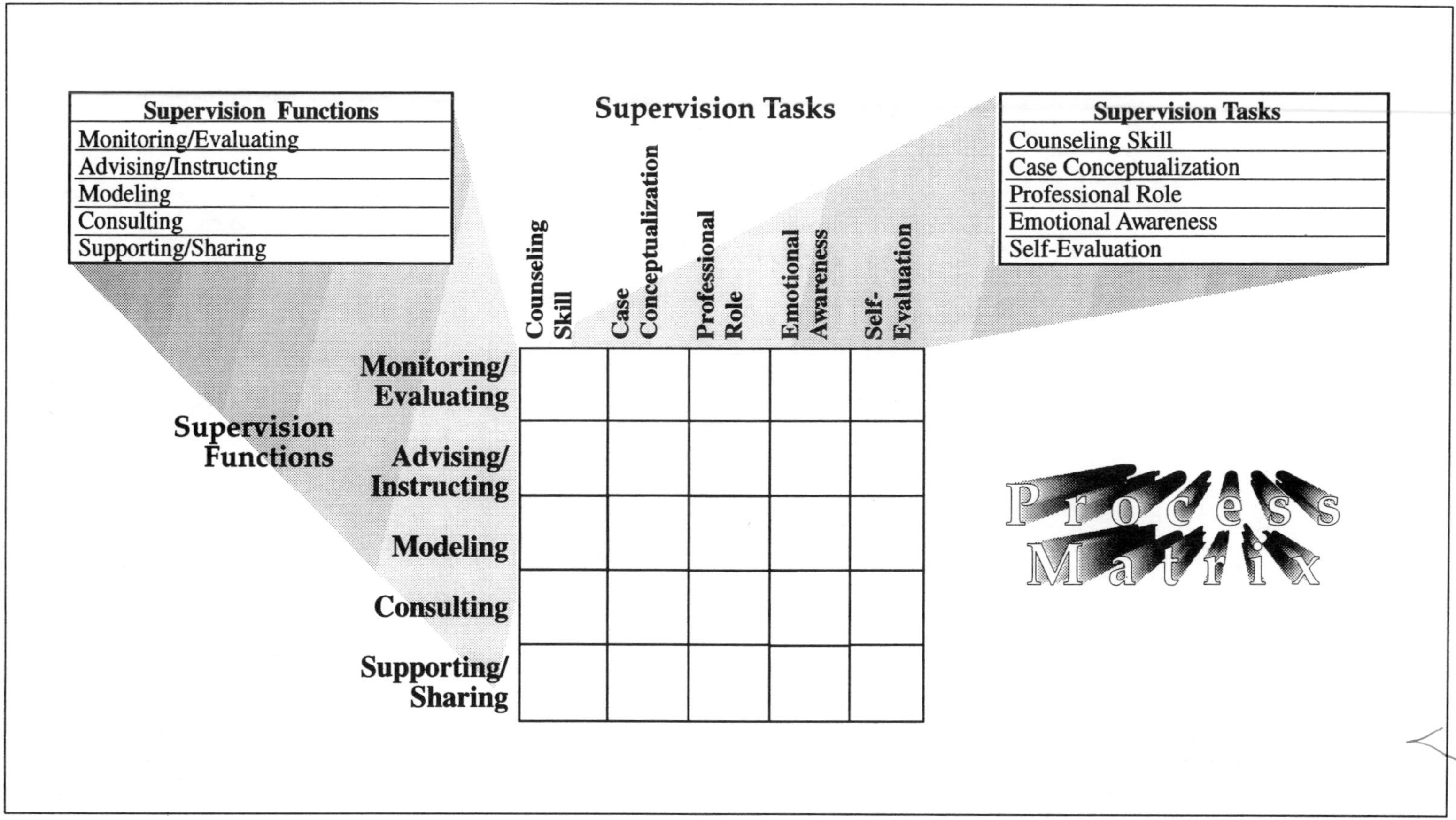

Figure 4.1. The Systems Model of Supervision: Tasks, Functions, and Contextual Factors (Continued)

Research Box 4.1

Supervisor's Work in Supervision

Poulin (1994) used dimensional analysis, a qualitative method in grounded theory (Schatzman, 1991), to examine the interviews and recall interviews of four expert supervisors working with one or two trainees of different levels of training experience. The dimensional analysis was used as an interpretative method to reveal the way in which supervisors construe their work in supervision. Poulin (1994) addressed her inquiry to three questions regarding the thinking of expert supervisors. What do supervisors notice? How do they come to direct their attention to the particular aspects within the supervision domain? What do supervisors do with what they notice to effect the work of supervision?

The findings in regard to the first question reflect those factors that make up the domain of supervision. The supervisee was the primary target of the supervisor's attention and was considered from the perspective of three primary roles: a person, a counselor, and a student. The supervisor attended to the supervisee's interpersonal style and personal interests as relevant to *person* of the supervisee, to counseling performance and comportment as relevant to the *counselor* role, and to his or her thinking abilities as reflected in the supervisee's thinking about and asking

questions about the work of counseling. The client was considered by the supervisor in three primary ways: (a) therapeutic issues and needs; (b) progress in counseling; (c) patterns of affect and behavior. The supervisor considered his or her own work in supervision, including reflections on feelings, performance, intention or goals, and strategies. The fourth factor of attention was the interactions of each of the other three factors. For example, the supervisor may attend to the relationship between himself or herself and the supervisee, client, or both or perhaps to the relationship between the supervisee and the client or perhaps all three. These findings are similar to the factors identified in the empirical and practice literature of supervision and introduced in the SAS model.

The findings relevant to the second question of the study illuminated those aspects of supervision that pull the supervisor's attention to the four primary factors. Poulin (1994) has suggested that "patterns may be recognized as repetition of a single element or a constellation of related elements; these patterns may be based either upon observations made across many individuals, or observations made of a specific individual—or, in the case of specific interaction, individuals—across time"

is, recognition or perception of what is "right" or "wrong" in practice—it seems important to assess such a knowledge base. Schon (1983) has discussed the possibility of describing tacit knowledge through a process of "reflection-in-action." For example, the supervisor can reflect on the values, strategies, and assumptions inherent in judgments of the supervisee's performance and thus more clearly guide the supervisee as well as uncover the "inside-the-head" thinking of a more experienced clinician. By examining the "thinking behind the words of supervision," the way in which these factors influence the supervisor's

Research Box 4.1

Continued

(p. 120). Additionally, supervisors notice different types of discrepancies in the patterns that might be generally categorized as discrepancies of (a) commission, (b) omission, (c) gradation, and (d) incongruency.

Finally, in seeking answers to the last question relevant to the actual work of supervision across time, Poulin (1994) identified five primary tasks: (a) framing a context for the immediate work, (b) determining a focal point to guide the inquiry, (c) identifying goals for the supervision immediately and in the long run, (d) choosing a supervisory strategy to achieve the goals, and (e) evaluating the process and outcome of the supervisory work. The most fundamental dimension of the supervisor's work in supervision is the evaluation of the supervisee. Although it isn't necessarily the focal point of the manifest conversation, it is always a basis for the assessment of the ongoing activity of supervision. The supervisor's attention to the supervisee's learning rests on two primary dimensions: the interpersonal and intellectual functioning of the supervisee. These dimensions guide the supervisor's focus and strategy in his or her work. The evaluation of the supervisee on these two dimensions influences the supervisor's focus on the intra- and interpersonal process of the supervisee or the supervisee's intellectual and conceptual understanding of the client.

Conceptualized broadly, the supervisor's evaluative efforts drive the supervisory process; these supervisors perform formative evaluations in the moment-to-moment exchange with supervisees. Based on assessment of various aspects of the primary dimensions of supervision over time, contexts are framed, focal points are determined, goals are identified, and strategies are chosen. As these processes occur, their consequences are evaluated, affecting further choices and decisions whose influencing factors and consequences, in turn, are assessed. Evaluation as practiced by these supervisors covers a wide range of outcomes, or consequences, across both the supervision and counseling contexts; the supervisor appears most likely to make evaluations based on the supervisee's in-session supervisory behaviors. The evaluative processes of these supervisors appear to be grounded in the recognition of both patterns and discrepancies relative to expectations and based on either immediate aspects of experience or comparison with similar situations in the past (Poulin, 1994, p. 124).

or trainee's immediate responses can be identified. Poulin (1994) used dimensional analysis, a qualitative method (Schatzman, 1991), to examine and recall interviews of four expert supervisors. Her analysis revealed that supervisors focus their attention on themselves, the supervisee, the client, and the relationships between all of these players in their various roles. Although the SAS model was not developed directly from this research, the contextual factors of SAS concur with these empirical findings (see Research Box 4.1).

In addition to being defined in the text, contextual factors are illustrated both by transcripts of supervision interviews and by reflected interviews of supervision. The reflected interview captures the meaning that the supervisor and supervisee attribute to the supervision interaction. These interviews are presented in the same format as in Chapter 3. Column 1 contains the transcript of the supervision interview; Column 2, the supervisor and/or trainee's remarks; and Column 3, the SAS analysis of the contextual factors. Notice that the words in boldface type refer throughout to various dynamics of the SAS model. Please refer to Figure 4.1 to explore the relationship of each bolded phrase to the model as a whole.

I have chosen to organize the transcripts by interview rather than by factors, to enhance the context of the dialogue. Several factors, however, are illustrated in any given interview and thus necessitate reading certain sections out of sequence. Note that some transcripts include excerpts that are not contiguous (designated by numbering the excerpts within the transcript). Read through each transcript in its entirety to become familiar with the context and flow, and then refer to it more specifically, as indicated in the text, for illustrations of the factors being discussed.

Supervisor Factors

The ideal supervisor has been described as a person who exhibits high levels of empathy, understanding, unconditional positive regard, flexibility, concern, attention, investment, curiosity, and openness (Carifio & Hess, 1987). Although such personal qualities are valuable in any relationship, these descriptors focus almost entirely on the intra- and interpersonal characteristics of an individual. They implicitly suggest that supervisors are born and not made. All individuals bring to supervision their own interpersonal characteristics, knowledge, abilities, and cultural values. Even so, supervisors express these characteristics uniquely as the foundation on which the supervisory role is built. Supervisors can enhance their own interpersonal style by the manner in which they use their repertoire of interpersonal skills and clinical knowledge to be deliberate, systematic, and relevant in their professional role.

Early researchers of supervision focused on determining the importance of supervisors' use of facilitative conditions in the supervisory relationship. More recently, gender, theoretical orientation, and experience level have been found to be related to trainee satisfaction with supervision and with supervisors' planning behaviors, in-session verbal behaviors, and preferred interpersonal power bases (for reviews, see Holloway, 1992b; Russell et al., 1984).

In SAS, five factors have been identified in the empirical or conceptual literature as relevant to the supervisor's performance: (a) professional experience in counseling and supervision; (b) expectations concerning roles for the supervisor and supervisee; (c) theoretical orientation to counseling; (d) cultural characteristics, including race, ethnicity, and gender; and (e) self-presentation. A brief definition and illustrative transcripts are included to clarify their functional meaning in the SAS model.

Professional Experience

It has been suggested in the supervision literature that the supervisor engages in a developmental process of change that unfolds as the supervisor engages in the unique demands of the supervisory role (for a review, see Walsh, 1994). Whether this is accurate remains to be determined. At least, empirically, the amount of experience in counseling and supervision appears to be related to the types of judgments made by supervisors regarding self-disclosure, trainee performance, and instructional approach to supervision (see Research Box 4.2). In Transcript 4.1 (col. 2, p. 67), the supervisor alludes to his years of professional experience, and this reference has a powerful effect on the trainee. Although the supervisor uses the mention of his expertise as a way to strengthen his conceptualization of the client, the trainee reacts negatively.

Roles

Social role theories outline the behavior considered to be a part of the supervisory relationship, specifically the role of the supervisor (see Chapter 1). The most frequently recognized roles are teacher, counselor, and consultant; however, the roles of evaluator, lecturer, and model of professional practice have been used to describe supervisor behaviors and attitudes (see Research Box 4.3). Notice in Transcript 4.1 (col. 2, p. 69) that the trainee refers to the importance of the supervisor's role, the extant power base of the supervisor as a professor, and its inhibiting effect on her interactions with him—that is, the difficulty in forming a collaborative relationship.

Theoretical Orientation

The supervisor has the task of teaching the trainee the application of theoretical principles of counseling as they are relevant to the individuals and cases that trainees will encounter. Thus, supervisors rely explicitly and implicitly on their own knowledge base to determine what to teach as well as how to teach it. Trainees sometimes state a desire to learn a particular approach to counseling; however, supervisors and trainees are often assigned to one another without any consideration of the background of the supervisor or the expectations of the trainee. Or supervisors of a particular theoretical orientation may choose to take only those trainees who want to learn their approach.

TRANSCRIPT **4.1**

Contextual Factors

Supervision Interview	*Recall Interview*	*SAS Analysis*
Trainee OK . . . I think what I want to dwell on today is what was going on for me in these two sessions . . . ah . . . probably as it relates to termination and exploring . . . what's happening as you are moving toward the end of your sessions, because I felt that both of these sessions were somewhat different than preceding ones.	**Supervisor** From the very outset of her presentation, I was impressed with her presence. She was articulate; she has thought about it. She seemed to me to be from the very beginning a couple of cuts above what I would expect somebody at that level of training to be. And that kind of cued me in to how to listen to her and how to relate to her. It was really beyond different, different than I would respond to a beginner, to somebody at that level of training, both in, ah, . . . the style I use and the content I would address myself to, and the extent to which I would be concerned with the process. I was clear from the outset that she was not a typical beginner.	Although in the interview the supervisor is consulting with the trainee about the client situation, he reflects about the trainee's presentation of information and is assessing her knowledge base (**trainee factors: experience level and self-presentation**).
Supervisor When you say two sessions? Did you have two sessions since we met last week?		
Trainee Two clients . . . You haven't seen my other videotape . . . so both sessions seem to have some things in common maybe, ah, that were confusing to me, and I didn't feel right about these sessions. There was something going on . . . I haven't quite pinpointed it yet. So what I'll do is start with the first client, who you saw last week.		
Trainee With this first client, I just want to show you the beginning of the videotape because it is what, ah, we left off at such a good place with the material about her father and her feelings of being vulnerable and weak and the sexual discomfort, and we started to explore that again here . . . And it was just like— ugh—being in quicksand for me, so I'll show you what happened.		In the supervision interview, the trainee discusses the **client factor (identified problem)** and includes her own personal experience of being in the **counseling relationship.**

(continued)

TRANSCRIPT 4.1   **Continued**

Supervision Interview	Recall Interview	SAS Analysis
Supervisor OK, now the last session was the first time she brought that material up, right?	**Supervisor** Whenever there is a indication of sexual content, ah . . . particularly sexual content that has some negative kind of implication, then I'm immediately oriented toward the sexual experiences of the counselor.	The supervisor reflects on his conceptual and **theoretical orientation** to the sexual content of the client's problem.
[Videotape of counseling session is begun]		In the supervision interview, the supervisor continues to probe for information on the **client's identified problem and the interpersonal process of the counseling relationship.**
	Supervisor I think my approach was not too dissimilar to that I would use with a more advanced student. And that was to look at her process. To orient her toward her internal process, her dynamics— the relationship between what she was experiencing and what she was doing. Probably, as much or maybe even more than the content of the interaction.	He continues his reflection, however, on the **trainee's experience level** and the **client's behavior in the counseling relationship.**
Supervisor Hold it for a minute. What immediately . . . Is this the very beginning?		
Trainee Very close to the beginning.		
Supervisor Oh, OK.		
Trainee And, ah, I'm asking her again what would happen and something to that effect and she is saying, "Well, if I wasn't wary of watching my father, something might happen," but then she immediately goes in and she says . . .		

(continued)

TRANSCRIPT 4.1   **Continued**

Supervision Interview	*Recall Interview*	*SAS Analysis*
Supervisor Oh, OK.		
Trainee . . . "But I am like that in all things."		
Supervisor Hold it, did you raise the issue when you started, reminding her of the last session?		
Trainee I asked her if she wanted . . . if she had something she wanted to work on today, or if she wanted to continue where we had left off. She said yeah, that's what she'd like to do.		
Supervisor Did you, ah, in the interim do any reading at all about incest or talking or thinking about it?	**Supervisor** I'm looking for some way to introduce what the counselor's own experiences attitudinally or experientially are with something similar—to get some sense of what the counselor may be communicating, both receiving from the client and what the counselor may be communicating about the content.	The supervisor is seeking to understand the **trainee's theoretical base** as well as **cultural values** and attitudes toward sexually relevant material. This is consistent with his view that sexuality is a culturally sensitive topic.
Trainee Well, I read some material, and I sorta reviewed those, and I had another book I started reading that she brought in for me.		
Supervisor . . . So she may be seeing things more sexually because of the state of her development rather than because of the accurate recollection of being in relationship with her father . . .		
Trainee You know, and I guess that kind of raises a kind of question in my mind . . . maybe I'm still doing it at this point but . . . is regardless of whether it really happened or not, isn't it still the impact it would have on you . . . whether, I mean if . . .		The trainee is expressing her orientation toward conceptualizing incest victims (**theoretical orientation**). Although she doesn't say, "This is my theory of counseling," it is her conceptual orientation toward the client problem.
Supervisor Yeah, a perception that . . .		

(continued)

TRANSCRIPT 4.1 **Continued**

Supervision Interview	*Recall Interview*	*SAS Analysis*
Trainee [overlap] If you can never remember, maybe you can never remember except through hypnosis or something or you are too young or whatever . . . but if you still felt that happened to you it's still going to have as big of an impact as if it did . .		
Supervisor It's going to have an impact, yes; depending on how concrete the recollection is, the impact may be different, and this is my impression last week . . . there is incest without physical contact, an incest impact without physical contact . . . but the point I'm making is not that whether it happened or not . . . but that her tendency would be to protect . . . her father or the relationship they had in her memory . . .		
I've worked with numbers of incest victims who've said, "I think it must all be a dream I had" or "I'm making it up; it couldn't have been like that . . ."	**Trainee** He is defending his point by saying how many clients he has worked with and that puts me (as a supervisee) in a position of having to listen to what he says and accept it without too much argument because I, obviously, don't have the same, umm, amount of expertise in this field, and I find that then it limits my freedom to be me, to argue back—perhaps, defend my position and explore it.	The supervisor explains his view of the issue of perception of versus actual occurrence of an event and refers to his **experience in counseling** with incest victims that reminds the trainee of his expert power. She is responding to his **self-presentation**—that is, how he chooses to present his position, rather than the information he presents.
Trainee Umm, huh, Well then, how do you distinguish, ah . . . you know, I am wondering if I'm being naive with her when she's saying nothing happened at all. The, ah, closest she could remember was just sorta wrestling around, nothing sexual in nature, so should I go with that or just keep it in the back of my mind?		The trainee's recall of this exchange reflects her attention to the supervisor's power and reflects that it inhibits her from being in the supervision

(continued)

TRANSCRIPT 4.1 **Continued**

Supervision Interview

Supervisor What could you do . . . ?

Trainee Well, I don't know everything yet . . . it's going to come out.

Trainee I was feeling very out of touch with her, and I think I wished I just stopped and said anyway, "Something just doesn't feel right here, ah, is something else going through your mind?"

Supervisor How could you do that?

Trainee "Are you talking or thinking something that we are not talking about?"

Supervisor Now, how can you do that neutrally?

Trainee Yeah, that's a good question.

Supervisor Do you understand what I mean by neutral, as compared to what you just said you might do?

Trainee Yeah, not putting it on to her, but owning it for myself, and say "I'm feeling like maybe there is something that could be going on?"

Supervisor OK, well, that's still not quite . . .

Trainee "I feel out of touch with you."

Supervisor Yeah, that's one possibility, but even more neutral . . .

Recall Interview

Supervisor I'm being fairly instructive and didactic with her, and I've done both with her. Probing at what I think is a more sophisticated level than I would with a beginner. Being more didactic because I think she can absorb it, without feeling directed. She has a critical enough capacity, and she is more advanced. I can be less didactic. But there are some areas, because she is a beginner, that she is not aware of. Some both conceptual and behavioral kind of modalities that she is not aware of. She's at a level of maturity and sophistication to be able to integrate those critically, and so I give them to her directly.

SAS Analysis

relationship more fully. In essence, she feels disempowered.

The trainee is reporting in supervision interview her experience of the **counseling relationship** and how it has influenced her conceptualization of the client.

The supervisor reflects on the strategy that he uses based on the **trainee's experience level** and **self-presentation**.

(continued)

TRANSCRIPT **4.1** **Continued**

Supervision Interview

Trainee Hmmmmm . . . give me a clue.

Supervisor [Trainee laughing] OK, you are saying, "I think you're thinking something else . . . something else is happening that we're not dealing with." A more neutral way is to ask, "What are you experiencing now?"

Trainee What's going on for you right now in this experience?

Supervisor Because you get a sense of something happening that isn't being made clear at all. That you know . . .

Trainee I get the part of trusting my own intuition about it too. Being an intuitive person, I don't always trust the process for myself. Since it's not always concrete or realistic, and has a nebulous feeling for me. I maybe try harder to hang onto something concrete, rather than saying, "Wait a minute, this is valid."

Supervisor Process is very concrete.

Recall Interview

Trainee I guess at this point supervision is different for me with this person than the preceding supervision, because we don't have a history together. He is not aware of the client, and I thought there were some really important factors in the way we were interacting here. I felt like a student in this relationship with the wise professor who had the answers and that made me somewhat inhibited and uncomfortable, and I'm aware of that happening in this supervision interview.

Trainee Yeah. When he stopped trying to be there for me and just told me what he had in mind, it made a lot more sense for me, and it was something that would stick with me. This is what you could do. And when he said it, it clicked for me. It was a good learning experience, then, just having him tell it to me directly.

SAS Analysis

The trainee reflects on the impact this **new supervisory relationship** has on her experience of the supervisor and her perception of **the role** he takes. She feels stuck by the formal nonpersonal role of the student and has not yet developed a more idiosyncratic and personal role set of the mature relationship.

The trainee reflects on her own learning needs in this interaction and the importance of the supervisor changing his strategy by giving her a suggestion on how to intervene rather than having her guess what he meant.

Unpublished supervision interview. Based on an actual transcript altered to protect the identity of the participants.

Research Box 4.2

Research on Supervisor's Professional Experience

Supervisor experience has been examined as it relates to supervisors' facilitative behaviors and judgments of trainee performance (Marikis, Russell, & Dell, 1985; Stone, 1980; Sundland & Feinberg, 1972; Worthington, 1984b). Sundland and Feinberg's (1972) study revealed that when given a positive view of the supervisee, supervisors with more experience provided the highest levels of facilitative conditions; however, when given a negative view of the trainee the experienced supervisors provided the lowest level of facilitation. Thus, the influence of both interpersonal attraction to the trainee and experience as a supervisor influenced supervisors' using their facilitative skills. Surprisingly, more experienced supervisors were more negatively influenced and thus less attracted to the "negative-set" trainees. The authors suggested that because the more experienced supervisors in this study were not trained in the experiential-didactic training model (due to historical cohort group), whereas the less experienced supervisor had been so trained and were also in closer proximity to the student role, the latter were more tolerant of the negative-set supervisee.

In another study that examined supervisor experience with supervisor's judgment of the trainee, Worthington (1984b) asked experienced and inexperienced counselors to assume a supervisor role and to rate counselors and clients, represented in a 10-minute excerpt from a counseling session, on eight personality trait labels. Experience level of the supervisor was defined by the amount of counseling experience of the participants ranging from "no experience" through postdoctoral experience. Half of the supervisors were led to believe that the counselor in the videotape vignette was at the beginning level and half were told she was at the internship level. The results indicated that supervisors with more counseling experience made fewer trait attributions to the counselor than did supervisors with little or no counseling experience. Theoretically, the argument was made that supervisors' experience in counseling promotes increased cognitive role taking (empathy) and thus they are better able to attribute the supervisee's behaviors to situational variables rather than personal traits. The "set" of counselor's level of training had no significant effect on the supervisors' judgments of counselor traits. Furthermore, supervisors, regardless of counseling experience, did not differentially attribute trait labels to the client. These findings, in contrast to Sundland and Feinberg's

---

The counseling-bound theories of supervision, described in Chapter 1, generally maintain that the supervisor's method is intrinsically linked to the counseling approach. Patterson (1983) maintains that this is the only way supervision can be considered. An example to consider is Albert Ellis's work in supervision (Transcript 2.5, p. 35), reflecting his efforts to teach the supervisee the thinking of a rational-emotive therapist.

The cross-theoretical approaches have tried to create theories unique to supervision that are not wholly dependent on theories of counseling. SAS would be classified in this latter group. This does not mean that an individual supervisor's theoretical orientation to counseling or

Research Box 4.2

Continued

(1972), suggest that experience in supervision frees the supervisor from making global personality judgments of the trainee and allows the supervisor to focus on the situational characteristics that might be influencing the trainee's performance. The supervisor's ability to recognize interpersonal and situational factors in counseling that may influence the counselor's behavior is salient to establishing an empathic relationship in supervision and assisting the supervisee to devise different counseling strategies that respond to contextual factors. Unfortunately, the definition of experience level in this study limits the generalizability of the results. Because most supervisors have some counseling experience, it is unlikely that "no experience" in counseling is a realistic alternative as a supervisor characteristic. Because many training programs use doctoral students to supervise beginning-level counselors, however, these results emphasize the importance of using more experienced counselors as supervisors and/or teaching supervisors to focus on situational influences on the supervisee.

Stone (1980) found that more experienced supervisors focused more on counselor behavior in their before-session planning statements than did inexperienced supervisors. Marikis et al. (1985) improved on Stone's (1980) study by including only participants with counseling experience and with at least a didactic course on supervision. Experience level of supervisors ranged from "no supervisory experience" to postdoctoral supervision experience. In addition, they compared planning behavior to actual in-session behavior of the supervisors. Their findings indicated that there were no differences on planning behaviors among the different experience-level groups and that the most frequent planning behaviors were counselor-oriented statements, followed by client, subject matter, and process statements. These results contrast with Stone's findings that there were significant differences in planning behavior across the different experience groups. Marikis et al. (1985) also found that there was little relationship between the planning process and in-session verbal behaviors. There were differences, however, in verbal behaviors between the "no experience" and the two experienced groups. Supervisors with some experience were more verbal in session, self-disclosed more, and provided more direct instruction of counseling skills.

particular aspects of human behavior would be unimportant when analyzing a supervisor's behavior. Process research has indicated that theoretical orientation to counseling appears to be related to the structure of the supervisory relationship (see Research Box 3.1). When a supervisor instructs on particular aspects of a personality or a counseling theory as they are relevant to client behavior, that supervisor's orientation is manifestly salient to his or her decision making in supervision.

The first indication of a supervisor factor influencing the supervisor's action in Transcript 4.1 occurs in column 2, page 65. This supervisor recognizes that his attention to sexual issues in the counseling relationship orients him to determining the trainee's attitude toward

Research Box 4.3

Research on Supervisor Role

Role theories of supervision outline the expectancies and behaviors that are considered to be a part of the supervisory relationship and, specifically, the role of supervisor. A few research studies have investigated the types of roles typical of the supervisor (Ellis & Dell, 1986; Ellis et al., 1988; Gysbers & Johnston, 1965; Stenack & Dye, 1982). In an early study, Gysbers and Johnston (1965) asked supervisors and supervisees to respond to the Supervisor Role Analysis Form (SRAF). Supervisees' expectations for supervisor behaviors changed across the 6-week practicum period from specific help, demonstration, and teaching behaviors to consultative and student-directed behaviors. Supervisors acknowledged their expectation to be responsible for structuring the learning experience but disagreed on the degree of specific direction or counseling support they should offer the student. Similarly, Stenack and Dye (1982) had both faculty and graduate students with supervision experience indicate the correspondence of a list of 60 supervisor behaviors to the roles of teacher, counselor, and consultant. They found that the teacher and counselor roles were clearly distinguished but that the consultant role overlapped with the teacher role. It appeared that any differences between teacher and consultant were related to issues of supervisor control of the interaction rather than with specific supervisor behaviors. A more shared approach to control was indicative of the consultant role. They concluded that

specific behaviors alone cannot clearly define supervisor roles; other elements of the interaction such as goals, control, and focus are also determinants.

Ellis and associates conducted three related studies in which the role model theories of Bernard (1979) and Littrell et al. (1979) were examined using a multidimensional scaling methodology. In the first study (Ellis & Dell, 1986), supervisors' perceptions of the supervisor role were characterized by three dimensions: process versus conceptualization, consultant versus teacher/counselor, and cognitive versus emotional (or nonsupportive versus supportive). The findings in the next two studies of counselor trainees' perceptions of supervisor roles (Ellis et al., 1988) corroborated the three-dimensional structure of supervision found in Ellis and Dell (1986). However, trainees' differentiated between the teacher and counselor role, whereas supervisors did not. The authors concluded that the results modestly supported Bernard's (1979) supervisor roles of teacher and counselor and supervisor functions of process, conceptualization, and personalization. There was little support, however, for the developmental dimension of supervision as posited by Littrell et al. (1979) because there were no differences across experience levels of trainees. The most apparent difference in the findings with the models was the emergence of an emotional-behavioral dimension.

sexuality. He takes this position grounded in his understanding of human behavior and the potency of sexuality both psychologically and sociologically. A review of the influence of the supervisor's theoretical orientation appears in Research Box 4.4.

Research Box 4.4

Research on Supervisor's Theoretical Orientation

The influence of the supervisor's theoretical orientation on supervisory behavior has been the subject of several studies. Sundland and Garfield (cited in Sundland, 1977), and Beutler and McNabb (1981) found that students tend to adopt the theoretical orientation of supervisors and/or the director of clinical training. In an extensive study of clinical psychology graduates in a medical school practice setting, Guest and Beutler (1988) confirmed that orientations of prominent supervisors were particularly important in establishing a trainee's viewpoint regardless of the correspondence between trainees' initial orientation and the supervisor's orientation. Furthermore, trainee locus of control and other personality variables did not contribute to changes in orientation or values over the course of one training year or in follow-up 3 to 5 years after training. Supervision as a powerful socialization factor in the profession is very evident from this study. The supervisor's importance as a model professional is reflected in the trainees' adherence to the values of their teacher. Although in this instance the researchers were interested only in the theoretical orientation of the supervisor and its adoption by the trainee, we can easily extrapolate from here and consider the implication such findings have for the transmittal of cultural values and professional attitudes. If the supervisor unwittingly or deliberately presents stereotypic, prejudicial attitudes toward other people or promotes disrespectful and exploitive behaviors toward clients, such influences will be difficult to combat. Goodyear and Robyak (1982) found that regardless of theoretical orientation, more experienced supervisors shared similar emphases in supervision, whereas less experienced supervisors were more divergent in ways consistent with their theoretical orientation. These results support similar studies in psychotherapy (Friedler, 1950) and an early study by Demos and Zuwaylif (1962) in supervision. In another study, Goodyear, Abadie, and Efros (1984) had experienced supervisors view supervision sessions of prominent supervision theorists working with the same supervisee (Goodyear, 1982). Findings indicated that supervisors of different theoretical orientations were rated differently in attractiveness (as measured by the Supervisor Rating Form; Heppner & Handley, 1982) and in their use of the critic, model, and nurturing roles. They also were perceived as different in their use of the counselor and teacher roles and in supervisory focus on such issues as case conceptualization, counseling skills, and transference. Holloway et al. (1989) also studied the Goodyear (1982) videotape series and concluded that although there were prominent similarities in patterns of verbal behaviors, there were also predictable differences among the theorists. Thus, in these two studies of the same data set, theoretical orientation of the supervisor was related to perceived differences in supervisory behavior and actual differences in supervisory discourse. Goldberg (1985) believes that the supervisor's personality or character style and theoretical orientation is the single most influential factor in the supervisor's behavior. Studies of the relationship between supervisor theoretical orientation and supervisor methods strongly support Goldberg's claim (Carroll, 1995; Putney, Worthington, & McCullough, 1992).

Cultural Characteristics

The supervisor brings to the relationship his or her way of viewing human behavior, interpersonal relations, and social institutions that is largely influenced by cultural socialization. Because cultural perspective is relevant to the conceptualization of both professionalism and mental health, the SAS model considers cultural values as salient to the supervisor's attitudes and actions. Cultural characteristics include gender, ethnicity, race, sexual orientation, religious beliefs, and personal values that strongly influence an individual's social and moral judgments. In the SAS model, the relationship of supervision is understood from a perspective of power and involvement—inherent qualities in cross-cultural and cross-gender interactions that indicate the complex, sometimes subtle, but always critical aspects of supervisory work. The relationship of race and ethnicity to supervisory process has been researched in the context of the supervisor and trainee relationship. McRoy, Freeman, Logan, and Blackmon (1986; see Research Box 4.9), in a survey study of field supervision, concluded that although there were numerous potential difficulties in cross-cultural supervisory relationships, only a few actual instances were reported. African American supervisors reported that language differences; communication styles; the role and authority of the supervisor; personality conflicts; and differences in opinions, backgrounds, and life experiences may be problematic. The interaction between power in role and power in society is evident in that African American supervisors experienced situations in which white students questioned their competency and were actually unwilling to accept supervision. White supervisors reported that lack of trust, poor communication, lack of knowledge of cultural differences, failure to clarify values, language barriers, prejudice or bigotry, differing expectations, and student defensiveness may all cause problems in the relationship. Unfortunately, it is often difficult for students and supervisors to identify such sensitive situations and discuss them openly. Because of the focus on the trainee in these studies, racial and cultural factors of supervision are presented in Research Box 4.9.

The relationship of gender to the perception of interpersonal power and interactional processes has been studied relatively frequently in supervision. In general, same-gender dyads have reported closer relationships. Women trainees were perceived to use more dependent styles to seek influence, but there was no difference in males' and females' use of power strategies to influence client change (see Research Box 4.5). Interactional analysis of matched and mismatched gender dyads in supervision (Nelson & Holloway, 1990) showed that male and female supervisors used more powerful messages (see Research Box 4.5) with female trainees, and female trainees were much less likely than males to use high-power messages. Nelson (1993), in a

Research Box 4.5

Research on Supervisor and Trainee Gender

The influence of same- and mixed-gender dyads has been the focus of three studies. Worthington and Stern (1985) examined a number of trainee variables, including gender matching of supervisor and trainee. They found that male supervisors and trainees thought they had better relationships than did female supervisors and trainees and that matching of gender was more important to trainees than to supervisors. Trainees felt that they had closer relationships with same-gender supervisors, and they attributed more influence to the same-gender supervisor than to other-gender supervisors. Goodyear (1990), using an analogue design, examined the extent to which gender of supervisor and supervisee was related to interpersonal influence strategies and global skill ratings of the supervisee. Both supervisors and supervisees perceived female supervisees to be more likely to employ a "person-dependent" influence style—that is, dependent on supervisor behaviors; there were no other significant main or interaction effects for gender on global skill ratings.

One study, Robyak, Goodyear, Prange, and Donham (1986) examined the relationship of gender, supervised experienced in counseling, and client presenting problem to students' preferences for using particular power bases to influence client change within an analogue study design. The findings indicated that experience level of the trainee was related to preferences' for legitimate and referent power bases, whereas gender and type of presenting problem had no significant effect. Students with less experience preferred the legitimate and referent power bases to a greater extent than did students with more supervised experience. The authors explain their results from the perspective of social influence theory, stating that the legitimate power base allows beginning-level trainees to use the socially sanctioned role of counselor to structure the relationship and gain credibility. In addition, the use of the referent power base mitigates the stiffness or formality of legitimate power by seeking to gain the client's confidence through personal qualities that will enhance interpersonal attractiveness. Although this

conceptual review, examines the importance of gender in therapeutic and counseling relationships.

Specific training in didactic and experiential curriculum is necessary to overcome cross-cultural barriers to communication. There are numerous writings on instructional approaches to sensitize students, educators, and supervisors to such issues in theory and practice (for a review, see Bernard & Goodyear, 1992). Specifically addressing cross-cultural events in practice, Pope-Davis, Reynolds, and Vasquez (1992) have developed a training program including videotapes to facilitate counseling and counselor training. The SAS model is meant to encourage supervisors to recognize the importance of cultural factors in supervision and to pay attention to how these issues interact with each of the other factors of the model.

research is limited by the analogue and survey approach to data collection, it does provide information regarding the role of experience in the choice of power base in formal, working relationships, such as counseling and supervision. The trainee's use of different power bases across these two relationships may be an interesting area for future research.

Robyak, Goodyear, and Prange (1987), drawing from the interpersonal influence model of counseling (Strong, 1968; Strong & Matross, 1973), examined the influence of supervisor's gender and experience and supervisory focus on his or her preferences for expert, referent, and legitimate power bases (French & Raven, 1960). The expert power base stems from specialized knowledge and skills. Referent power is derived from interpersonal attraction. Legitimate power is a consequence of perceived trustworthiness, in that the professional is a socially sanctioned provider of ser-

vices. In this analogue study, male and female supervisors ranging in supervision experience from 1 month to 40 years, read a typescript of a female supervisee's comments and then selected from three possible supervisor responses. Each response reflected the use of one of the three power bases by the supervisor. The results indicated that both gender and amount of supervisory experience had significant main effects on the supervisor's preference for the referent power base but not on the expert or legitimate power bases. It appeared that males and inexperienced supervisors preferred the use of the referent power base. Supervisors who focused on self-awareness of the supervisee showed a greater preference for the expert power base than the supervisors who focused on client conceptualization; and the legitimate power base was not significantly related to any of the three independent variables.

Not surprisingly, it is difficult to make available a transcript of supervision that illustrates the issues in cross-cultural or same-nonminority cultural interactions. As reported earlier, supervisors and supervisees, particularly in the cross-cultural situation, are unlikely to speak directly about these problems. Second, many of the issues of power and race are undetectably subtle in such contexts or remain only "inside the head" of the participant.

Transcript 4.1 (col. 3, p. 66) presents an opportunity to consider how personal values or cultural factors in the supervisor's own development and experience might influence his views on incest and sexuality. He mentions the importance of the trainee's own sexual values as instrumental in her treatment of the client as an incest victim and, in turn, it can be inferred that his cultural values toward sexuality are equally important.

Another example of cultural factors toward sexuality is evident in Transcript 4.2 (col. 1, pp. 77-78). In this interaction, both the trainee and the supervisor acknowledge the existence of a mutual attraction

TRANSCRIPT **4.2**

Contextual Factors

Supervision Interview

Supervisor How is your sense of being flattered by her attention preventing you from being therapeutic to her?

Trainee I think that is it. I think it would almost be "Well, do I want to say something that would dispel this whole flattery, you know, something that would dispel it?"

Supervisor So you are liking it. There is something about it that is enjoyable to you? Are you aware of any risks in this situation?

Trainee Oh, definitely. I think that getting into that sort of mode is not therapeutic, and I think that it impedes objectivity on my part. And maybe I think that is what I am really becoming aware of. I think I question more what my motives are for asking a particular question. Just because I sort of see myself more involved in this underlying play.

Supervisor You're really aware that there is something going on with you that may be influencing the way you act. So your sense of what is going on, does it stop with flattery? Where does it stop?

Trainee Well, I think either, as we have talked about before, one of the issues has been right up front with us, that's been Jill's issues on sexual orientation, sexual preference and, umm, I think there is some attraction going on.

SAS Analysis

Supervisor begins by consulting with trainee around the dynamic in the **counseling relationship** and the therapeutic implications of this dynamic.

The trainee focuses on the counseling that might correct this problem in the **relationship.**

The supervisor again focuses on the **counseling relationship** and explores the possibility of a mutual attraction and the risks involved, perhaps implying that there are **professional or ethical** concerns in this situation.

The trainee returns to focus on her therapeutic effectiveness as it relates to the situation in the **counseling relationship** rather than addressing directly the ethical standards that may be in jeopardy.

The supervisor now appears to be collecting information on the trainee's **interpersonal behavior in the counseling relationship** and whether anything other than flattery has taken place. Again, perhaps she is seeking information that will help her to determine if an ethical breach in the form of a sexual relationship has taken place already.

(continued)

TRANSCRIPT 4.2   **Continued**

Supervision Interview	*SAS Analysis*
Supervisor On both parts?	The supervisor is willing to consider sexual orientation of the counselor. Her own values regarding sexual orientation could become important in this context (**supervisor factors: cultural characteristics**).
Trainee I think so. I think so. And it's very scary for me because I think I'm recognizing that. Well, I am recognizing that. And I don't want to cover it up, and I also do not want to withdraw completely, neither do I want to continue in this sort of seduction or this, this courtship that I sort of see her moving toward at a more rapid rate.	The trainee expresses her concern with what is happening in the **counseling relationship** but does not explicitly comment on her own **values** and attitudes toward lesbian relationships. She focuses her concern on the therapeutic issues that are jeopardized from the mutual seduction between herself and the client.
Supervisor How might you work so you don't continue that with her?	The supervisor is guiding trainee to change the **counseling relationship** so that she can remain therapeutic and not engage in a seductive process. The supervisor does not deal explicitly with the **ethical concerns of dual relationships** at this point.

This transcript is taken from the videotape series *Engagement and Power in Clinical Supervision* by Martin Acker and Elizabeth Holloway, University of Oregon, Eugene, OR, 1988. Used by permission of Martin Acker and Elizabeth Holloway. (Videotapes not available for distribution.)

between the two women in the counseling relationship. However, the sexual orientation does not become the focus of the conversation. Rather, the supervisor guides the trainee to work on ways to remain therapeutic with the client and thus stop the seductive process that is unfolding in their relationship. Thus, although there is tacit acknowledgment of the sexual orientation between the trainee and client, the supervisor chooses not to pursue this line of inquiry. The salient issue here is not the supervisor's values in regard to lesbian relationships; rather, the larger issue of mutual attraction and seduction in therapy takes precedence.

Self-Presentation

In SAS, the term *self-presentation* is used to refer to each participant's interpersonal presentation of self. This term originates in the social-psychological literature concerned with impression formation. Although, initially, there was some suggestion that self-presentational behaviors were restricted to those activities that an individual deliberately regulated to communicate a particular image of oneself to others (Baumeister, 1982), it has been suggested more recently that this definition is too narrow (DePaulo, 1992). DePaulo (1992) argues that verbal and nonverbal behaviors in interpersonal contexts can include more than superficial concerns and are important in developed relationships (Schlenker, 1984). In addition, self-presentation is seen to include behaviors that are produced automatically; these are expressive behaviors that have become habitual and are no longer deliberate but that were originally purposefully regulated. In the interpersonal psychotherapy literature, such behaviors are referred to as "a person's style of relating," habitual ways of behaving that have been learned early in life and are maintained through adulthood (Teyber, 1988). It might be argued that in supervision, self-presentational style is always a factor; however, it is under particular conditions that style becomes prominent and decidedly the primary factor in the course of the communication.

Schlenker and Leary (1982) have studied the relationship of social anxiety to self-presentational behaviors. In the situations in which individuals want to create a favorable impression, as certainly any trainee being evaluated will want to do, they will experience some level of social anxiety. This anxiety will be affected by their expectations for success, their degree of social uncertainty regarding expectations, and the importance they attribute to the person they are trying to impress. Schlenker and Leary concluded that under conditions of high social anxiety, where there is an overriding concern of evaluation, individuals will display changes in their communicative style; they will display greater cognitive withdrawal coupled with increased self-preoccupation, thus interfering with the effectiveness of information processing, sensitivity to ongoing events, and self-monitoring and self-control. For example, individuals may resort to approaches that are "reticent or reserved or withdrawn," "pleasing, compliant, and dependent," or "aggressive, hostile, or defensive."

Friedlander and Schwartz (1985) reviewed the social-psychological literature on self-presentation and from it drew those principles that were particularly relevant to the therapeutic context (see Research Box 4.10). In supervision, Ward, Friedlander, Schoen, and Klein (1985) used the self-presentation construct to examine supervisors' judgments of trainees in relation to trainees' self-presentational style. The self-presentational construct has not been used in the study of the supervisor's behavior. Studies have focused on the supervisor's perceived style specific to supervisor roles (Friedlander & Ward, 1984) and the characteristics of the supervisory relationship (Efstation et al., 1990; see Research Box 3.2). The supervisor's pattern of verbal behavior in the process of supervision has also been examined (Holloway & Poulin, 1995; see Research Box 3.1).

In SAS, self-presentation is used to refer to the affective, verbal, and nonverbal behaviors that the participants engage in to convey a particular desired impression on the other; these behaviors may be habitual and require no conscious monitoring or may be purposely regulated. They characterize the individual and become the supervisor's individual manner of enacting his or her role.

In Transcript 4.1 (col. 2, p. 67), the trainee reflects her reaction to the supervisor's referencing his amount of experience with incest survivors rather than her viewing his experience as an asset to her learning. She says his perception limits her "freedom" to learn. The manner in which he presents his knowledge (self-presentation) is the primary influencing factor, although she chooses not to share this reaction with the supervisor. Transcript 4.3 offers an example of the parallel process of supervision and the supervisor's reenactment in supervision of the trainee's problem-solving approach to the client's hopelessness and resistance to change. The supervisor (col. 1, p. 82), becoming increasingly frustrated with the trainee's enactment of the client's resistance, appears defensive (self-presentation) with the trainee. This response escalates the trainee's resistance to change, and the supervisor appears to be almost pleading (self-presentation) with the trainee to accept her intervention (col. 2, p. 84).

Trainee Factors

Who is the ideal supervisee? The psychological health and personal character of the therapist have been considered to be of primary importance in the traditional training of the analyst. In-depth personal therapy has been regarded as a critical element in the training process to (a) enhance the therapist's ability as an unbiased clinical observer and mitigate the effects of countertransference, (b) demonstrate experientially the validity of therapy as a treatment, (c) model firsthand the techniques of psychotherapy, and (d) improve the psychological health of the therapist and ameliorate the stresses of practice (Wampler & Strupp, 1976). However, as training programs in psychology have become more competency based in their approach to evaluating trainees' appropriateness for the counselor role, researchers have focused on those characteristics that potentially influence the acquisition of behaviors deemed necessary for effective counseling. In particular, the facilitative conditions, as assessed in simulated or actual counseling, have become the target behaviors for assessing the influence of personal factors such as cognitive structure and experience level (for reviews, see Hansen, Pound, & Petro, 1976; Hansen et al., 1982; Holloway, 1984; Holloway & Wampold, 1986; Russell et al., 1984).

TRANSCRIPT **4.3**

Contextual Factors

Supervision Interview

Supervisor What . . . How are you . . . have your feelings toward him just as a person changed any since the session started and where you are now with him because of his "yes, but"?

Trainee When I'm in the session with him I don't usually get particularly frustrated. I seem to be able to exercise a certain amount of patience with him, but I find myself after the session or when viewing the tape, and occasionally in the session, getting real frustrated. Just kind of getting to that point where, you know, "Shake yourself, Jerry."

Supervisor You want him to move and part of you knows what he needs, but he's not letting you help him.

Trainee Right, right. Yeah, and I really do feel like, I'm not sure that I feel anything personal towards me, but I really feel like he has a real active role in sabotaging his own well-being. And he isn't responding to any help. At least I feel like that.

Supervisor So you haven't . . . he's not reporting to you any difference in how he feels or in how his days are going.

Trainee Not at all.

Supervisor So then, you've tried both the behavioral approach and the cognitive approach with him?

Trainee Umm, at least tried to, tried a couple of different angles, a couple of different approaches.

SAS Analysis

The supervisor probes for the trainee's feeling about the **client and the interpersonal dynamics of the counseling relationship.**

The trainee continues to describe his experience of the client in the **counseling relationship.**

The supervisor helps the trainee to focus on the dynamic in the **counseling relationship.**

The trainee begins to conceptualize the **severity of the client's problem** and then moves back to his frustration of not being able to get the client to accept his help. The trainee's message is that he has tried a number of different ways to deal with the depression and has been unsuccessful.

The supervisor and trainee continue to discuss the **client's problem and its severity** and the interventions that have been used in the **counseling relationship.**

(continued)

TRANSCRIPT 4.3 Continued

Supervision Interview

Supervisor Have you explored that with him at all? Just to pull out more information to see if that is on the right track?

Trainee We've explored a lot about what it feels like for him. We've explored a lot about just what it's like for him and maybe the progression and how it is getting worse. As far as exploring my hunch that he is becoming over-involved, I don't think I've had a real good sense of how to do that really without seeming like confronting him with my hunch, my interpretation of what is going on.

Supervisor I wasn't suggesting that as a strategy, I was just trying to get some sense of your intuition and what that might be based on. So it seems like your sessions are, correct me on this then, like he comes in and talks about the depression and on your part there is a lot of empathy, a lot of expression of the feelings, but when you try getting too close to him, asking more about feelings or suggesting this or that, that's when he starts the "yes, but" to keep you away. Does it feel like he's pushing you away?

Trainee As a personal thing, pushing me personally away?

Supervisor Not personally, but as you suggest ideas to make it better.

Trainee With my other clients, when I ask "Well, do you have any insight into this situation?" they give me something that is down below this line, and I'm immediately sensing that Jerry is going to "yes, but, that thing."

SAS Analysis

The supervisor begins to explore with the trainee other interventions that he might have used. Again, the trainee reports feeling that he has tried a number of things and now doesn't really know how to proceed without **confronting the client (client factor: counseling relationship)**.

The supervisor appears to **defend (self-presentation)** her intentions for asking the trainee about his work and then returns to summarizing the client's situation, including her analysis of the **dynamics of the counseling relationship.**

The trainee is really letting the supervisor know that her ideas for intervention will probably only result in the **client's continued resistance (client factor: counseling relationship).**

(continued)

TRANSCRIPT 4.3 **Continued**

Supervision Interview	*SAS Analysis*
Supervisor Right. If you can be Jerry and you just imagine Greg starting to intervene or one of your friends starting to intervene, what comes up?	The supervisor tries another approach by asking about the trainee's understanding what the **client might be feeling (client factor: identified problem).**
Trainee Fear.	
Supervisor Fear.	
Trainee I think so. And . . .	
Supervisor We were just talking about that.	
Trainee Yeah, I don't know that for sure, but I would say that, it's like it's a scared animal. That's the sense that I get; I don't mean to be patronizing to Jerry, but it's like that's something that I'm not able or wanting or capable or I don't want to deal with that. I can't handle the change or I can't handle exposing myself to anything different than what I am experiencing right now. And I hate this, but at least its familiar. You know . . . kind of that same.	Continued discussion of the client's dynamics and problem.
Supervisor So there is this weary gray path.	
Trainee I think so . . . I think that is where he is at.	
Supervisor What do you think he risks?	
Trainee Umm, I really don't know. You know and maybe that goes back to what we talked about earlier about that I don't know really why he's doing the things that he is doing. Why he is sabotaging this . . . this situation. But . . .	The trainee returns to the dynamic of the **counseling relationship,** and essentially his frustration with the client's sabotaging the trainee's efforts to help him.
Supervisor If you were able . . . if you can just right now take on Jerry's role and it doesn't mean that you come up with the correct feeling, but just explore some alternatives . . . umm, and	The supervisor tries another intervention with the trainee to help the trainee break through the impasse with the client. The emergence of the process in the **supervisory relationship as**

(continued)

TRANSCRIPT 4.3 Continued

Supervision Interview

you imagine Greg sitting here and coming up with an intervention, you're aware, you've shared with me the feeling of fear. Take it one step further; were you hearing yourself saying that you agree to try an intervention? See if that gives you any more information about what he may be risking.

Trainee OK, I'll try and practice being Jerry at that critical point.

Supervisor And going a step further then, he's gone so far.

Trainee Yea, I feel Jerry saying . . . I'm having trouble kind of putting this thing in to play, but, umm, I feel Jerry saying, "Yeah, yeah, OK but, it's hopeless, you know. I can understand what you're saying, I can understand talking about this stuff, but it's hopeless. I mean if . . . OK so if I do this and so I try doing this stuff, something else is going to come up. You know, so if it's not one thing it's another."

Trainee Yeah, as you say that I'm starting to get skeptical whether he would acknowledge that coming into counseling would identify for him that he does have some hope in there even if it's only this much.

Supervisor What are you feeling?

Trainee I feel . . . I sense that he would try and be skeptical about that too, and respond by saying like, I mean if I gave the question just directly like that. That he would respond by saying something like "You know I didn't come here because I thought

SAS Analysis

parallel to the counseling relationship is becoming more evident as the supervisor continues to seek solutions for the trainee. The supervisor is asking the trainee not to remain stuck like the client in the role-play.

The **trainee sabotages (self-presentation)** the supervisor's efforts to move him past his impasse with the client as he takes on the client's sense of hopelessness and inability to change.

The **supervisor presents an almost pleading (self-presentation)** response to remind the trainee to do something different in the role-play. She is acting out the trainee's attitude to the **counseling relationship** in the **supervisory relationship.**

The parallel process continues as the trainee presents the client's hopelessness

The trainee continues to reflect the **client's hopelessness and his own sense of hopelessness** about the client's depression.

(continued)

TRANSCRIPT 4.3 **Continued**

Supervision Interview

SAS Analysis

that I could change. I just came here because people usually do before something really bad happens."

Supervisor And so if you were to say to him, ask him, "Does that mean you are ready to give up?" or "Would you be willing to make one more small try?"

Ostensibly, the supervisor is pleading with the client in role-play to make an effort; but in actuality, with the trainee. The parallel process is full-blown as the supervisor finds her efforts being sabotaged by the trainee through the role-play situation.

Trainee He would probably . . . I don't know, I don't know for sure, because I don't think I've ever posed that exactly to him. But I'd guess he would say something like "No, I think I've tried almost everything or at least something close to it, and they are not fitting, they're not working."

Supervisor And that would be frightening, because are you saying that he might right in the session say to you, "It makes sense to give up"?

The supervisor changes the focus to the **client's level of severity** in respect to suicide potential, and the trainee assures her that there is no potential threat. It appears in some ways that the trainee is really speaking about himself and the fact that he wants to continue with this client in spite of the frustration and anger that he feels toward the client.

Trainee But that he would say that it makes sense for him to give up.

Supervisor Yeah, is that a concern?

Trainee If you say give up, you mean, like commit suicide or something like that?

Supervisor Right.

Trainee No, I don't think he wants to do that at all personally.

This transcript is taken from the videotape series *Engagement and Power in Clinical Supervision* by Martin Acker and Elizabeth Holloway, University of Oregon, Eugene, OR, 1988. Used by permission of Martin Acker and Elizabeth Holloway. (Videotapes not available for distribution.)

In the 1980s, as models of supervision began to attend to the actual process and strategy of supervision (Goodyear & Bradley, 1983; Hess, 1980; Loganbill et al., 1982; Stoltenberg, 1981), researchers became interested in characteristics of the supervisee that may influence the supervisory relationship (for reviews, see Holloway, 1984; Russell et al., 1984; Worthington, 1987). The trainee's cultural experience, gender, cognitive and ego development, professional identity, experience level in counseling, theoretical orientation to counseling, and self-presentation were identified in the empirical and conceptual literature as important factors in supervision. In SAS, these characteristics of the trainee have been grouped into five trainee factors: (a) experience in counseling, (b) theoretical orientation in counseling, (c) learning style and needs, (d) cultural characteristics, and (e) self-presentation. Transcripts 4.1 and 4.3 illustrate the functional meaning of these factors, and Research Boxes 4.5 through 4.10 present empirical findings relevant to each factor. Refer to Figure 4.1 for the factors within the SAS model.

Experience

Experience level has been a frequently studied factor in supervision research (see Research Box 4.6). The trainee's familiarity with the professional role and tasks of counseling appears to be related to the supervisor's expectation of trainee competence and the trainee needs. The experience of the learner has also been connected to need for support and structure in supervision. Experience in counseling should not be confused with cognitive or ego developmental factors that may influence the trainee's performance or the supervisor's choice of supervisory method. In SAS, developmental cognitive and ego characteristics of the trainee are discussed under learning style and needs, and self-presentation, respectively.

There are two instances in Transcript 4.1 in which the supervisor attributes his behavior to his judgment of the trainee's experience level. He discusses the influence of her presence and articulation as more advanced than someone of her level of experience (col. 2, p. 64). Again, his consideration of her level of maturity in combination with her experience is used as a basis of determining how to deliver information (col. 2, p. 65).

Theoretical Orientation

The theoretical orientation of the trainee has not received much attention in the research literature (see Research Box 4.7); most supervisors, however, would concur that the views a trainee holds about human behavior and change will certainly be a part of supervision. Perhaps because much research in supervision has been about supervisees early in their professional training, there is not a clear theoretical designation expected of these individuals. Instead, the focus is on the development of a personal model of counseling that matches generally expected principles of personality and counseling theory. Several of the illustrations in the transcripts refer to instances in which the trainee is

Research Box 4.6

Research on Trainee Experience in Counseling

Experience level of the trainee has been related to perceived supervisory needs and satisfaction with supervision. The predominant findings between the expressed needs of very beginning-level and intern-level trainees include relationship characteristics (Heppner & Roehlke, 1984; Miars et al., 1983; Reising & Daniels, 1983; Wiley & Ray, 1986; Worthington, 1984b; Worthington & Stern, 1985). For example, initial-level trainees appear to require more support, encouragement, and structure in supervision, whereas interns demonstrate increasing independence from the supervisor (Hill et al., 1981; McNeil, Stoltenberg, & Pierce, 1985; Reising & Daniels, 1983; Wiley & Ray, 1986; Worthington, 1984b; Worthington & Stern, 1985) and more interest in higher-level skills and personal issues affecting counseling (Heppner & Roehlke, 1984; Hill et al., 1981; McNeil et al., 1985; Stoltenberg, Pierce, & McNeil, 1987; Worthington & Stern, 1985).

Since 1986, a few researchers have examined experience level of trainee and other personality factors to uncover the relationship of trainee characteristics and supervisory needs. Borders, Fong, and Neimeyer (1986) examined the relationship between student counselors' experience level (practicum versus intern level) and ego development (Loevinger's, 1976, scale) to perceptions of their clients. Their results indicated that ego development levels were more predictive of descriptors used by students than were experience levels. Lower-ego-level students tended to use more simplistic, concrete descriptors, whereas those at higher ego levels used more sophisticated, interactive descriptors. These results support the work of Holloway and Wolleat (1980), which investigated the relationship between conceptual level (CL), a construct related to social perceptual development, experience level, and clinical hypothesis formation. Although student experience level was not a significant factor, students with higher CL asked more divergent questions and had greater clarity in their clinical hypotheses than did low-CL students.

---

remarking on his or her thinking about theoretical principles of counseling in relation to a particular client issue. These instances may be considered a part of the "theory to practice" and "practice to theory" learning that occurs in the professionalization process.

In Transcript 4.1 (col. 1, p. 66), the trainee describes her beliefs on issues of incest. She is conceptualizing the client's behavior based on the trainee's theoretical orientation. Notice here that the supervisor's psycho-sociological understanding of human sexuality, as discussed under Supervisor Factors, has an important bearing on his determination that he understand the trainee's orientation toward sexuality. Although this is not an example of a more fully developed statement on her approach to counseling, it does demonstrate how conceptual beliefs with regard to human behavior are influential in the thinking about a specific treatment of a client.

Research Box 4.6

Continued

Tracey et al. (1989) designed an analogue study in an effort to examine the central tenet of developmental models of supervision—namely, that the degree of structure provided in the supervisory relationship is central to trainees' learning needs. Specifically, beginning-level trainees are said to need more structured environments than do more advanced trainees. Tracey et al. were interested in how counselor trainees' preferences for varying levels of supervision structure may be moderated by experience, reactance potential, and the content of supervision. Reactance potential was described as a personality variable related to an individual's need to resist or comply with imposed structure or direction in interpersonal contexts. The content of supervision was described as either a noncrisis situation or a crisis situation that involved a suicidal client. The findings of this study revealed several interactive effects of the independent variables on trainees' preferences for supervisory structure. The authors concluded the following:

(a) structure was important for beginning trainees and less so for more advanced trainees; (b) urgency of the client condition had a strong moderating effect on the experience-structure preference; and (c) in the noncrisis content condition, reactance accounted for structure preferences of advanced-level trainees. These findings support some of the previous work that has indicated that as trainees progress through levels of practice experience, their need for supervisory structure diminishes (McNeil et al., 1985; Reising & Daniels, 1983; Stoltenberg et al., 1987; Wiley & Ray, 1986). The structure-experience relationship, however, is moderated by both personality variables of the trainees (in this case reactance potential) and the situational determinants of the supervisory focus (crisis versus noncrisis client). This well-designed study presents a strong argument for researchers to include personality characteristics, experience level, and content conditions of supervision in studies of supervisory environments.

Another example of the importance of the trainee's theoretical orientation is in Transcript 2.5 in which the trainee is at a distinct disadvantage in collaborating with the supervisor in the conceptualization of the client because of the trainee's lack of adherence or knowledge of the rational-emotive approach. The supervisor lectures the trainee on a different theoretical approach to the client situation.

Learning Style and Learning Needs

In the SAS model, *learning style and needs* refers generally to that identified group of developmental factors relevant to the trainee's approach to and perception of the supervisory experience (see Research Box 4.6). Developmental characteristics, such as conceptual level (Harvey, Hunt, & Schroder, 1961) and ego development (Loevinger, 1976), have been examined in light of the acquisition of counseling skills, such

Research Box 4.7

Research on Trainee Theoretical Orientation

Sundland and Garfield (cited in Sundland, 1977) and Beutler and McNabb (1981) found that students tend to adopt the theoretical orientation of supervisors and/or the director of clinical training. In an extensive study of clinical psychology graduates in a medical school practice setting, Guest and Beutler (1988) confirmed that orientations of prominent supervisors were particularly important in establishing a trainee's viewpoint regardless of the correspondence between trainees' initial orientation and the supervisor's orientation. Furthermore, trainee locus of control and other personality variables did not contribute to changes in orientation or values over the course of one training year or in follow-up 3 to 5 years after training. Supervision as a powerful socialization factor in the profession is very evident from this study.

Supervisor/Trainee Interactions

The influence of matching of supervisor and supervisee individual characteristics on trainee satisfaction and performance has been the approach of several investigators. Hester, Weitz, and Anchor (1976) looked at attitude similarity-dissimilarity, as measured by Byrne's Attitude Scale (Byrne, 1971) on trainees' attraction to the supervisor. Findings indicated that the skill level of the supervisor was a greater determinant of attraction than was attitude similarity. Lemons and Lanning (1979) found that similarity in value systems, as measured by Rokeach Value Survey (Rokeach, 1967), was not related to the quality of the relationship or satisfaction of the trainee; however, level of communication in supervision was related to these same variables. Kennard, Stewart, and Gluck (1987) found that theoretical similarities between supervisors and trainees enhanced trainees' perceptions of the quality of supervision.

as empathy and clinical hypothesis formation (see Research Box 4.8). Stoltenberg and Delworth (1988) prescribed matches between the developmental characteristic of conceptual level and the degree of structure in supervision. For example, the greater the tolerance for ambiguity and the more relativistic the thinking, the greater opportunity for the supervisor to offer a more unstructured approach to supervision. Unfortunately, there are few empirical findings to guide the supervisor in choosing those strategies that would reflect a structured versus unstructured learning environment. At this point, reflected interviews of supervision may offer the greatest insight into the relevance of such factors to actual decision making and to the practice of the trainee or supervisor. Poulin's (1994) dimensionalization of reflected interviews of expert supervisors found that the supervisor thought of trainee characteristics in three categories: as a person, a counselor, and a student. Within these categories, the supervisor counseled trainees' learning needs within the context of the style in which they learned

Research Box 4.8

Research on Trainee Learning Needs

Several measures of counselor's cognitive functioning have been of interest to researchers. In particular, conceptual systems theory (CST; Harvey et al., 1961) has enjoyed considerable popularity since the early 1970s. The studies of conceptual level suggest that matching learning environment to trainee's cognitive characteristics may be fruitful in creating facilitative supervisory environments.

Cognitive constructs related to CST such as ego development, dogmatism, and locus of control have also been investigated in relationship to counseling skills and cognitions. Although none of these studies took place in the context of the supervisory situation, they do suggest that certain cognitive constructs may influence the learning and performance of counseling-related skills. Winter and Holloway (1991) completed an analogue study that examined the relationship of supervisees' conceptual level (CL), experience level, and perception of supervisory approach to their choice of audiotaped passages to be presented for a simulated supervisory interview. Cognitively complex supervisees were more likely to choose passages with a counseling skills focus over passages that focused on client conceptualization or personal growth. Descriptive data showed that nearly 75% of complex supervisees made explicit requests for supervisor feedback as compared to 50% of middle-CL group and 35% of low-CL group. Thus, cognitively complex counselors preferred to focus on passages that would encourage the supervisor to provide feedback on their counseling skills. The authors interpret this finding in light of the higher personal responsibility generally demonstrated by complex individuals in interpersonal situations. That is, high-CL participants selected segments that focused on their skills and actual behav-

iors in the counseling passages, thus inviting the supervisor to provide direct feedback on their work and allowing trainees an opportunity to improve their skills. Experience level was a significant influence in the choice of passages. The greater the counselor experience, the less the focus on client conceptualization and the more the focus on personal growth issues, such as countertransference, self-efficacy, and self-awareness, and the more willingness to choose passages that reflected less favorably on them as counselors. There were no interactive effects of CL and experience level nor did supervisor approach influence the choice of counseling passages. As discussed earlier, the results regarding experience level of trainees are consistent with numerous other studies that have examined supervisory needs at different levels of practical experience (Heppner & Roehlke, 1984; McNeil et al., 1985; Miars et al., 1983; Rabinowitz et al., 1986; Stoltenberg et al., 1987).

A series of investigations by Borders and associates have examined the relationship of trainee's ego development to (a) beginning- and advanced-level counseling skills (Borders & Fong, 1989), (b) perceptions of clients (Borders et al., 1986), and (c) in-session cognitions about actual counseling events (Borders, 1989; Borders, Fong, & Cron, 1988). In each of these studies, with the exception of Borders et al. (1986), experience level of the participants was controlled by examining only one level of counseling experience. However, trainees at the same level of experience produced different types of cognitions relative to their level of ego development. Thus, preexisting personality constructs seem to interact with the influences of experience level.

and their readiness to assimilate and make use of the knowledge (see Research Box 4.1). In Transcript 4.1 (col. 1, pp. 68-69), the trainee reflects on how the supervisor's teaching strategy affected her and how she believes she learned best from him. The supervisor has been exploring her coming up with the "right answer," and she has previously commented on her frustration with this tactic. Finally, she asks him for a "clue," which appears to clue him into the fact that they are playing detective and she needs to learn in a different way. Another example occurs in Transcript 3.1 (col. 2, p. 48) in which the supervisor reflects on what the trainee needs to learn (learning needs) and how he will best teach her without activating defensiveness.

Cultural Characteristics

Cultural characteristics include gender, ethnicity, race, sexual orientation, religious beliefs, and personal values that may be central to an individual's group identity and relevant to supervision. In SAS, cultural values are seen as salient to trainees' attitudes and actions toward their clients and supervisors—that is, in any interpersonal situation. Research in this supervision area is relatively limited, although there has been significantly more research on the relationship of cultural variables to the counseling relationship and effectiveness (for reviews, see Atkinson, Morten, & Sue, 1989; Pedersen, 1985; Sue & Sue, 1990; Tyler, Brome, & Williams, 1991). Bernard and Goodyear (1992) present an excellent chapter on the multicultural context of supervision and extrapolate findings from the counseling literature to issues of training. Tyler et al. (1991) address the issues of training in multicultural supervisory dyads and offer ways in which both supervisor and trainee can take responsibility for discussing issues of power and culture as they relate to their interactions with the trainee's clients. The structure of power and involvement in the supervisory relationship may be particularly complex in a cross-cultural context because of the added complexity of power in the general society between minority and nonminority groups (Solomon, 1983). There has been limited research on the relationship of gender and role (supervisor/supervisee) to the process characteristics of power and involvement (Nelson & Holloway, 1990). Female trainees are less likely to be encouraged to use higher power responses in their interactions. These responses include giving of opinions and ideas, thus resulting in a decided disadvantage in the opportunity to receive feedback. Although similar studies examining ethnic or racial minorities in cross-cultural situations do not exist at this time, it is likely that positional power of the supervisor or trainee might be in contradiction to the usual social arrangements and thus, conceivably, be problematic.

In Transcript 4.2 (col. 2, p. 78), the issue of the sexual orientation of the client and the trainee emerges but does not become the focus of the supervisory discussion. In a broader societal culture where sexual orientation is the subject of discrimination and prejudice, it is interesting to note that neither the trainee nor the supervisor choose to discuss this topic directly. This omission may be a consequence of the sensitive nature or hesitancy about discussing sexual orientation, or it may be an implicit decision that the more important focus is the client seduction and the possibility of a sexual relationship between the client and counselor. (For further discussion of cultural elements see Research Box 4.9.)

Self-Presentation

Self-presentation is a social-psychological term that refers to the regulation of one's behaviors to create a particular impression on others (Jones & Pittman, 1982). A brief discussion of this construct appears in the Supervisor Factors section on self-presentation on page 78. The trainee's interpersonal and emotional characteristics in supervisory and counseling relationships have been included in the research of self-presentational behaviors (see Research Box 4.10). Constructs such as interpersonal patterns, reactance potential, defensiveness, and counterdefensiveness have been studied in relation to the process of supervision and relationship variables (see Research Box 3.1). Poulin (1994), in her dimensional analysis, concluded that a primary dimension in the supervisor's understanding and judgment of the trainee's behavior in supervision was the trainee's interpersonal behaviors as reflected in the roles of person, counselor, and student (see Research Box 4.1).

In Transcript 4.1 (col. 2, p. 64), the supervisor attends to the trainee's level of maturity and presence in the session and describes these characteristics as a central aspect of his deciding how to approach the teaching situation. In Transcript 4.3 (col. 2, pp. 83-84), the emergence of the parallel process in supervision clearly illustrates the importance of the trainee's self-presentation (that is, his resistance to changing his approach to and sense of hopelessness about the client) in the supervisor's attempts to find solutions to the problematic client situation.

Client Factors

The client is always present in the supervision. Indeed, the supervisor's raison d'être is to ensure that the trainee can deliver effective service to the client. Yet, ironically, there is little research that examines client change or characteristics as an outcome or in relation to the supervision process (see Research Box 4.11). In SAS, there are three client factors: (a) client characteristics, (b) client identified problem and diagnosis, and (c) counseling relationship (see Figure 4.1).

Research Box 4.9

Research on Trainee and Supervisor Cultural Elements

Although the investigation of cultural and racial characteristics on the counseling relationship has generated considerable research in the last decade (for reviews, see Helms, 1984; Parham, 1989), only a few empirical studies were found in the supervision literature. Cook and Helms (1988) were interested in the predictability of satisfaction with cross-cultural supervision from relationship dimensions as measured by the Barrett-Lennard Relationship Inventory (BLRI; Barrett-Lennard, 1962), the Supervision Questionnaire (Worthington & Roehlke, 1979), and a personal data sheet. They asked four culturally diverse groups,—Black, Hispanic, Asian and Native Americans—to respond to a survey regarding their supervision experiences. The results indicated that only supervisor liking and conditional liking relationship dimensions were related to satisfaction with supervision. In addition, supervisees' perceptions of their supervision relationships varied according to their race or ethnicity: (a) Blacks, Hispanics, and Native Americans felt lower levels of liking from supervisors than did Asians; (b) all groups but Native Americans felt that supervisors were emotionally comfortable with them; (c) Blacks and Native Americans perceived the highest mean levels of unconditional liking; (d) Blacks perceived significantly higher levels of unconditional liking than did Hispanics; and (e) Native Americans perceived significantly higher levels of discomfort than any other group. The limitations of this study warrant mention: the sample size for Native Americans was 8, only 51% of potential participants choose to respond, and the dependent measures reflected perceptions of the supervisor's attitudes rather than actual behaviors of the supervisor. It is important, however, given the paucity

of research on this topic that future researchers use diverse methods to understand the role of ethnicity and race on relationship dimensions in supervision.

McRoy et al. (1986) studied racial and power dynamics in supervisory relationships in an exploratory survey study. Although respondents identified few actual problems, they identified many potential areas of concern. Because the field supervisor's role is perceived as powerful by supervisors and supervisees alike, there appeared to be few actual discussions about potential cultural conflicts, despite the fact that students perceived their supervisors as sensitive to cultural differences. The unwillingness to talk about these issues in relation to the counseling relationship as well has serious ramifications for culturally appropriate treatment. It seemed that participants were willing to identify the potential of cross-cultural problems in the abstract but not able to discuss these openly. Gutierrez (1982) has addressed the ways in which cross-cultural sensitivity and practice can be incorporated into the entire counseling curriculum. Building a program that enhances open communication and knowledge among minority and nonminority students and faculty is a beginning to directly confronting these issues in the supervisory relationship.

Zuniga (1987) developed a culturally focused supervision experience with Mexican American supervisees. The trainees' feelings of inadequacy and competence, not unusual for beginning-level counselors, were processed within a cultural context. The trainees developed insight into not only their own issues of working with Mexican American clients but also the relevance of their own experience in dealing with a sometimes hostile and discriminatory environment in developing strong survival skills.

Research Box 4.10

Research on Trainee Self-Presentation

Ward et al. (1985) examined the influence of different self-presentational styles on supervisors' judgments of counselor competence. Their study addressed an important and rarely examined area, the evaluation of trainees based on their in-session supervisory behavior. In this analogue study, the investigators created stimulus conditions in which trainees were viewed taking a defensive or counterdefensive interpersonal style. The defensive trainee was evaluated by supervisors as more self-confident, whereas the counterdefensive trainee was evaluated as more socially skilled. When the client was reported to have improved, trainees were judged as more competent, self-confident, expert, and attractive than when the client worsened, regardless of style. It appeared from this study that supervisors base their judgments of the trainee's professional skills on client progress. This is particularly salient given the lack of attention to client outcome in evaluating supervisory methods. Tracey et al. (1989) used the construct "reactance potential" to examine supervisors' teaching response to trainees' behavior. Reactance potential was described as a personality variable related to an individual's need to resist or comply with imposed structure or direction in interpersonal contexts. The authors concluded the following: (a) Structure was important for beginning trainees and less so for more advanced trainees; (b) urgency of the client condition had a strong moderating effect on the experience-structure preference; and (c) in the noncrisis content condition, reactance accounted for structure preferences of advanced-level trainees.

Client Characteristics

An important and frequently researched area has been the variety of client characteristics in relation to the process and outcome of psychotherapy. Characteristics and variables that have been studied include social class, personality traits, age, gender, intelligence, race, and ethnicity. Some of these characteristics have some real practical value in determining the appropriateness of brief versus long-term therapy and premature termination (Garfield, 1994). The relevance to these general client characteristics, rather than specific diagnostic attributes, has not been studied within the context of supervision, training, or both. Pragmatically, however, the supervisor frequently considers client age, ethnicity, gender, and race in determining the appropriateness of the match between counselor and client as well as in looking for solutions to various difficulties that may emerge in the counseling relationship. The literature on matching client gender, ethnic minority status, or both with therapists suggests that, although there appears to be a preference for ethnically similar counselors, this is not consistently evident in the empirical literature (Coleman, Wampold, & Casali, 1994). It behooves the supervisor to recognize that

Research Box 4.11

Research on Client Factors

Only a few studies have examined client outcome measures in relation to supervision.... Dodenhoff (1981) found that direct instructional methods were positively related to trainee effectiveness and client outcome as rated by the supervisor. Steinhelber, Patterson, Cliffe, and LeGoullon (1984) evaluated the effects of supervision variables on client outcome. They found that there was no relationship between the amount of supervision and changes in ratings of clients on the Global Assessment Scale from pretherapy to posttherapy. There was a relationship, however, between those changes and trainee-therapist reports of congruence of their theoretical orientation with their supervisor's orientation.

The complexity of using client outcome measures as a standard of supervision effectiveness is reflected in those studies that have compared ratings of client change from multiple sources. Similar to Dodenhoff's (1981) findings that supervisors' judgments of client change differed from other ratings, Najavits and Strupp (1994) found that supervisors were not able to differentiate more effective from less effective therapists (based on outcome measures and length of stay), whereas therapists,

independent observers, and clients were able to do so. On the other hand, Rounsaville, Chevron, and Weissman (1984) found that evaluations of therapists based on self-report differed sharply from evaluations of therapist competence based on viewing videotapes of actual sessions. Ratings of therapist competency are further complicated by client characteristics. Both Rounsaville, O'Malley, Foley, and Weissman (1988) and Strupp et al. (1988) found that evaluations of therapist competence at performing manualized treatments were confounded by patient difficulty; those therapists with the most difficult clients were rated as less competent than those with less difficult clients. Although an analogue study, the Tracey et al. (1989) study . . . lends support to the findings that client severity is related to trainee preferences in supervisory approach; the suicidal client condition had a strong moderating effect on the trainee's preference for more direction from the supervisor regardless of trainee experience level.

In the psychotherapy literature, discrepancies between clients', therapists', and trained observers' perceptions of process and outcome variables are

variables such as social desirability, attitudes, and or values may play an important role in a counselor's potential effectiveness. The attribution of therapist ineffectiveness may be erroneously placed on the lack of similarity between client and therapist rather than on other characteristics of the client, the counselor, or both that may be inhibiting progress.

The Identified Problem and Diagnosis

The identification of the client's problem is often the first topic for discussion in supervision. This might include a formal *DSM—IV* assess-

Research Box 4.11

Continued

generally found (Orlinsky, Grawe, & Parks, 1994); however, it is disconcerting that supervisors, who have the responsibility to ensure the therapist's competent practice with clients, are perhaps more influenced by the trainee's interpersonal involvement in supervision than their effectiveness with the client.

Friedlander et al. (1989) used the Interpersonal Communication Rating Scale (ICRS), the Relational Communication Control Coding System (RCCCS; Ericson & Rogers, 1973), Hill Counselor Verbal Response Category System—Revised (HCVRCS—R; Friedlander, 1984), and a rating system, developed for the study (Supervisory Feedback Rating System; SFRS) to study the parallel process in counseling and supervision as manifested in one case. Friedlander et al. (1989) argued that the relationships often mirrored each other by citing the parallel nature of the self-report data and verbal communication patterns across nine concurrent supervisory and counseling sessions. They concluded that supervision and counseling seem to be reciprocal and interlocking processes and that trainees are in a highly vulnerable position as the linchpin between both relationships. This is one of a few

studies (Doehrman, 1976; Wedeking & Scott, 1976) that has investigated the effects of the supervisory process on the trainees' process with their clients.

Tracey et al. (1989) designed an analogue study in which they examined the relationship of severity of client problem to the degree of structure provided by the supervisor. More generally they were interested in how counselor trainees' preferences for varying levels of supervision structure may be moderated by their experience level and reactance potential. The content of supervision was described as either a non-crisis situation or a crisis situation that involved a suicidal client. The findings of this study revealed several interactive effects of the independent variables on trainees' preferences for supervisory structure. The authors concluded the following: (a) Structure was important for beginning trainees and less so for more advanced trainees; (b) urgency of the client condition had a strong moderating effect on the experience-structure preference; and (c) in the noncrisis content condition, reactance accounted for structure preferences of advanced level trainees.

ment and diagnosis or a more problem-solving description of the client's presenting concern. New clients may be introduced to the trainee's caseload after careful screening by the agency, the supervisor, or both. Supervisors in practice often screen clients for beginning-level trainees to ensure that trainees will be assigned only cases appropriate to their level of competence. Supervisors also may choose cases for trainees based on the supervisor's areas of expertise. Occasionally, clients may be dealing with issues that are similar to a life circumstance that the trainee has not yet resolved, and the supervisor then refers the client rather than risk the almost certain countertransference that would emerge in the therapeutic relationship. In addition, other characteristics of the client are relevant to the supervisor's and trainee's choice of topic of supervision and the manner in which they engage one another.

There is evidence of this focus on client concerns in almost all of the transcripts presented in this book. Typically, these examples involve the trainee's describing for the supervisor the details of the symptomology, significant historical events, contemporary events, and the assessment and diagnosis of the client. In Transcript 4.3 (col. 2, p. 81), the trainee and supervisor focus on the client's behavior and the trainee's conceptualization of his behavior in counseling. Again in column 2 on page 83, the conceptualization of the client's behavior dominates the session.

The supervisor is responsible for ensuring that the client receives adequate treatment from the supervisee. In part, this assessment of the match between the supervisee's area and level of competence and the client's needs will depend on the severity of the client's problem. Axis IV of the *DSM—IV* is reserved for rating the severity of the psychosocial stressors in an individual's life. To determine the course of treatment, the degree of stress is then examined in light of the client's mental condition or the nature of the problem and past adaptability to living. If a client is severely depressed or aggressive and is experiencing an unusually high number of stressors, then the supervisor and counselor may need to do a specific assessment for suicide or homicide potential or both.

Note in Transcript 4.3 (p. 81) that the supervisor is initially attempting to get a clear assessment of the client's level of depression and, specifically, to find out if the trainee is concerned about the client's suicide potential. Level of severity of a client's problem has been related to the degree of structure in a supervision interview (Tracy et al., 1989). Notice how the supervisor in Transcript 4.3 asks very direct questions regarding the client's change in regard to the depression (col. 1, p. 81) and then returns to the suicide potential again through questioning (col. 1, p. 85). It is interesting to see that the supervisor readily accepts the trainee's judgment that the client does not present a grave suicide risk. Other supervisors might have pursued this line of questioning further and helped the trainee create a clear suicide assessment procedure with the client. This supervisor redirects herself to the counseling relationship.

Characteristics of the Counseling Relationship

The counseling relationship is an important basis from which to understand the effects of different treatment strategies as well as the effectiveness of the trainee in creating a therapeutic relationship (Holloway & Neufeldt, in press). The reenactment of the relationship dynamics in the supervisory situation is a familiar phenomenon to supervisors and has been named the *parallel process* (Dodenhoff, 1981; Ekstein & Wallerstein,

1958). Parallel process occurs when the central dynamic process of the counseling relationship is unconsciously acted out by the trainee in the supervision relationship. The trainee may be experiencing difficulty with the client and feels powerless to change the situation therapeutically; subsequently he or she takes on interpersonal strategies similar to the client's form of resistance. If the supervisor does not recognize the dynamic as a part of the counseling situation and the trainee's feelings of powerlessness, then the supervisor may collude with this reenactment by adopting a role similar to the trainee's in the counseling relationship. The obvious result is an impasse in supervision. A supervisor who recognizes the parallel process can intervene directly with the trainee, thereby breaking the impasse in supervision while concurrently modeling effective interpersonal strategies for the trainee. Thus, with effective supervisory intervention, the trainee begins to understand, both experientially and conceptually, the meaning of the client's behavior and is able to resume a therapeutic approach to the problem.

Transcript 4.3 is an example of parallel process (p. 83 and following, p. 84). Notice how early in this excerpt the trainee begins to "yes, but" the supervisor. In the same way that he experiences his client sabotaging his own efforts to be therapeutic, the trainee works to discount the supervisor's ideas and suggestions. As he describes the client's lack of energy and motivation to change, the trainee acts resigned and helpless in the face of the client's symptoms. The supervisor, like the trainee, in the counseling relationship, offers suggestions or gives advice on how to handle the client only to encounter the trainee's resistance to any proactive approach. The ironic moment comes (col. 1, p. 83) when the supervisor asks her trainee to be the client, and, of course, he does so quite successfully. This excerpt does not give us the advantage of the supervisor's breaking the impasse by not colluding with the "yes, but" sabotaging of the trainee and trying to solve the problem. The teaching moment is available, however, as the last exchange of the excerpt is completed.

Institutional Factors

Supervision, whether a part of a training program or continuing professional development, takes place in the context of institutional organizations, such as in-house departmental clinics, university counseling centers, hospitals, or community mental health and other service settings. The role of supervision in respect to the service demands of the organization is an important consideration in establishing goals and functions of supervision. Yet the influence of organizational variables on supervision has rarely been investigated or discussed in the professional literature (see Research Box 4.12). Institutional charac-

Research Box 4.12

Research on Institutional Factors

The influence of organizational variables on supervision has rarely been studied. In a survey that asked interns to indicate their level of readiness for the professional demands of the internship, participants most frequently expressed concern over their lack of preparedness for dealing with organizational politics (Cole et al., 1981). Dodds (1986) has summarized the different goals and roles of training institutions that can place the supervisor and supervisee in conflict. He has provided a framework to understand the stresses that emerge from the overlapping systems of a training institution and a service agency. Ekstein (1964) described the clinical rhombus as the interactions between the four roles that were necessary to ensure the effective functioning of an agency with training involvement—the agency administrator, the clinical supervisor, the supervisee-therapist, and the client. The need to maintain a relationship between all of these participants (not always face-to-face) is critical to the quality of professional training. The director of internship training or supervisor often has the responsibility of orienting the trainee to the agency, the training program, and the various personnel, service functions, and goals as an important beginning step to integrate the intern into the agency (Holloway & Roehlke, 1987). Although surveys of professionals suggest that institutional variables are critical to maintaining an effective supervisory program, there is no research that specifically examines the relationship of certain institutional policies, procedures, or goals to trainees' learning.

teristics are defined in SAS as (a) agency clientele, (b) organizational structure and climate, and (c) professional ethics and standards (see Figure 4.1).

Agency Clientele

The clientele served by the agency is relevant to the trainee's type of clinical training and, in some instances, perhaps to supervisory strategies. There has been little research on this topic, but a number of supervisory articles discuss the specialized training needs of trainees working with different types of clinical groups—for example, incest survivors, male perpetrators, substance abusers, medically related syndromes, and many more. Often, clientele in the program are required to have specialized knowledge, certain personal experiences, or, in some cases, membership or former membership in the clinical group. There are also more informal ways that the predominant clientele may affect the program. Fredenberger (1977) noted that clinics that offer services exclusively to a particularly disturbed psychiatric population may find that job-related stress and staff burnout are abnormally high among the staff. Agencies that work with specific age groups or developmental stages (e.g., adolescents, families, children, and the elderly) may also have specialized requirements for admittance to training or for specifically endorsed supervisory techniques.

In Transcript 4.4, the trainee's client is a volunteer from a college course on interviewing. Students received extra credit for projects such as seeing a counselor-in-training for four sessions. Notice how frustrated the counselor is because the client doesn't seem to have a "real" problem (col. 1, p. 101). The supervisor reconceptualizes the client problem by applying a developmental perspective that is consistent with the client's needs and thus allows the trainee to understand more fully the role of the counselor with this type of clientele (col. 1, p. 103).

Organizational Structure and Climate

Ekstein and Wallerstein (1958) depict the many roles necessary for the supervisor to work in an institutional setting. Their clinical "rhombus" concept consists of six interactions between the four roles of the supervisor—agency administrator, clinical supervisor, supervisee-therapist, and client. Each of these roles suggests different motivations and goals, yet all four must seek to accommodate the goals of the other three. Dodds (1986) discussed the necessary balance between goals and motivations of the training institution and the service agency. He suggested that the success of the supervisor-supervisee relationship would depend on the degree to which the supervisor could function as a teacher and the supervisee could function as a staff (albeit less experienced) professional. Both participants of the training dyad must understand and be motivated to function in roles prescribed to them by their organizations. Organizational norms and politics often intrude on the supervisory relationship. In a survey that asked interns to indicate their level of readiness for the professional demands of the internship, participants most frequently expressed concern over their lack of preparedness for dealing with organizational politics (Cole, Kolko, & Craddick, 1981).

An overwhelming amount of stress in the workplace may lead to burnout of the staff members, a process whereby professionals disengage from their work (Cherniss, 1980) due to emotional exhaustion, depersonalization of the organization, and a reduced sense of accomplishment. Counselors caught in this state begin feeling "compassion fatigue" and drastically reduce their involvement and emotional contact with others. They begin to view the client as an object, not an individual (Jackson, Schwab, & Schuler, 1986). Cherniss (1980) suggests that the environment within an agency can lead to the transmission of burnout between workers and thereby influence the training program. Because of the close, ongoing relationship between supervisor and supervisee, it is likely that this environmental stress will be carried into the supervisory relationship. Supervisors and supervisees

TRANSCRIPT **4.4**

Contextual Factors

Supervision Interview

Trainee I don't know what to do with this client. Basically she said that she just came for the credit. No problems.

Supervisor Did she spend the entire time with you? I mean, the full 50 minutes?

Trainee Well, almost. I'm not actually sure when we ended, but I think that it was pretty close to the hour.

Supervisor What happened during that time?

Trainee There were a lot of silences it seemed, especially at the beginning. She just sort of sat there expecting me to do something. So I began asking her questions about her current living situation, school, things like that, to get to know her.

Supervisor Umm-hmm, that seems like a pretty good start. Did she seem particularly interested in any aspect of this conversation?

Trainee Well, it was kinda interesting. When we started talking about her living situation, I discovered that she was living with her folks but wasn't entirely happy about it. She has a boyfriend that she has been seeing for about 6 months and going home to her parents every night is not very convenient.

Supervisor How has she dealt with the situation so far?

Trainee She really hasn't dealt with it. She is actually afraid to bring up moving out to her parents. She doesn't want to be ungrateful and actually has a pretty good deal . . . free rent and board. So it's sort of complicated, I think, but she says it'll take care of

SAS Analysis

The supervisor is collecting information on the counselor-client interchange. The trainee is reporting the **client's no-problem** approach to the session.

The trainee continues to elaborate on the client's situation and the specifics of the client's report on contemporary and familial relationships.

(continued)

TRANSCRIPT 4.4 **Continued**

Supervision Interview	*SAS Analysis*
itself. So basically I guess that she doesn't want to talk about it. I mean it isn't a big enough problem to warrant her attention.	
Supervisor It sounds as if it is something that she is concerned about but maybe just a gnawing sort of concern not dramatically interfering with her life.	
Trainee That's probably it. The real problem is how am I going to talk to her about something. Maybe I should just have her terminate now if there isn't anything to deal with. You know that is one of the problems of having these volunteers—they don't have "real" issues. I don't know how I'm going to learn how to do this unless I have a real client.	The trainee describes the client as not really being a client because of her volunteer status. The implication here is the **clientele** in the training situation is the source of the trainee's dilemma.
Supervisor I can see you are frustrated with not having a person who is eager to solve a problem and get your help in doing it. You know it isn't always as clear-cut as that in counseling. Sometimes a client is confused about the problem they want to work on or perhaps just have been trying to put it aside because they don't see any easy solutions. In the case of your client, it sounds as if she is going through some pretty predictable developmental issues. She's what, 20?	The supervisor briefly introduces the theoretical concept of developmental counseling.
Trainee Close, she's 19 and will be 20 in April.	
Supervisor Counseling might be very helpful to her in solving her developmental issue of separating from her parents.	The supervisor and trainee focus on the client's problem and severity in these first few interchanges. The issue is the status of the client as a volunteer and the seemingly lack of an issue for her to talk about in counseling.
Trainee Right, but I don't think that she wants it to be defined as a problem. I think that she just would prefer to	

(continued)

TRANSCRIPT 4.4 **Continued**

Supervision Interview	*SAS Analysis*

chat with me as a friend and not think of herself as being in counseling.

Supervisor In some ways it appears that she's trying to play down any difficulties she might have for fear that she'll be seen as sick. Does that make any sense to you?

Trainee Maybe, she did say a couple of times that she has never been in counseling and neither has anyone in the family. Although at one point she mentioned that her parents did have some marital problems during her early teenage years and that they probably could have benefited from some help. She just sees herself as the problem solver in the family, so it seems strange to her to be asking for help.

Supervisor Well, there are a couple things you've said that I think might be useful for her to talk about—her parents' relationship, her role in the family, and the relevance of both of these factors to her leaving home. But first, I think that you need to help her understand what counseling is and how it can be helpful to problem solve everyday events and especially during times when we're going through developmental transitions, like leaving home, forming and breaking serious relationships, having children, et cetera.

> The trainee's experience level seems to necessitate the supervisor's explaining the scope of counseling.

In this way she might be freed up to talk about her specific issue without feeling like you are labeling her as "sick."

Trainee Actually I realize that I wasn't thinking about counseling in a very developmental way myself. I have been so focused on needing someone with a really big problem so I could learn how to deal with it.

> The trainee returns to her concern that the agency **clientele** is not going to meet her needs in learning to be a counselor.

(continued)

TRANSCRIPT 4.4 **Continued**

Supervision Interview	*SAS Analysis*
Supervisor Well, we are in a special circumstance having volunteer clients, but it doesn't mean that they can't teach a lot about identifying issues to work on and how to form a relationship. Believe me that the difficult situations in life will be presented to you only too soon. Let's focus on some hypotheses about her difficulty in leaving home.	The supervisor gives attention to the **trainee's emotional state (self-presentation)** and then goes on to discuss a developmental orientation to counseling **(supervisor factor: theoretical orientation)**.

Unpublished supervision interview. Based on an actual transcript altered to protect participant confidentiality.

are subject to bringing environmental norms and stressors into their relationship and ultimately to transmitting these attitudes to the counseling situation; thus, it seems important for them to understand their roles and behaviors in the context of organizational conditions.

In Transcript 4.5 (pp. 105-106), the frustration that the trainee is experiencing in not having an ongoing client soon becomes a discussion of the organizational climate. Both the trainee and supervisor seem helpless in dealing directly with the negative atmosphere and inefficiency around the intake assignment procedure. The supervisor chooses to solve the problem by intervening at a level in which she has control and assigns a client to the trainee from her own caseload. Although the organizational situation is the focus of conversation, it is not the focus of the solution.

Professional Ethics and Standards

The supervisory relationship is considered a critical component of professional training, and yet, until the 1990s, specific guidelines for the practice of supervision were almost nonexistent. The "ACES Ethical Standards for Counseling Supervisors" (Supervision Interest Network, 1993) is the most comprehensive set of guidelines directed specifically at the supervisory relationship. This document addresses the supervisor's responsibilities with regard to client welfare and rights, supervisory role, administration of supervision, and training program requirements in universities and agencies (Dye & Borders, 1990). The *American Psychological Association Ethical Guidelines for Practice* (American Psychological Association, 1992) also addresses the ethical issues in supervisory relationships. Professional standards for training provide guidelines

TRANSCRIPT **4.5**

Contextual Factors

Supervision Interview	*SAS Analysis*
Supervisor Well, Sandra, I understand that you were assigned a new client yesterday . . . that's the good news.	
Trainee Not so good news. This client didn't show up, and I waited for an hour. This has happened now for the second time. I'm really frustrated. Everyone else in my group has four clients, and I have none.	
Supervisor It is frustrating since it makes it difficult for us to work on actual material. Have you told the intake worker that you haven't had anyone who's shown up yet?	The client's no-show quickly becomes an issue of the trainee's disgruntlement with the **client accessibility in the agency.**
Trainee I have. I've been down there every day, maybe twice a day, for the last week. I am starting to get paranoid about them overlooking me on purpose. You know, the system is pretty disorganized. It really just depends on whether they remember to assign to you over anyone else. Can't you do anything about this? I mean do senior staff have to put up with this situation, too?	The trainee continues to express her frustration with the intake procedure in the agency.
Supervisor Well, umm-hmm, well, it is possible to intervene, but I'm . . . it is difficult to make a change . . . the staff person has been there for a long time and it is something of a time-sink to try to change her ways of doing things.	The supervisor begins to acknowledge the negative feelings and **atmosphere that surround this issue in the agency.** Because of this general **organizational climate,** the supervisor chooses not to intervene with the intake worker.
Trainee She is such a problem. I mean you have to try to figure out on a daily basis what kind of mood she is in to know whether or not you should ask her for something. Basically, I think that she blames me for my assignees not showing up. I've never even met	The supervisor's responses seem to invite the trainee to continue with her complaints about the staff person rather than try to problem-solve her situation.

(continued)

TRANSCRIPT 4.5 **Continued**

Supervision Interview	*SAS Analysis*
these people. She is the one doing the telephone interview. You're right about people just giving up. I swear half the senior staff just goes around her or does it themselves.	
Supervisor We've been trying to ease her out, but it is extremely difficult. I just can't waste anymore energy on it and I . . .	The supervisor continues to focus the discussion on the **organizational situation** and her personal resolution of withdrawing from it.
Trainee Do you truly think she has something against me? I mean it isn't that I have any history with her, but she is so rude to me.	
Supervisor I really don't know, Sandra. To have to take her on just to get you a client is not a pleasant prospect. I think that I'm going to assign you someone out of my intake caseload. Let me take a look to see who I have today. Can you meet with someone this afternoon?	The supervisor stops the speculation regarding the trainee's personal effect on the intake worker and circumvents the organizational problem by finding a different way to assign the trainee a client.

Unpublished supervision interview. Based on an actual transcript altered to protect participant confidentiality.

for the frequency and duration of supervision and supervisor qualifications. Examples include the American Psychological Association *Accreditation Handbook* (Accreditation Committee, 1986) for academic programs and internships in professional psychology, the *American Counseling Association Ethical Guidelines* (American Counseling Association, 1981), the *National Association of Social Workers Published Guidelines* (National Association of Social Workers [NASW], 1980), and *Standards for the Private Practice of Clinical Social Work* (NASW, 1981). See the Appendix for the Association for Counselor Education and Supervision Standards for Counselor Supervision.

Professional organizations charge supervisors with the responsibility of the treatment of the client by the supervisee, the teaching program for the supervisee, and the protection of the profession from incompetent or impaired professionals or both. Within an agency or organization, the supervisor must also work within specific obligations, standards, and rules regarding client service and training programs. Supervisors often find themselves balancing the standards of the profession with the immediate service needs of the agency. Thus, supervisors must consider all levels of standards and ethics as they relate to their responsibilities. First, as a representative and model of the profession, they must act in compliance with the ethics and standards for delivery of services. Second, they must oversee the trainee's compliance with these ethics. Third, they must act ethically in the role of supervisor. Finally, they must teach ethical standards and guide the trainee in making ethical decisions.

A number of ethical issues pertain to the supervisory relationship, and several good sources of information for studying these issues exist (see Bradley, 1989; Harrar, Vandecreek, & Knapp, 1990; Tannenbaum, Green, & Glickman, 1989; Whiston & Emerson, 1989). For the purpose of describing SAS, this discussion is limited to defining and illustrating examples of the teaching of ethics as it emerges in the practice of supervision. The teaching of ethical decision making often occurs when the supervisor and trainee are dealing with ethical concerns of (a) dual relationship, (b) confidentiality, and (c) the limits of professional competency (Rinas & Clyne-Jackson, 1988).

Dual relationships represent one of the most problematic ethical issues facing supervisors. The supervisor must not only ensure that the trainee not engage in a dual relationship with the client but must also maintain the primacy of the supervisory role over any other role with the trainee. Transcript 4.2 presents an example of the supervisor's dealing with a potential dual relationship—a sexual relationship between the counselor and the client. In column 1, page 77, the supervisor asks if the relationship goes beyond "flattery"—implicitly asking if there is a sexual relationship. Because a dual relationship of this nature is in clear violation of the ethical code, the supervisor needs to establish enough trust within the relationship to encourage the trainee to discuss such issues and events, and if a violation has occurred, the supervisor to needs take action in compliance with professional guidelines against the trainee. The complexity of this role in supervision is illustrated in the gentle yet persistent manner in which the supervisor collects information from the trainee regarding the flattery and mutual attraction in the counseling relationship. This example underscores the importance of the supervisor's maintaining a relationship of referent power and trusting involvement. By doing so, the supervisor gives the trainee a safe place to discuss her concerns and empowers the trainee to take appropriate action, with the supervisor's guidance, before the situation damages either the client or the trainee.

Just as any sexual contact is prohibited between client and counselor, any form of sexual contact between supervisor and trainee is a violation of the ethical code (APA, 1992, Principle 1.19; Supervision Interest Network, 1993, Principle 2.15). Although I do not have a transcript depicting this type of relationship (for obvious reasons), in a survey by Pope, Levenson, and Schover (1979) of those students who reported having had a sexual contact with an instructor (10% of sample), the majority indicated that the sexual relationship was with their supervisor. Because of the evaluative power of the supervisor over the trainee, there is the potential for exploitation of the trainee, the resultant risk of inadequate supervision of cases, and a serious breach in the teaching contract with the trainee (Bartell & Rubin, 1990).

A dual relationship between supervisor and trainee may also be a consequence of the supervisor's engaging the trainee in personal therapy concurrent with a supervisory relationship (Supervision Interest Network, 1993, Principle 2.16). The distinction between the process of counseling and that of supervision may sometimes appear similar, especially under circumstances in which the trainee is working through an emotional issue as it relates to the client, the counseling relationship, or both. The supervisor first and foremost must uphold the supervisory contract and deal with personal issues of the trainee only as they are relevant to the provision of clinical services and professional function. In addition, any examination of this process should reveal the relevance of all discussion to the supervisory goals.

In Transcript 4.6, the supervisor and trainee are discussing the client's dependency needs and the trainee's very emotional and rejecting response to these needs. Notice how the conversation moves back and forth between the trainee's awareness of her own emotional response in the counseling relationship (col. 2, p. 109), the historical precedent of these feelings in her own life (col. 2, p. 109), and the application of this knowledge to the client situation (col. 1, p. 110). The supervisor encourages her to become aware of both her feelings and their origin but then deliberately asks her to anchor her thinking and conversation to her professional function (col. 1, p. 110). If this talk were taken out of context, it could just as easily be part of a counseling conversation; however, the intent of the supervisor in engaging in this discussion is clearly for the purpose of teaching the trainee how to be with her client. Although the trainee may take her awareness of these personal issues to therapy, and in fact the supervisor suggests this course at a later point, it is not the supervisor's role to pursue the trainee's treatment.

In Transcript 4.7 (col. 3, pp. 111-112), there is an excellent example of the supervisor weighing the issues of confidentiality in the profession, the dynamics and needs of the counseling relationship and treatment, and the policies within the agency.

Conclusions

Chapters 2, 3, and 4 have described the seven dimensions of the SAS model used in analyzing the supervision process. These include the task and function of supervision, the relationship of supervision,

TRANSCRIPT 4.6

Contextual Factors

Supervision Interview

Supervisor I think you might be on to something. Let me tell you what I understand from your experience with the client. You felt that as we talked about the client's dependency needs that maybe what you hadn't discovered was the fact that you can give to someone and it won't take away her self-sufficiency. It won't mean that you're being overprotective of her. It won't mean that you're taking away your respect of her as a person who can take care of herself.

Trainee Yeah, my hunch is that my experience of what that should have been was something that penalized me at times and therefore that's the way I sort of think about it.

Supervisor And it sounded like it had some of those strings attached just, someone overprotecting you, someone taking away from you something. Is that right?

Trainee Yeah.

Supervisor Taking away those things from you by saying, "I'll take care of you because you can't take care of yourself, nor will you be able to."

Trainee Yeah, yeah. It was really dumb. It was a really contradictory message. It was on one hand you're not handicapped, you're going to live like a nonhandicapped person; you have all those expectations. Plus you're the first child and you're not the boy you were supposed to be. But on the other hand, you really can't go outside and walk around on your own.

Supervisor So you were both things.

SAS Analysis

The supervisor starts by connecting the trainee's experience of the client— that is, her fear of the client's dependency. Thus, the **trainee's interpersonal style (self-presentation)** of dependency and counterdependency is being activated in the **counseling relationship.**

Here, the trainee is alluding to her personal history with this dynamic.

The supervisor continues with the trainee's personal historical experience in the development of this dynamic.

The trainee begins a more detailed and in-depth account of her familial experience around the issue of dependency and counterdependency.

(continued)

TRANSCRIPT 4.6 **Continued**

Supervision Interview

Trainee There's a real lack of trust.

Supervisor How were you ever going to be independent within that frame, and yet to be loved you had to be. So you were stuck.

Trainee Well, I got a different person.

Supervisor Well, in that moment, it was a way of not being stuck. And with this client, then she's asking, she's touching upon something that is not clear within you. We can't articulate exactly what she is asking, but it is something to do with "taking care of me." Something to do with dependency. Maybe why you're saying "I don't want to give her that" is perhaps because you're afraid it will put her in a bind, she won't be able to grow and develop and be that independent, self-sufficient person.

Trainee Let me tell you a keyword that my mother uses—"duty." This is what you do because you have to do it. I don't want that type of relationship either. I don't want to do certain things because I have to.

Supervisor Uh, but translate that to the client now. What do you not want to do for her because you think you might be obligated out of duty as the counselor?

SAS Analysis

Continued focus on the dynamic facilitated by the supervisor's empathy and reflection of the trainee's concern.

The trainee makes a confusing comment that refers back to her history.

The supervisor does not clarify the meaning of this comment, but rather pulls the trainee back to the meaning of her **emotional awareness within the context of the counseling relationship.** The supervisor makes the connection between what the **client is asking for** and why the trainee may be afraid to give it. The supervisor is anchoring the interpersonal dynamic with the counseling relationship.

The trainee, however, continues with a discussion of her familial experience.

Again the supervisor returns to the client factors, and now directly asks the trainee to **conceptualize her role with the client** based on her awareness of a sense of duty. The supervisor uses the bridge of "duty" to connect the familial history with the **professional role.**

Unpublished supervision interview. Based on an actual transcript altered to protect participant confidentiality.

and the contextual factors (supervisor, trainee, institutional, and client). Each of these factors has been illustrated in transcripts of supervision and the importance of each discussed in relation to the empirical

TRANSCRIPT **4.7**

Contextual Factors

Supervision Interview	*Recall Interview*	*SAS Analysis*
Trainee Last week or the week before we had this session, the reason why I had so much doubt is because it was the very end of the session and he just sort of threw out that he wanted to be able to play these (counseling) tapes for this religious counselor. I didn't get any more information.	**Supervisor** Well, again, here's another problem . . . ah, that has come up in my experience over the years a number of times, but it's fairly rare. That is, the client wanting to take tapes out on themselves and their counselor and play them for somebody else or even for themselves. And again, I have conflicting feelings about it. I can't just give . . . well, we don't do that here . . . although sometimes I think its a terribly appropriate and efficacious thing for a client. So, again she is bringing me a problem of ah . . . not only do I think of, as pedagogically meaningful, instructionally meaningful for me to have something to say to her about. Ah . . . perhaps even a policy decision to make here in some or some policy guidelines. But I also think she has great difficulty deciding even among those kinds of things . . . what she wants to do and so again it's . . .	Although the supervisor does not comment in the supervision interview very much, it is clear that he has a lot of thoughts about the trainee's issue with the client's taking the tape. Notice that he considers factors of the trainee's difficulty in making decisions **(self-presentation), her learning needs, the needs of the client, and the agency standards or policies.**
Supervisor Umm-hum.		
Trainee . . . and when he wanted to play the tapes and I would still have difficulty with that I wouldn't want him to play these with that man.		
Supervisor Umm-hum.		
Trainee I wouldn't feel good about that at all.		
Supervisor What would bother you about that?		
Trainee Because then it would be too much like, umm, like that man would be interpreting what I was saying.	**Supervisor** Ah . . . I think it puts me in an interesting self-debating state about how to deal with that. I mean it's almost like I'm predicting what I'm going to say.	His self-debate on whether or not to tell the trainee what to do brings up the issues of her **learning needs** and his **own biases.**
Supervisor He would be superior, superordinate, talent-wise.		

(continued)

TRANSCRIPT 4.7 **Continued**

Supervision Interview	Recall Interview	SAS Analysis
Trainee Kind of giving final, final say. And then it seems like at that point it would be real detrimental to my work with George. I mean, it's like too many, too much input.		
Supervisor Yeah.	**Supervisor** I think that I'm open enough to different kinds of solutions. You know there is no absolute policy here, and I haven't made one, and there isn't one published yet in the agency, so I'm free to roam the territory of possibilities and decide with her what we think is best for her and this client and the agency.	He uses the **lack of policy at the agency** as a way to consider the ramifications for all the parties that might be affected.

Unpublished supervision interview. Based on an actual transcript altered to protect participant confidentiality.

literature. Although, for purposes of explication, these factors have been explicated in isolation, it is evident from the transcripts that they are indeed interrelated, often occurring together in the same supervisory session. The factors move in and out of the participants' interactions as well as their awareness of the interaction in which they are engaged. At times, the influence of the factors can be inferred from the language and context, and at other times they are manifestly present in the interaction itself.

Those who would understand the "big picture" concerning the process of supervision will likely continually probe for evidence to answer the following questions:

- What factors are influencing the participants' judgments in guiding the supervision process?
- What characteristics of the contextual factors have they relied on in their decision making?
- What characteristics have they not considered but on reflection seem important in designing a teaching approach in supervision?
- What kind of roles do they tend to manifest in supervision, and are these the most beneficial for learning to take place?

- What tasks of supervision do they focus on with particular trainees?

The next chapter contains an entire transcript of a supervision session with the participants' reflections of their work and my analysis of the presence of the influencing SAS factors. By this process, it is hoped that readers will see a model of how to (a) apply SAS to their own work in supervision, (b) begin to ask the questions that can guide their practice, and (c) use a common language to contemplate their answers.

5

Uncovering the Words of Supervision

⊘ Chapter 5 presents a supervision interview between an experienced supervisor (20 years teaching and practicing supervision) and a postdoctoral resident in clinical psychology. Both agreed to be videotaped and then each to be interviewed by me about the supervision interview as we watched the interaction. They had been working together in supervision for over 6 months, although this was the first time they had videotaped their work.

The supervisor, Martin Acker, and I worked together for several years in teaching supervision. Our relationship of professional collaboration in supervision is evident in my interview of him in this transcript. Because the origin of the Systems Approach to Supervision (SAS) model came from our initial work together, you will notice that his reflection of the supervision interview contains some of the language and thinking of the SAS model. The advantage of such an interview is the opportunity to demonstrate how experienced supervisors knowledgeable in the model can describe and make sense of supervision using SAS language and concepts. In this way, the nature of our interaction is different from my interview with the supervisee with whom I did not have a prior relationship and who did not know the SAS model.

The interview with the supervisee is not unlike the interpersonal process recall (IPR; Kagan & Kagan, 1990) approach in which a supervisor asks the supervisee to reflect on the counseling interview. Here, of course, it is the supervision interview that is the focus of the supervisee's reflections, and the interviewer is a third party to the initial supervision interaction.

The transcript is arranged so that you can read a segment of the supervision interaction, followed by the participants' reflections, and, finally, my ongoing reflection of both the supervision session and the recall experience. You will notice that sometimes both supervisor and supervisee comment on the same item, whereas at other times only one of them might make a comment.

Unlike the previous examples in this book, which were done for research purposes, these recall interviews were an effort to uncover, retrospectively, the thoughts and feelings of the participants. My own comments often reflect an effort to conceptualize what it was they were saying in our interaction and to begin a process of analysis of the original supervision interview. During this process of discussion and analysis, we developed a relationship that allowed critical elements of the participants' thoughts and feelings to be divulged.

There are seven levels of meaning in this analysis:

1. The ongoing intent and meaning implicit in the supervisor's and supervisee's supervision interaction
2. The supervisor's perception of meaning as he reflects on the supervision interaction
3. The supervisee's perception of meaning as he reflects on the supervision interaction
4. The ongoing intent and meaning implicit in the supervisor's and interviewer's reflected interview
5. The ongoing intent and meaning in the supervisee's reflected interview
6. My analysis of the intent and meaning as a participant-observer of all three interviews
7. Your perception of intent and meaning as an observer of the interviews and reflections on the interviews

The levels of meaning are a rich, albeit complex, source of information for understanding the interaction of the primary factors of supervision as defined by the SAS model. The use of multiple sources of information relating to the understanding of meaning in supervision contexts has been discussed by Holloway and Poulin (1994). They classified supervision studies, using Poole, Folger, and Hewes's (1987) taxonomy on structure and meaning for social communication (see Research Box 5.1) and concluded that the majority of empirical information on supervision is generated from observers rather than from participants of the process. The inclusion of "subjectively" based or participant-based information is needed to understand the decision making of both the supervisor and the supervisee to the teaching-learning process.

There is one more dimension to my commentary. I have organized the three interrelated interviews into seven broad themes and omitted

Research Box 5.1

Meaning in Social Communication

Supervision is a shared, interactional phenomenon that unfolds moment by moment, and in each moment the relationship creates or restricts the opportunity for teaching and learning by participants. The primary task is to create a mutuality of understanding both about the process of psychotherapy and the ongoing teaching and learning processes of supervision. In this context, shared understanding is tantamount, yet few observational methods have explicitly investigated the degree and processes of "shared understanding."

The understanding of "meaning" has been of considerable debate in the use of interactional data. Poole et al. (1987) have distinguished between the domain of meaning and the degree of intersubjectivity, or shared understanding (meaning), created by the interaction. Domain includes both observer-privileged and subject-privileged perspectives of the interaction. Each of these domains can generate *generalized* knowledge of the interaction that is available to anyone who might observe the event or *restricted* meaning that is reserved for those observations that are directed by knowledge of a special theory or framework from which to attach meaning to the events.

Observers' general knowledge of the language and cultural context of a conversation allows them to attach meaning to an interaction. It is meaning derived from the general cultural context that has been of interest to researchers of personal relationship. Supervision is a specialized institutionalized activity, and researchers have been less interested in the general observer's understanding of the event than in the understanding of those observers who are a part of the institutional context. Consequently, restricted observer-privileged observation techniques have been very popular, and researchers have used them to analyze the local, sequential structure of supervision discourse (Holloway & Poulin, in press).

Subject-privileged meanings of a generalized nature are those meanings to which anyone from the participants' same cultural or subcultural group has access. The only microanalytic study in supervision to access this domain of meaning was Holloway et al. (1989). In a multiple-case study, experienced supervisors' and trainees' judgments of supervision interviews (Goodyear et al., 1984) were related to the patterns of discourse. It is unfortunate that observations generated from members of the same institutional or cultural group of supervision have not been more consistently accessed. Because the researcher draws meaning from individuals who

---

a few sections from them because of an overlap in issues or to protect the anonymity of the client. I have indicated the occurrence of any major omissions. I have also edited the transcripts to make them more understandable in the written form. The editing included removing minimal encouragers, repetitions, and hesitations. In no instance was the message or meaning substantially changed or omitted.

My commentary during the recall interviews themselves represents my first, spontaneous analysis of the supervision interview and, in some cases, of its relationship to the relevant reflective interview. When

Research Box 5.1

Continued

practice, findings from studies that focus on the generalized, subject-privileged domain of meaning may be more pragmatic and may effectively bridge the gap between science and practice.

Restricted subject-privileged meanings refer to the participants' unique or idiosyncratic meanings that develop from the relationship and are not available to outsiders. An exception to this trend is the study by Strozier, Kivlighan, and Thoresen (1993) in which the supervisor and trainee coded their intentions and reactions, respectively, on a researcher-devised checklist as they watched their previously videotaped supervision interview. Shared understanding is defined as the state "wherein people share common understandings generated by cultural or interaction processes" that Poole et al. (1987) have labeled *intersubjectivity.* Intersubjectivity has been studied as a particular *state or outcome* that may be characterized on a continuum representing the *degree of intersubjectivity* or as the interactive processes that generate shared understanding.

Participants' shared meaning of a supervision interaction has been measured primarily with global, syntagmatic, restricted subject-privileged techniques. In these types of studies, each participant is asked to judge the quality of the

interaction along dimensions such as supervisory style (Supervisory Styles Inventory [SSI]; Friedlander et al., 1989), the immediate impact of each session on participants (Session Evaluation Questionnaire [SEQ]; Friedlander et al., 1989; Martin et al., 1987; Strozier et al., 1993), and judgments of best and worst sessions (Martin et al., 1987). The judgments of each participant are then charted on graphs and compared heuristically to determine the degree of "shared understanding or meaning."

The interactional events that generate intersubjectivity in supervision have been relatively ignored. Few studies in supervision have identified the processes that are related to participants' shared understanding. One exception is Martin et al.'s (1987) intensive case study, which compared the supervisee's and supervisor's shared judgments of best and worst sessions and then examined the type of interactional activity that might relate to differences in their global judgments. In this study, the global, subjective meanings of participants converged on best sessions but diverged on worst sessions. Investigators examined the interactional events, "the processes of intersubjectivity," that might explain their global judgments.

I have shown the videotape, audiences have commented on the complexity of the three different interviews, their relationship to one another, and the undeniable effect on all of the participants. I leave to you, the reader, the task of unraveling the layers of meaning in order to arrive at your own understanding of these supervisory experiences.

The interview is keyed as follows: S = supervisor (Marty); T = trainee (Phil); I = interviewer (Elizabeth).

Beginning the Interview: Focus on the Client

Supervision Interview

T OK. can we start?

S Yeah, what do ya got?

T OK. This is a 27-year-old man [client] . . . mmm . . . whose **presenting problem** is that he couldn't tolerate his wife's marijuana use . . . and it wasn't that . . . it wasn't a health concern. It wasn't that he was concerned about her health, or inhaling the smoke himself, it had some other meaning. . . .

Function: Case Conceptualization	Task: Counseling Skill
Supervisor Recall Interview	**Trainee Recall Interview**
	T Umm, I guess watching myself I can see how I was, you know, feeling then. I can sort of feel it now, which is kind of tight. Umm, what is that feeling? Just kind of a bad feeling inside like, well, self-conscious. I recognize it as something I do to myself when I get anxious . . . kind of tighten my face . . . my body is kind of tight and this sort of creeping starts coming up in my chest, and I think I sort of see that.
	I You can see that right as you begin the interview?
	T Umm hmm. **I think I was pretty anxious beginning, and it was kind of interfering with my concentration.**

SAS Analysis

Trainee factor: self-presentation

Client factor: identified problem

Although the supervisee's attention is to the client in the actual interview, he is actually preoccupied with how his anxiety is interfering with his presentation of the case.

Supervision Interview

T Just feeling a kind of panic, let's see, about his words . . . Umm, let's see, he would get stressed out and tense and the whole world would go sort of limp.

S I take it then that he started his relationship with her not knowing she was a smoker.

T That I'm not sure about. But it's sort of become a preoccupation for him. So one of the things that we focused on initially was his trying to understand what this meant. He saw that it was irrational and that it wasn't really about, you know . . . he didn't really understand what it meant, but he was tired of kind of freaking out every time he heard that she smoked or was gonna go have a joint with a friend. He said that he sometimes felt like she would kind of sneak off or go somewhere and smoke and it felt kind of deceptive.

He was also very worried that his wife was having an affair. He sometimes would follow her around in his car, if she was out with a friend, for example, to make sure that she wasn't cheating on him. She would sort of go off and, you know, smoke, and he would feel like when she was going off and getting something that he wasn't providing. And in those moments, he would feel panicky, become flirtatious with female colleagues, get together with them, and resolve to leave his wife.

S Umm hmm.

T It was kind of a punishment, umm, if he got together with other women. He just kind of felt bad, you know; it just didn't feel good, but at least he said that he, in those moments, felt more independent and that he could sort of get along without her, you know.

S If he saw other women?

T Yes, then, it's like "Well, this doesn't feel very good but to heck with you, you know, I'm OK."

Function: Consulting	Task: Case Conceptualization
Supervisor Recall Interview	**Trainee Recall Interview**
S Phil . . . I'm aware there were moments when I thought I might intervene for either further clarification or even to begin some interpretation, but up until this point, I am not clear about **what issues are most difficult for Phil himself** or what issues he's directing toward, where his energy is, so it was important just to allow him to almost ramble on in this historical way, not so much for the information that I needed about the case,	
I Umm hmm.	
S . . . but rather to get a sense of where his energy was, where he was focusing, what, if anything, might be troubling him about the situation since he's brought this for supervision.	

I So that one of the things that you're clearly not doing here is following up on the diagnosis of the case and the case conceptualization. He really is moving toward that—talking about the client. But what you're saying is that at this point you're interested in the kind of factors in the case that are affecting him.

S Correct. I didn't lead him in any particular direction at this point . . .

I Umm hmm.

S . . . but to wait and follow his direction.

SAS Analysis

Trainee factors: self-presentation and learning needs

In the supervision interview, the supervisor stays with a consulting function to uncover the essential elements for the supervisee. Notice, on reflection, that he brings up issues that may be influencing the supervisee's direction with the case and his learning needs with regard to the supervision. Both the supervisor and supervisee at this point have reflected on trainee factors but have not brought them up in the supervision interview.

Supervision Interview

T Umm, let's see, then we started talking some. Oh, he made an interesting slip, I guess, during the third session. Let's see, he was talking about . . . oh, what was that? Oh, I'll just see if I can get that. (Phil begins to look through his notes on his lap).

Supervisor Recall Interview	Trainee Recall Interview
	T Umm, I guess what I'm thinking now is similar to what I was talking about before.
	I Umm hmm.
	T Which is, the way I'm holding myself I'm so, you know, looks like my shoulders are curled over and **I'm kind of tight, still kind of an anxious**

**response. Concentrating a little bet-
ter, but, umm, still having some
trouble concentrating I think.**

I Do you think, as you look back, that
the supervisor understands that or perceives that at all? That you're feeling
this anxiety?

T Umm, I think he might. Yeah,
'cause I think **there's a kind of a softness.** Actually, I'm not sure if Marty
does or not, but, I **guess I'm thinking
my experience with him generally is
that, you know, he's pretty soft and accepting.** No matter what my reactions
might be or whatever difficulties I
might be having, it's always OK. I'm
not sure if he senses it or not, but it's
always **easy to share that kind of stuff
with him.**

I So he hasn't done anything yet that
would tell you directly that he . . .

T That he saw it.

I . . . That he perceives it, that he understands, but based on your relationship with him, you have an expectation that it's OK.

T Right.

SAS Analysis

Relationship factors: phase and interpersonal structure

Supervisor factors: self-presentation

Trainee factor: self-presentation

During the reflected interview, the supervisee continues with his
attention to his anxiety and how it is manifested in his body. After my
query of his perception of his supervisor's role in this anxiety, he
speaks of the supervisor's self-presentation of acceptance and the
expectations he has of Marty, given the history of their relationship. He
also talks about the easiness of sharing sensitive topics in their relationship, which implies a relational structure of positive involvement.

Supervision Interview

T I want . . .

S Before you get to that. How did you begin to think about the presenting situation? What kind of conceptual options occurred to you?

Function: Consulting	Task: Case Conceptualization
Supervisor Recall Interview	**Trainee Recall Interview**
S Yeah, again that's a more explicit expression of what I was trying to do earlier. What my approach was to him earlier was for me to wait until he made clear, or more clear, what his directions were. What he was focusing on. And, I guess at this point, it seemed reasonable for me to move that a little faster than it was moving and **to direct his attention now to think about what he was thinking about,** rather than to continue just with the anecdotal presentation of the case.	
I Well, one of the things that I noticed here was that he started shuffling through his papers to find the exact phrase and he previously had looked at his papers. Do you recall whether that was influencing your pacing at that point, that you would choose that moment to bring him to his own thinking?	
S Yeah, umm, he seemed to be getting partly lost in the anecdotal material, but partly, I think, needing the structure of the anecdotal material. That suggested to me, perhaps, **he was getting somewhat anxious and it might be helpful for him for me now to provide a little structure.** Not pointing him in any direction but giving him a point of departure to examine his own focus.	
I Umm hmm.	

SAS Analysis

Trainee factors: learning needs and self-presentation

Although in the supervision interview the focus remains on case conceptualization, on reflection, the supervisor comments on the supervisee's anxiety and takes this as a cue to provide some structure to the interview. He is changing his strategy due to his perception of the trainee's learning needs and that the anecdotal material has served its function.

Supervision Interview

T Umm, well, first I was just kind of focused on what the symptom meant, and maybe I got too caught up in it, in that I wasn't focusing as much as I might on **our relationship or what the energy was like between us.**

S Umm hmm.

T It was more like he came in and provided information, and we were both trying to understand, you know, what this . . .

S So you put it out there; both of you were looking at that.

T Yeah, we both sort of looked at that. The things that we were thinking about was, one, that somehow this represented sex. He wasn't providing something for her and somehow her going off and smoking . . . she was getting something that he couldn't provide. Then we talked some about their sex life. That was one aspect, and the other was that somehow it represented independence, that she would get along without him. And somehow smoking meant that she was autonomous and that threatened him. And he'd talked some about an earlier girlfriend where he was kind of controlling and kind of clutching, and when he got into this relationship, he was real determined not to be so controlling and not to need a lot, not to ask for a lot of reassurance.

S What suggested the sexual image on that . . .?

T What it was like for him when she smoked, and then how he would go out, to me it sounded sexual. It sounded like she was going off with another lover, and he would get her back by going off and sleeping with someone. And then it wouldn't feel very good, but at least he would be OK on his own, he would have someone else. And I suggested that analogy, and he said that it did have that quality to it, that there was something about that. She has to have sexual relations, have intercourse, and he's been too frightened. The only times that he's had sexual contact, intercourse, in his life were when he smoked marijuana, and so, there's kind of this pressure now to be sexual and he's real anxious about that.

Function: Consulting	Task: Case Conceptualization
Supervisor Recall Interview	**Trainee Recall Interview**
S I'm struck with, too, the **change in his energy** after I provide the focus for him. **I** Yes.	**T** I think I said something about this later on in this meeting with Marty, but I think there is some interference? **At some point between me and the client in terms of the kinds of things that maybe we struggle with or that**

S Which is a clue that he's more engaged in that now. And perhaps somewhat more comfortable. The sexual issue I raised with him; because **I know from my history with Phil, that isn't a threatening issue,** that he can deal with that without it feeling any way threatening to him.

I So that knowing something about him and his own thinking around issues of sexuality and your relationship allowed you to move in fairly directly on that issue, and that appeared central to you.

S Yes . . . and the fact that **his energy picked up and the pace picked up** suggested to me that my intervention at that point was probably an appropriate one and a helpful one.

I Umm hmm.

I'm maybe acting a little bit like him here. Umm, not the . . . not so much, uh, the sexual stuff or the symptoms— you know. I had trouble identifying with that, but there was a kind of **the tightness, you know, the kind of defensiveness that's manifest in the body . . .**

I Umm hmm.

T . . . that I see myself, here, and I think he had kind of that quality, too. I'm not sure what more to say about it, but I think there's something.

I There's some connection, there's some resonance between you and the client, sort of almost a style or a feeling.

T Yeah, yeah, kind of the way we're guarding against something.

I Umm hmm. Up until this point in the supervision interview you have focused primarily on the client and the symptoms and the treatment, and now a little bit about your case conceptualization, and as you reflect on it, the attention has been for you, in these moments, on the inner self, the inner feelings. Do you recall in any way, what might have stopped you from seeing these things that you've said here today, in the interview?

T What things might have stopped me? Let's see, the first thing that comes to mind, it has to do with talking a lot about my inner workings. I have a tendency to kind of scare myself. I mean, there's something that makes me anxious, and I'll come to that situation and kind of scare myself as a way to deal with it. It makes things worse. I don't know if that makes sense to you. **I think I was just sort of interfering with kind of having a more spacious and open response to**

the process. I was more anxious and concerned about the camera. Was I familiar enough with the case and all that kind of stuff. **I think I had kind of a narrow, anxious, thing going.**

I So you really enacted, in a sense, outwardly what you're talking about now on the inward side.

T Right. Yeah.

SAS Analysis

Relationship factor: phase

Trainee factor: self-presentation

Client factor: counseling relationship

The supervision interview continues the focus on understanding the client and gathering information; but subsequently, with reflection, both participants are involved in much more complex issues.

The supervisor reflects on three different elements: the supervisee's self-presentation—specifically his energy; his level of engagement in the supervisory relationship, and his cultural values specifically related to sexual matters.

The trainee begins to make the connection between his client's anxiety and "tightness in the counseling sessions" and his own discomfort and bodily defensiveness in supervision. The reflected interview makes explicit the parallel process emerging in the supervisory relationship. The factors of parallel process are (a) client factor: interpersonal relationship in counseling; and (b) relationship factor of supervision: interpersonal structure. To this point, however, only the self-presentation of the client and supervisee are articulated; the supervisor's recognition of this dynamic has not yet been uncovered nor has the supervisee acknowledged the supervisor's role in the parallel process.

Supervision Interview

S Yeah, I was gonna ask you . . . good thing you brought that up . . . about how that relates to your sense of both what he needs to control and why he needs to control it and what the fear is all about.

T Umm hmm. Uh-hmm, yeah. Well, the . . . there's something about the way he carries himself.

Function: Consulting	Task: Case Conceptualization
Supervisor Recall Interview	**Trainee Recall Interview**
S The sexual issue is obviously an important one, but my intention at that point was to help him place that in a much broader context of the clients' perceptions, behavior, and history, so that while it is important, it has to be seen in a broader context, and Phil was getting . . . in a sense, involved in some of the details of the sexuality which were not unimportant, but still, I thought it was important to broaden that context. **I** Well, it seems like you're really wanting him to move now to **case conceptualization,** in a broader sense . . . **S** Right. **I** . . . than just sort of the anecdotal case, so let's see if he follows up on that.	

SAS Analysis

Client factor: identified problem

The supervisor is interested in having the trainee connect his theoretical orientation to his conceptualization of the case.

Impasse in the Supervisory Relationship

Supervision Interview

T There's something real tight about him. When he comes in sometimes, he'll just be shaking a little bit and he'll tell me that he's shaking a little. He's not sure why. And then that'll dissipate some, but there's something tight about him. He kind of makes an effort to normalize things with us. He's glad to see me. There's something real kind of friendly about things, and I think that maybe he does that to kind of make himself more comfortable or kind of help dissipate some of the anxiety. So I think he has this feeling like he's gonna break apart if he gets a little too anxious.

S How do you experience him when he talks about the sexual aspects of the relationship or his feeling? What do you experience from him and how do you experience the interaction?

Function: Consulting	Task: Moves From Case Conceptualization to Emotional Awareness
Supervisor Recall Interview	**Trainee Recall Interview**
S Interestingly enough I've come back to the sexual here, but for two reasons. One is for him to think more about the client as a total personality. What energy he's getting from the client, but the other is an opening to allow for the possibility of exploring **the meaning to Phil himself as a person.** To help him explore if in fact there are some aspects of the **issue of sexuality that are personally impactful on him that might interfere with or disturb his work with the client.** I have no specific reason to believe that might be the case, but with the **power of sexuality** being as it is, it seemed important to me to open that up sufficiently to move into it if it became apparent that was an important issue. And in a personal kind of issue, so it opens the possibility for a therapeutic-like intervention with him.	**T** Umm, I can see I'm not really answering the question. I think it all has to do with the same thing I've been talking about, **about feeling anxious and being so caught up in protecting myself that I'm not really with the process that's going on with Marty and I.** At least when I hear the question now about what goes on . . . how do you experience him when he's talking about it . . . he's talking more about what goes on here. How I feel and what's going on, and I'm still kind of a little bit too focused on understanding the client as opposed to what's going on between Marty and I.
I I think it's the way that you phrase the question. How do you experience him talking about sexuality and your experience? His experience in the relationship as he talks about that—you begin now **to move from the distance of case conceptualization to the intensity of the impact of the counseling relationship.** He has a choice; he can go with the client and how he perceives the client, or himself. And that's what you're leaving open to him.	**I** And you're seeing now that perhaps your motivation was to protect yourself from getting into your own experience with the client, with Marty . . . **T** Umm. Yeah, that's . . . **I** It seems like that's tough to think about right now. **T** I'm hesitating because my guess is that it's not so much what particularly was going on between the client and I at that moment that's making it hard for me to look at that, but probably that, **under the circumstances here about being videotaped.** Probably I would have some difficulty doing that with whatever the content of the question

S Right, and the choice of the words of that question is an advised choice for that reason.

was. If I were to really let go and get into what I was feeling with the client.

I So there are lots of different factors still influencing you as this interview unfolds.

T Yeah.

I **And one of them being sort of the context of how we're doing this, and another being your own resonance with some of the client's style. But to this point, I don't hear you saying that Marty, the supervisor, is doing anything to exaggerate that.**

T No.

I OK.

T No, I think if anything, umm, if any-thing, you know, **his softness is help-ful. I think what might have been in-teresting would have been for him to ask me about just the process of su-pervision. What was going on right now with us, with me, and attend to my anxiety about this process.**

If we just talked about that a minute, that might have alleviated some of it for me. 'Cause I was struggling with it while we were talking about some-thing else.

I So that he might have used a strat-egy that would pay attention to the **su-pervisory relationship and that would have uncovered some of this emotional reaction you are having to the context.**

T Right.

SAS Analysis

Relationship factor: interpersonal structure

Trainee factor: self-presentation

Client factor: counseling relationship (interpersonal structure)

In the supervision interview, the supervisor moves the trainee from conceptualization of the client's symptoms to the dynamic in the counseling relationship. He carefully invites the trainee to think about his relationship with the client. In the reflected interview, he comments on his consideration of two aspects of the situation contributing to his decision making: his own theoretical orientation of the importance of sexual issues and his attention to the supervisee's emotional awareness in the counseling relationship.

The supervisee is able on reflection to understand what it is the supervisor is asking him to do. However, he continues to focus on his experience in supervision and the supervisory relationship. He explains his lack of response to his own feelings of anxiety in the supervisory relationship. Although at first he does not acknowledge his supervisor's role in the development of his own anxiety, he finally indicates that he needed the supervisor to provide him a way to talk about his emotional awareness in the supervisory session and to deal directly with the interpersonal dynamics of the supervisory relationship before he could address the counseling relationship. Notice also that the context of videotaping in a studio has heightened his anxiety in the interview.

Supervision Interview

T He's a little hesitant, but then, umm, I think he's fairly open about it, I was . . . Umm . . . Let's see . . . I guess he, you know, he feels a little embarrassed, but I think he's pretty forthcoming about it. He kind of gets a little . . . you know . . . he giggles a little when . . umm.

Supervisor Recall Interview	Trainee Recall Interview
S A critical aspect of this as well, that, umm, is, brought to the fore by sexuality but isn't a sexual issue, really, and that's my understanding of **the difficulty men have in relating to each other seriously about sexuality.**	
I I see.	
S And so it wasn't just a matter of whether Phil might be uncomfortable with sex, the sexuality, but how the relationship with another man about this, ordinarily, not terribly open issue between men, might be impacting the relationship and in a way he addresses himself toward that a little bit now.	

I Well, you're really, uh, in the back of your mind is, is this **broader understanding of sexuality in our culture and the kind of cultural values are brought into that, and also the issue of gender.**

S And the issue of gender, and the issue of . . . and the, uh, the rules, in a sense, that men live by, in certain areas, in relation to each other. One of them relates to how they relate to each other, how we relate to each other about sex and sexuality.

I Well, I can't help but remark, Marty, that here we have Phil talking about a relationship with a male client, and here you are another male talking to Phil about that male relationship.

S Right.

I And so we have two levels of this same gender, umm, uh, relationship.

S Uh-huh.

SAS Analysis

Trainee factors: learning needs and self-presentation

Supervisory relationship: interpersonal dynamics

The supervisor articulates the influence that cultural values related to gender and, specifically, male-to-male relationship have on his thinking and the direction he takes in the supervision session. Notice that the trainee and the supervisor are on very different tracks at this stage of the interview—the supervisee, still preoccupied with his anxiety in his relationship with the supervisor, and the supervisor, thinking of the theoretical and cultural issues related to the client and counselor relationship.

Supervision Interview

S Have you asked him how he was, what he was experiencing as he shared some of this with you, at all? I mean, his perception of what was happening with him in his interaction with you as he shared some of this material about which, as he reports it, from what you say, he's quite fearful.

T Mainly he just said that, umm, you know, he starts feeling anxious. I don't know if I asked him directly what it was like to talk about it, but I think he said he felt anxious, and he giggled. No, he did get pretty anxious, and sort of needed to slow down and calm down. Yeah, he sort of got a little panicky.

Function: Advising	Task: Counseling skill
Supervisor Recall Interview	Trainee Recall Interview
	I Well, I guess I can't let that pass, you're sort of shaking your head.
	T Yeah, I think I didn't ask him. I didn't ask the client what it was like to talk about it. Or if I did, well, I can imagine myself asking that, but I don't remember what he said. I don't think we explored it. So I may have asked him and then maybe he steered elsewhere and I didn't stick with it. That's my guess.
	I So what is your feeling when Marty probes about whether you've done that, and in your mind you're thinking, I didn't do that. What's the next reaction to the fact? "I didn't do that and my supervisor's asking me."
	T Yeah, umm. Well, some, **some hesitation to acknowledge** it and thinking kind of, oh yeah, that would've been a really ripe area to pursue. Or thinking that maybe I asked about it and he got uncomfortable, and then maybe I reacted to the client's discomfort and didn't confront him and **not feeling good about that.**
	I So it really, in some ways, helped you to focus on that process with the client. In sort of unraveling what you did and if you did it, then maybe you got sidetracked and how that then relates to you and your discomfort with the client, or whatever. Or your own discomfort with self—I think that might've been more accurate—at that moment. And on the other hand, it also brought in some vision of "It I didn't do that, maybe I should've thought of it."
	T Yeah, **making a judgment about myself. It's like "Oh, man, I didn't do**

that again." I backed off in response to the client's discomfort. And I'm so sick of doing that. I wish that I had just acknowledged that. Marty, you know what happened. I think I asked that but I don't remember exploring it, because I can't recall what he might have said. It was probably another time when I was feeling not good about it.

SAS Analysis

Supervisory relationship: interpersonal structure (power)

Trainee factor: self-presentation

The supervisor is probing for the client's interpersonal behavior and the emotional tenor of the counseling relationship. The supervisee answers hesitantly and on reflection talks about his concern with his presentation in the supervisory session. He comments that the supervisor asks him something that he didn't do, and his embarrassment and self-deprecation as a result of this query reflects the referent power he attributes to the supervisor. He wants to please him by having the right answer. Notice throughout this interview that he has largely taken responsibility for the supervision and doesn't address his emotional needs. Only once did he mention that he wanted the supervisor to initiate talking about the ongoing supervision relationship. Even though the supervisor at this stage is beginning to open the emotional issues in the counseling relationship, the trainee does not seem ready to engage in this conversation.

The next five double-spaced, typewritten pages of transcript have been deleted. In the next section, the supervisor moves away from the discussion of the supervisee's emotional experience in the counseling relationship and returns to the conceptualization of the client's identified problem.

Emergence of the Reflective Relationship

Supervision Interview

T Sounds like . . . he describes his mother as hard . . . What else can I say? That's what comes to mind.

S That's an interesting kind of issue. How much of the interaction is more gender related than, of which sexuality is an expression, rather than essentially sexually linked? What do you think?

T Meaning that he's more anxious just around women period, than around a particular woman.

S Some aspect of that, yeah, what do you think of that?

T I think that's certainly a part of it . . .

Function: Advising Followed by Consulting	Task: Emotional Awareness Case Conceptualization
Supervisor Recall Interview	**Trainee Recall Interview**
S A further refinement of the **case conceptualization.**	**T** One reaction I'm having now is **how distant I feel from Marty in this whole thing.** Somehow, that I . . . create in part just because of my anxiety. But Marty seems way over there and kind of making comments, and I try and respond to them, but it's like he's off in a corner of the room somewhere. **I didn't feel that close or that connected.**
I One of the things I particularly liked in that intervention you gave . . . you gave your opinion first. And then you said, "What do you think?" You didn't show any hidden agenda that you were trying to get him to think about it in the way that you were thinking.	**I** Which is different from what you would expect from your relationship? That you have felt close to him in the past?
S It is possible for me to offer opinions and interpretations **without fearing they'll overwhelm him.**	**T** Yeah, **I have felt closer and I think that a lot of it, some of it has to do with the context here,** for me, that can be a struggle. He seemed a little removed, too. Kind of sitting back, and making some comments, asking questions. I guess we were just in an initial exploratory phase of things, and, I don't know if what I've presented really stimulated something for him or we were just kind of exploring around.
	I I understand what you're saying, and I guess I'm thinking that in some ways it sounds like perhaps the exploratory time, the conceptualization of the client, the planning of strategy, or treatment with the client, has gone beyond its usefulness. **That there's a real press inside of you to talk about the process between you, to talk about your own anxiety.** Did you feel free to initiate that discussion?
	T I think then, you know, during, when we did this interview, I had

some other things going on in my life and probably it would've been more difficult at that time—I mean today. I think I'm doing more of that with you . . .

I Umm hmm.

T . . . and probably could've done that . . . but didn't, so, yeah I . . . **it's certainly something that I . . . was aware of and probably could've initiated.**

I So you have an awareness and the skill, but the context of what was going on at this time in this relationship and your own personal life stopped you from taking that leap or risk or change in the direction of the interview.

S Right, I think it might've been, given what was going on, it might've been harder to tolerate than it would be today, under the same circumstances.

SAS Analysis

Supervisory relationship: interpersonal structure (involvement), phase of relationship

Trainee factor: learning style

The supervisor is conscious of the relationship created by his choice of teaching strategy and trusts that the supervisee will be able to offer his opinion forthrightly even if he is not in agreement. The reflective interview with the supervisee, however, uncovers his concern with pleasing the supervisor and with being caught "unaware" about a counseling relationship issue that he may not have addressed adequately or effectively.

The reflective interview with the supervisee represents a beginning of his using this interview almost in a supervisory way. Notice that he comments that he is feeling distant from his supervisor and follows with a comment on the personal situation he was in at the time of the supervision; then he connects to the current time and that it would be easier to engage in a more involved process in supervision. His entire reflection is on the nature of the supervisory relationship and his role in it. He appears troubled, in part, about this situation because the supervisory relationship has not always felt this way. It has been closer, and this is a quality he has come to expect in his work with this supervisor. Again, he mentions the context of the interview as affecting his focus and level of anxiety.

Supervision Interview

S How would you conceptualize and where do you think you might take it with him? What would you look at?

T Well, I think he probably has to somehow get more in touch with how easily he feels threatened. What he goes through . . . what he must go through around fears of being left. Maybe just memories and associating to his mom. There's very little negative, there's very little negative feelings about her and what transpired, even though he says she was hard or just an enforcer, not comforting. I imagine there's a lot of . . . he's probably pretty angry. One, that he has to go through so much turmoil now around women, and this mainly . . . then, just that feels so . . . the image that comes to mind for me is kind of "thin" emotionally, like he could . . .

S He's fragile.

T Yeah, fragile. There's not a lot of warmth or kind of . . . doesn't have the capacity to nurture himself or soothe himself or . . . when he gets in such a panic. There's a lot of feelings around that kind of stuff . . . that he's unaware of, and he's still a pretty young guy.

S How is he with men?

T Well, with me, I guess I mentioned before, I think he was working at being liked . . . likable. And kind of normalizing things, and "Hey, how's it going, Phil?" and "Good to see you" and, beyond that I, let's see . . .

Function: Consulting	Task: Case Conceptualization
Supervisor Recall Interview	Trainee Recall Interview
	T Couple reactions. One is, I'm just aware of how much I infer about him.
	I Umm hmm. About the client.
	T About the client, right. I guess it's **probably true with all therapists. How much of therapy is colored by how we understand our own process.**
	I Yes.
	T So, I think some of this fits for the client, but it sounds like things I've said about me. And sort of to separate those two out, is a pretty difficult process. I think there's a tendency to at least for me here **to understand his process in a way that I understand mine.** As opposed to waiting for more evidence and seeing how I react and what I think and what emerges. And I jumped the gun a little and try to conceptualize things the way I understand me, a little bit just because some of the things I said fit. Another reaction I had a minute or two

ago was how I feel about **this whole process that we're up to. Seeing, seeing myself there and having some feelings about my anxiety and then sharing my reactions to that with you.** I don't feel as bad about it as I might have a year or two ago . . .

I Umm hmm

T And I feel like, oh no, talk to Elizabeth about this and, I don't know who's gonna see this. Why do I talk about myself like that . . .

I Umm hmm.

T There's other things about me and stuff. I think I'm more accepting now but still, I'm not sure about how much, about my boundaries around that and how much to share and not share. How much of it is just healthy and how much of it isn't . . .

I So even engaging in this process, wondering about the self-disclosure that goes on and your openness and how healthy that is or not.

T But **it feels good just having said that to you, right now.** But yeah, sometimes, I feel like I'm more open about stuff.

I Than you should be.

T Than I should be or that other people would be. I remember a year or two ago, sharing some of this stuff with somebody I met while I was traveling. And they said, "You're not like that, you have this attribute and that attribute, and why do you think of yourself like that?" and he had some difficulty tolerating it. But, on the other hand, I do talk too much about that, or I'm too, I don't know . . .

I I guess what I understand you saying is that there's something inside yourself that's the censor and the judge. That you haven't talked about experiencing that with Marty. What I'm reflecting on is the fact that you are concerned about self-disclosure and at the same time one of the things you want in supervision is to break through the anxiety by talking about it. It hasn't happened at this point in the supervision. You can stay protected by your anxiety, but at the same time, you are not breaking through to some of the important material.

T   Yeah, yeah. It subverts things a little. **I feel more connected with you right now after having said what I just did, and similarly, it would've happened with Marty had I talked about my anxiety about the supervision.** If I had said, "I feel anxious because of the context," then I would've been more in contact with Marty 'cause that's what's going on with him and I.

I   Yes, yes.

T   That's what we've talked about. And **having had the contact, then I think I would've been more relaxed and more responsive to some of the questions that he was asking about my connection with the client. That's interesting. It's hard for me to talk about how I was responding to the client because I wasn't even responding to Marty.**

I   Yes. And you needed to establish that connection in this context before you could move forward.

T   Yeah.

I   And deal with the client. And it's always in the forefront of your mind as you look at this.

T   Yeah. And it got in the way of a more open kind of exploration, I think.

I   Well, I guess one of the things as we watch it, is to see whether Marty, as a supervisor, perceives that and explicitly uses strategies to open that kind of discussion.

SAS Analysis

Client factor: counseling relationship

Trainee factors: learning needs, self-presentation

Institutional factor: climate

Relationship factor: interpersonal structure

The supervision interview continues to focus on case conceptualization, but notice that the topics of sexuality and gender are the focus.

The emergence of an almost supervisory experience in the reflective interview continues as the supervisee reveals the meaning of his anxiety in how he thinks and feels about himself. He comments on how talking about it in the reflection frees him, in a sense is therapeutic. As he begins to discuss some of the historical events connected with his experience of self, I bridge back to the supervisory relationship and begin to analyze the function of the anxiety in that relationship. He collaborates in that process with me and reflects on his role in keeping the anxiety underneath the talk of supervision. He analyzes what his needs are in the supervision process and concludes that breaking through his anxiety about the situation would have allowed him to fully attend to the client. This process in the reflected interview is a representation of what the supervisee wanted to occur in supervision and anticipates unfolding in the supervision interview. Ironically, the validity of Marty's hypothesis regarding men talking to men particularly about sexuality (read, emotionality) is playing itself out in the reflective interview with the trainee. In this cross-gender relationship, the supervisee has more quickly engaged with me at an emotional level. Of course, there are numerous factors as identified in the SAS analysis that may be influencing his choice; however, the gender factor in the development of the reflective relationship seems worthy of some attention.

A section of the supervision and reflected interview that contains a continued discussion of the case conceptualization task and the supervisor's attention to the theoretical issues in male-male relationships has been deleted here.

Supervision Interview

T Beyond that, let's see, he says he gets along better with his father. The things that I remember about his relationship with his brothers is that his older brother would kind of beat up on him and tease him and would beat up on his little sister . . .

S Umm hmm.

T I don't really have sense about the difference, though between . . .

S It doesn't sound as though there was much comfort in his relationship with his siblings.

T No.

S From what you're saying . . .

T No.

S What's his relationship with men now; has he talked about that?

Function: Consulting and Advising	Task: Case Conceptualization
Supervisor Recall Interview	**Trainee Recall Interview**

S This is for me a real critical kind of juncture. And it's a rather personal kind of issue that my focus very intensively, theoretically and clinically, is on masculinity and maleness, and I'm at the point here of choosing between pursuing that because of my **theoretical interest** in it, on the one hand, and being careful about whether my pursuit of it is helpful and germane to his particular situation. So in effect, I have a personal hobby horse to ride and have to be sensitive to whether I'm using him to exploit that interest of mine, or whether I'm using my understanding and interest to enhance his work with his client. And this is sort of a critical point in that internal deliberation for me.	**I** Do you have any sense of what Marty's getting at here, where he's leading you or do you feel like he's leading you somewhere?
	T What comes to mind is just what we were talking about before, **the client's relationship with me and Marty's asking about his relationship with men.** What was going on with the client, and I don't know if I wasn't so much aware of my relationship with the client or I had some difficulty getting in touch with it. **I was disconnected from Marty.** I've got like three thoughts going at the same time right now, but I think where Marty is leading is, on one level, asking about his relationship with men, but then also what was my experience of him? What kind of inferences was I likely to make about how he related to men in the context of my relationship?
I Do you know or do you have a sense of what you were looking for from him that would give you some indication if you were leading him to some knowledge that would be of use with this client?	
S I raised the question because he seemed **to be hesitant or stumbling.** It wasn't clear to me whether I was therefore moving him beyond the case and that was the reason he was having difficulty with it. I was looking for some clarity, as though my question has real specific meaning for him in the context of this case. And it was questionable to me about whether or not it had. Conceptually, what I was trying to help occur here is his broader understanding of this personality in relation to the world. You know, how narrow was the area of concern or dysfunction. Was it strictly with women? Was it gender, generally, or was it something beyond gender?	**I** So if you reflect on it then you might see some connection between what happened much earlier when he asked about the experience—your experience between you and the client—and it was at that point you diverted, you said, "I don't think I answered that question." And now here he's talking about the relationship with men. Men with men, and so what you're saying is implicitly that draws to your mind your relationship with the client because you're both men, and perhaps your relationship with Marty because you're both men. I'm the only woman in this whole group.
I His hesitancy was very apparent compared to the smoothness that he kept up in questions when you were really dealing with the sexuality and with the specific things the client	**T** Right . . . right.

brought around his relationship with
women. His hesitancy here is a distin-
guishing feature in the intervention.
As you said there are different interpretations of that. One of the things that
occurred to me is that it hadn't occurred to him—to understand the
same gender relationships and that in
itself might have been worthwhile.

S Right. So there are a number of pos-
sibilities which cause me to stop in this
process—that is, continue but inter-
nally to stop and ask myself the motivation for doing this and being real
sensitive to the feedback that **I get as a
basis for making decisions about the
appropriateness of the direction I'm
taking.**

SAS Analysis

Supervisor factors: theoretical orientation and cultural values

Trainee factors: self-presentation and learning needs

In the last segment, the supervisor is commenting on how he
monitors his process and the direction of the conversation with the
supervisee. Because he is unsure about the relevancy of the cultural
issues to the client situation, he watches carefully for the supervisee's
feedback, wondering if he should focus on the trainee's "hesitancy" or
on the more conceptual aspects of gender in relationships.

The cultural issue of masculinity and male relationship is made
very explicit in this last segment of recall with the supervisee. The
theoretical discussion about men's relationships that occurred earlier,
the connection between the supervisor's query of his relationship with
the client, and, finally, his anxiety and concern with his dynamic
process with the supervisor all are threaded together by the supervisee.
His awareness of these connections happens in the reflected interview
but has not yet appeared in the supervisory interview itself.

I have deleted a section (two double-spaced, typewritten pages)
here that describes further the client's symptoms in the supervision
interview. In the reflected interview, the supervisee comments that he
believes he has been distracted by the client's "classical" symptoms.

Beginning of the Metaphor

Supervision Interview

S It might be interesting to look for metaphors with him. Metaphors about the image and the mechanics of smoking, perhaps, as well as some of the implications of it, and see what he does with that. Do you get a sense of his aesthetic sense or quality? Is he an artist? . . . Or is he a mechanic?

T He's a good little boy. That's what comes through the most . . . uh . . . I guess there's something of an artist there, but I don't know if either of those come through that strongly. He just seems young to me, which doesn't mean you can't be an artist, or . . .

Function: Advising and Consulting	Task: Case Conceptualization
Supervisor Recall Interview	**Trainee Recall Interview**
S I was distracting myself a little bit there, too. My focus here, momentarily at least, was on counseling skills. With him, but challenging his creativity.	**I** Any sense of what that sigh meant for you then?
I Phil's creativity?	**T** I was kind of at a loss in response to that question. I didn't really know; that's all I can really come up with. I didn't have the sense that he was really one or the other. I mean, I wasn't sure. That's not the main thing in the case. He didn't really strike me as an artist or a mechanic. He struck me as frightened.
S Phil's creativity. Using a creative approach to the client's characteristics or the client's skills or talents and using that as a medium to enhance the client's understanding and insight. I think I was probably more distracted by that clever piece.	**I** Uh-huh. What would you have liked Marty to do at this juncture?
I Your own cleverness!	**T** I don't know if I wanted anything in particular. I don't know that I'm answering your question, but the thought that comes to mind is that this is something **that I think Marty's interested in. Is someone an artist or a mechanic.** I really didn't have an answer for him, I didn't really get a take either way. I don't know if there's anything in particular I wanted. You mean in response, on this issue about artist or mechanic?
S My own cleverness!	
I Let's see if Phil thinks you're clever.	**I** What did you need from your supervisor, at that moment?
	T Well when I say I was at a loss, I was at a loss in response to that question. I didn't have anything to draw on

that went either way. I guess the main thing which we've been talking about all along is how it was sitting with him here. That would've been helpful. **And also to talk about how I felt about not having focused as much on the relationship with my client.**

I Umm hmm. To sort of push you a little more around your experience of the counseling relationship, to maybe catch you in your digression into the symptoms.

T Yeah, so that I could address my anxiety by talking about it. **It's not that it's up to Marty. If that had been talked about and if I had shared my feelings about having missed some of the stuff about the relationship, we would've made contact and that would've been essentially out of the way. Then I could've really gotten into the client material more and been more responsive to Marty's questions.**

SAS Analysis

Trainee factor: learning needs
Client factor: identified problem

The supervisor appears to be looking for relevant material to change the focus from the client's symptoms to his way of being in the world. This has been a continued focus for the supervisor as he has brought in cultural issues of sexuality, maleness, and male relationships. He now is trying to understand the client's style in the world. The reflected interviews show that both supervisor and supervisee were disconnected during this segment. The supervisor admits the influence of his own distraction and the supervisee acknowledges that he understands this segment as having more to do with the supervisor's needs than his own needs. He returns to his concern for the supervisory relationship and points out that he thinks that he is ready to talk about both his relationship with the client and with the supervisor but is waiting for the supervisor to bring it up. However, he analyzes his role in supervision and does not think that the supervisor is responsible for directing him to this material. Finally, note the comment in the supervisory interview that the supervisee makes to describe the client: "He's a good little boy." It will be relevant later in the interview.

A segment is deleted that includes further elaboration of the use of metaphor to understand the client.

Breaking Through the Impasse in the Counseling Relationship

Supervision Interview

T Umm. Somehow be more three-dimensional and fuller. Somehow, I was distracted by the sexuality in his life.

S Why, what about you, as you reflect on yourself, made that a distraction or a diversion?

T That's a good question, yeah. [long pause]

Function: Consulting and Supporting	Task: Emotional Awareness in Counseling Relationship
Supervisor Recall Interview	**Trainee Recall Interview**
S To me, obviously, that's very critical, that the counselor look at his contribution, and from an introspective perspective. But it's important to do that not as the central focus of the interaction, which is why it comes so late in our discussion. I've opened it a little bit earlier to the focus on **Phil as a person,** but just opened and didn't pursue it. And now that we've worked some and to considerable effort on case conceptualization, skills, various aspects of his work with this client, **the foundation is laid for this to be an appropriate but not an intrusive kind of an intervention.** He can look at this the way he's looked at the other aspects we've talked about, and he's quite open to it.	**T** It's still a good question. [laughs] **I** That's the moment you've been talking about. You experience a frustration about it as you sit here. **T** Let's stick with that for a second. I mean I think I answer that here—I think I remember what I said, but . . . I think there is something about really being with the client, and opening up, that I was avoiding. **I** And do you have a sense of your experiential feelings in the moment you were finally asked the question? As you sit there in that role and your supervisor is asking you about your emotional awareness with the client
I I'm wondering whether there's something **in particular with this therapist you're working with, that would lead you to think that this is a very important question to ask,** or you want to be sure you get this question in?	**T** Yeah. What my reaction is some fear, or just, I don't wanna feel that. There's a feeling about my client, that he's incomplete in some way, that there's something missing, that he's fragile . . . **You know, but fragile** isn't

ever quite descriptive enough, there's like a piece missing, that's more descriptive for me. **And that kind of resonates with that feeling I have in me sometimes and I don't really wanna feel that.**

I And that's what Marty is asking you to do?

T Umm hmm.

S Partly, certainly theoretically on a number of levels. One is because the therapist does make a contribution as a person to the therapy, and it's my function as a supervisor to not obscure that, to make it possible for that to be examined. **With the understanding that once we raise it and examine it that we're not involved in a therapeutic relationship if there are issues to be worked on.** The other is my understanding of gender relationships and the issue of sexuality. And the third, there was something about his talking, his response to my question, my comment, that the girlfriend had a lot of power, that the man gives women a lot of power. **Something in the energy I got from him about that suggested that this may be an issue for Phil.**

I So three different levels, three different reasons or rationales to pursue this.

S Right, so I opened it to allow that to emerge if it's going to emerge. I didn't have a strong sense that it was a critical issue at this point, but it might be an issue, and therefore it has to be given an opportunity to emerge.

SAS Analysis

Supervisor factor: theoretical orientation to supervision

Trainee factor: self-presentation

Client factor: identified problem

The supervisor has moved from the distraction of the symptoms in the supervisory relationship to the focus on the supervisee's self-awareness. This is a return to the earlier juncture where the supervisor asked the question, but the supervisee evaded the question; only in the reflected interview was he able to recognize that he was not ready to respond. The supervisor provides a rationale for pursuing the supervisee's self-awareness also from his theoretical orientation, from his understanding of the supervisee's change in energy (self-presentation), and from his role as a supervisor to help the supervisee become aware of his personal reactions in the therapeutic relationships.

The supervisee shares in the reflective interview the meaning behind the "energy" that the supervisor is picking up. His acknowledged fear of dealing with his own material in relation to the client speaks to the difficulty he has had in responding earlier to this question and feeling distracted in the supervision, as well as to his inability to ask the supervisor to address this issue with him. Recall that earlier in a reflected interview the supervisee commented that it wasn't only the supervisor's responsibility to draw attention to the relationship of supervision, and yet in the supervision interview, it is the supervisor's question that opens the opportunity for this discussion.

Parallel Process Emerges: Return of the Metaphor

Supervision Interview

T The thing that comes, that jumps into my mind, is that he and I are similar in some ways. That maybe it was a kind of collusion, I don't know. [laughter]

S How, what do you see as the similarities?

T I can see, well, the thing I was thinking was, just the concern about being overwhelmed by feelings sometimes, or . . .

Function: Supporting	Task: Emotional Awareness
Supervisor Recall Interview	**Trainee Recall Interview**
S All right, just stop it just for a minute. With that silence, on his part, there's **a choice point about whether to somehow help him, facilitate him, even subversively, coerce him to make what he's thinking explicit, or to decide that if he's aware of it, internally, that that's sufficient, that it doesn't have to be shared with me.** And I opted for the latter, rather than to somehow intervene at that point to encourage him. When he said, "Could that be it?" he was talking to himself. To make that explicit. **It wasn't necessary, in my opinion,**	**T** I'm kind of dreading what I'm gonna say right now. Not so much, I'm not dreading that I'll say what I just said to you. But I roughly remember some of the things that I said, and, it doesn't feel good . . . **I** To hear it? **T** To hear it, or for you to hear it, or for Marty to hear it, for anybody else to hear it. **I** Umm hmm.

at that point, for him to make explicit to me. He was obviously allowing himself to be aware of his own process.

I Is there anything in particular about Phil, or the situation with this client, or other kinds of factors that had you go with the second decision, to **essentially trust him with his internal dialogue?**

S In my experience with Phil, he's very forthcoming **in our relationship, apparently. It is comfortable enough for him and safe enough for him to share with me quite openly.** So I can trust that he's not withholding from me material that would be important for us to share, for the purposes of his continued development with a client.

I So by not demanding or pushing him to share, in fact, you're thinking he can handle that on his own. That, in fact, you're empowering him, in a sense, to make that decision without your intruding in that internal dialogue.

S Yes, and it also **further enhances the sense of security in our relationship.**

I So then the relationship, there is the primary factor that would lead you to that decision is what I hear.

T Yeah, just there's some bad feelings. **And then that issue about well, am I revealing "too much"? And I would feel that way whether we were taping or not, I mean, just to tell Marty that in supervision, I go . . . uhhhhg . . .**

I It almost in some way speaks to the reason why you focused on the symptoms and that the supervision session has taken some time to get to this juncture. And now it's here; you wanted it. You said you need to focus on this; you've been telling me, and now the moment's come and what you're experiencing, I think, is that recognition that, I know why, perhaps, the moment didn't come earlier.

T Boy, that's a big issue. What I'm thinking is yes, **it didn't come earlier because it's an important thing, but also it didn't come earlier because, I think, of my anxiety about being here.** So, I wouldn't say that the anxiety about being here was ultimately a concern about talking about this issue although maybe, in part, it was.

I Or compounded it, certainly.

T Yeah, it was a part of it, yeah.

I It didn't make the issue not real outside of here; it is real, but this compounded it. Sort of multiplied the effect.

T I was probably defending against other things** in addition to maybe not even being in touch with this issue. I think it was more just a characteristic way that I respond in a situation like this. I think there's more to this that I'm not quite seeing. It's just interesting that **I wasn't making much contact with Marty. I wasn't making much contact with you, here, until we talked about that and now I'm talking about not making contact with the client. That's the parallel, although it feels like they're much different issues. With you and I, with Marty and I, just this context. And with the client it was some similarity between us.**

S It's certainly a very critical aspect of it, yes.

I Well, what I'm struck with is that this is a critical juncture.

T Yes, that's true.

I Are you prepared to listen to it?

T Sure.

I Plunge in, huh?

SAS Analysis

Trainee factor: learning needs

Relationship factors: interpersonal structure of both supervisory and recall interviews

Client factor: counseling relationship

This reflected interview with the trainee is the culmination of his levels of anxiety in the counseling relationship, the supervisory relationship, and the reflective interview. He articulates the connections between these three contexts perfectly. He begins to unravel his own emotional issues around the client and understands their impact on his involvement in the three relationships.

This is a critical juncture for the supervisor because he needs not only to decide how much to know of the supervisee's emotional awareness, but also to define his role within the supervisory rather than the counseling relationship. This might be an example of the distinction between encouraging personal awareness as relevant to the counseling situation and delving very deeply into the personal significance of the emotions in the supervisee's personal rather than professional life. In other words, here the supervisor stays within the boundaries of the role expectations for the supervisory relationship rather than moving into a counseling relationship.

The supervisor identifies two factors that influence his decision to not push the supervisee: his trust in the supervisee's ability to divulge what is necessary for his own learning (learning needs) and his trust in the supervisory relationship's mutuality or capacity to encompass self-disclosure. Certainly, earlier in the interview the supervisee was not able to share his anxiety in the counseling or supervisory relationship; the emergence of this material at this stage in the interview, however, may justify the supervisor's trust. That is, the interview itself has a rhythm to it; because the supervisee withheld his feelings early in the interview does not mean that the material may not emerge later, as we are beginning to see in this last segment of dialogue. The supervisee's fear of what he might say to the supervisor, how he might expose himself to all of us, and the supervisor's unerring trust of his supervisee's ability to deal candidly and openly, poignantly depicts the issues of power and vulnerability in the supervisory relationship.

Supervision Interview

T ... And breaking apart. Typically, when I can ... identify with things that the client is struggling with I think I'm more effective, so, I don't know what it is about ...

S About this.

T ... About this presentation that might have led one to want to somehow avoid him, but ...

S Something got too close?

T Maybe.

S You can get close and that's useful, but there may be a line over which you go and that somehow gets in the way.

T Maybe.

S Nice little boy?

T Yeah, I think it's true. Yeah.

Function: Supporting	Task: Emotional Awareness
Supervisor Recall Interview	**Trainee Recall Interview**
	I As I saw that expression, Marty sort of put his head forward and said, **"Nice little boy?"** and then you sort of chuckled with that, and now as you watched in this moment you chuckled, and what was that about, for you, the feeling level, of that very brief interchange?
	T It wasn't as bad as I ... I was expecting that I said something else, so, right now it's, it didn't feel like much; it was "Oh, nice little boy." One or two friends of mine have showed a perception like that of me recently. I run a nice little boy number, so it was like "Oh, yeah."
	I So you were laughing, and when you heard it here you laughed.
	T Marty hadn't said that to me before, but someone else had, so it's interesting **that he picked that up. He**

picked that as opposed to something else we were talking about. Boy, I'm tired of that one.

I Right, well I am going to suggest something, and that is, in that moment I sensed some connection in the tape. As I watched it, that little interchange, even the slight movement of his head and you kind of chuckling . . .

T Between Marty and I . . .

I . . . Yes, the two of you connected in some way that I hadn't been able to recognize earlier. Does that make any sense to you?

T Yes, yeah, I think it's true.

I So at this juncture in supervision, Marty pressed the experience of you and the client, and what that led to was a moment of expression between the two of you that spoke of the connection . . . a positive connection.

T Yeah, maybe this was the first moment that I really felt seen. I'd been saying, "I wish we'd talked about my anxiety, I wish we'd talked about this and that, but then he said, 'oh, you mean like a little boy.' " Then he saw me, it wasn't like he was in the corner asking more general kinds of supervision questions like "Did you talk about family?" I mean he did ask, that's not fair, I guess, he did ask about what it felt like being with him. But those questions are questions that you would be asked in any supervision session about my client. Somehow when he said, "You mean a nice little boy?," I was being seen, and somehow it was more immediate.

SAS Analysis

Client factor: identified problem

Relationship factor: interpersonal structure

Trainee factor: self-presentation

The supervisor uses the words earlier used by the supervisee to describe the client, in order to gently confront the supervisee with his similarity and identification with the client.

The supervisee's reflection of the meaning that the interchange had for him is a powerful reminder of the influence of the supervisor and the importance of developing a relationship that has personal meaning and involvement. He articulates so clearly the importance of being "seen" as a person who is the professional and its impact on the supervisory relationship. The supervisor in this one phrase, "nice little boy?," hooked together the similarity between the counseling and supervisory relationships without ever intruding into the supervisee's private world. The supervisor stayed within the boundaries of the relationship of supervision and did not enter into a therapeutic process with the supervisee.

Supervision Interview

S How do you feel about my raising this with you, about our talking about it?

T I feel OK about it, as long as people looking at it don't . . . No, I feel OK about it.

Function: Consulting	Task: Emotional Awareness in Supervisory Relationship
Supervisor Recall Interview	**Trainee Recall Interview**
I Seems like a very critical interaction, these last few seconds. You're sort of chuckling a little bit and very intensely watching. What kinds of feelings were being brought up for you as you watch it now?	
S Well, first of all, I'm very fond of Phil as a person, for many reasons. He's warm, he's forthcoming, and he's open to examining what's happening with him. However, it also **continues to be important for me to reinforce the security in the relationship and the positive feelings by not pushing him. I, toward the end, was teaching, in a sense.**	
I In this moment?	
S In this, just before that when I talked about how important it is to be aware of when the identification	

becomes so intense and so exclusive that it interferes with the professional relationship. I did it sort of in the form of a question, but in effect, actually I was always paraphrasing him. I think I extracted that from what he said, but it made it more explicit.

I Well, what I noticed there was a very exquisite use of a teaching strategy around an emotional issue. I think, as an outsider watching this, it's very apparent to me that there's a lot of emotion going on with Phil. Some hesitancy in sharing all his internal feelings and dialogue, and what I felt was that you gave him the distance to have that privacy. And that, in part, said to him, "I trust your ability to handle some of this on your own." And then you gave him some information that could stimulate his own internal dialogue. **But based on what you've described as the relationship, Phil's experience level, and the clinical expertise, that this perhaps was the most empowering thing to do for him.**

S Yes, and I think for me that's a critical concept. In addition to anything else that's happening, I work with him and work with other supervisees, the question I ask is **what can I do now that's most empowering? How do I respond? How do I interact in the way that helps the person I'm working with feel their personal, professional competence and power . . .?** And the feedback that happens, when it happens, is a payoff for the work.

I Yes.

SAS Analysis

Trainee factors: experience level, learning needs, self-presentation

Relationship factors: interpersonal structure, power and involvement

At this juncture, the supervisor asks a question related to the supervisory process. The question directs the supervisee to give feedback about his work.

The supervisor reflects the importance of the interaction and his care in not intruding on the supervisee's privacy in an unnecessary way. He talks about both the supervisee's personal attributes, his experience in counseling, and his relationship as the determining factors in his choice of teaching strategy.

Supervision Interview

T Maybe that's . . . I don't know the feeling . . .

S Right now?

T Yeah, the feeling of being more direct with him, when I think about it now, I start feeling a little depressed if I was to be more direct. So by going over here I could avoid feeling depressed.

S And how would you understand your feelings of depression under these circumstances?

T Hmmm. Boy, in terms of me. I guess having to do with similar issues around women in some ways. It's possible that I just didn't want to face that head on with him.

Function: Supporting and Consulting	Task: Emotional Awareness
Supervisor Recall Interview	**Trainee Recall Interview**
S There's an opening there. I asked him a question that's clearly related to an **emotional state,** but I tried to put it in a cognitive frame,—"How do you understand what you were feeling?"— so that he could respond intellectually or cognitively, which would have been a legitimate response to my question, or respond as he did by reflecting on his own emotional state. And **he's forthcoming, he's open, he's secure enough and professional enough to want to examine his state, and so he took that route.**	
I Umm hmm. And although the question, in structure, is similar to a question which you used some time ago, his response is different.	
S Yeah.	

I . . . that the interview has unfolded and it's gathering in intensity as it moves toward Phil's involvement as a therapist in this case . . .

S Umm hmm.

I And so his response is different.

S Yeah, the quality, the whole emotional quality is different.

I **And I can't help but remark that your hypothesis that you generated some time ago around perhaps him wondering about the power of women, and the power of women in his life, has now surfaced for us in his response.**

S Yeah.

SAS Analysis

Trainee factors: experience level, self-presentation

The supervisory interview has broken through the supervisee's anxiety and begins a discussion of his emotional similarity with the client and its relevance to the therapeutic relationship.

The reflected interview provides an analysis of the growing intensity of the supervisory relationship and the effect that it has on the supervisor's choice of strategy. He again uses his knowledge of the supervisee's experience (professionalism), self-presentation, and the relationship to decide how to phrase the question and probe the counseling relationship. The involvement between the two has increased positively since the nice little boy intervention, and thus the question regarding the therapist's involvement in the case is *considered* in a more meaningful way. Notice, too, that issues of gender relationships that were earlier treated more theoretically have now become relevant in the discussion of the supervisee's identification with the client.

Endings

Supervision Interview

S As I understand depression, at least to some extent, depression is a manifestation of kind of hopelessness, weakness, inability to cope with something that was really important. And you mentioned that he appears fragile, so, confronting him possibly would assault his fragility in that he'd feel, in a sense, helpless to do anything about it, and then if you project it back on to yourself. At least it's an interesting kind of perspective for you to keep in mind.

Function: Advising	Task: Case Conceptualization and Emotional Awareness
Supervisor Recall Interview	**Trainee Recall Interview**
I Did you want to comment on that? **S** Yeah. I wanted very much for this not to be understood by him as a diagnostic comment I was making about him. And so **I brought it back to the client, and then tied it back to him, but not in a diagnostic way, by suggesting that this is an interesting thing to speculate about.** **I** Then again, I think that the sequencing of your message to him is important. Because although he left you with an inward focus on himself, you related it to the client interaction, then you moved back to him. You really created the bridge from his response to your response at the end of your message. **S** Umm hmm. **I** The impact of that strategy appears that you give him more distance, more room again. **S** Yes, without minimizing the importance of his introspection.	**I** What do you think Marty was doing there? **T** Umm. Just to try and explain or shed some light on why I might have reacted the way I did. I think you're suggesting something beyond that. **I** Well, maybe the other part of it is, how did you experience that comment? **T** Well, as he was saying it, I got a little fuzzy-headed, so **he was probably onto something.** And then I started thinking well, he talked about depression or hopeless, some hopelessness about not being able to do something, and so then I was **thinking about just what was going on with me then and, actually, has been always going on with me and how that might fit.** And, I have a sense about it, about what has felt hopeless or what has felt hard or what I might've been depressed about. **I** So that outwardly he was making a comment that seemed to me could've been sort of this general psychology comment, "This is the way I understand depression." And you say, "Well, I think he's sort of shedding light on what depression does to feeling." And when you reflect on your experience of his comment, it's much more to do

with you, to do with what depression is personally.

T Yes.

I What I'm struck with is the different levels in which that comment influences. One is you can know what his, you can guess what Marty's intention is, but it has nothing to do, necessarily, with your experience of it or the importance of it. I'm really struck with the complexity of how the comments are received.

T So he's saying something that might be more general, but I really take it in a specific way.

SAS Analysis

Relationship factor: contract

Trainee factor: learning style

As the interview draws to a close, the supervisor explains his strategy of using a somewhat distancing strategy (advising) to encourage the supervisee to continue working on his identification with the client. The supervisee clearly experienced the complexity of the message as he reports his fuzzy-headedness and then proceeds to unravel his perceived meaning in the reflected interview.

Supervision Interview

S Well, you got a couple things to chew on with that, even though you're not seeing him.

T Yeah, I mean I did feel kind of like I was spinning my wheels a little just focusing on the symptom, and it felt kind of unidimensional, and it's interesting to think about what I might have been doing. So maybe I was colluding with him.

S The thought that occurs to me right now as we finish is that if the symptom obscured the view of the problem that in fact what was happening was that he was blowing smoke at you.

T Umm hmm.

S Just a kind of metaphor. Well, we'll leave it at that.

T OK, anyhow, so in some ways I wonder if I feel a little bit like him now as we talk about it—a kind of tightness that he had . . .

S Maybe a little uncomfortable but also maybe important data that you're providing yourself now to work on.

T OK.

Function: Advising and Modeling	Task: Case Conceptualization and Emotional Awareness
Supervisor Recall Interview	**Trainee Recall Interview**
S What I tried to do at the end was bring it back to the clinical, to the interaction with the client, again as a way of emphasizing that **the reason we're together is his work with the client, that's the focus of our work.**	**I** Any final reflections on the feeling of the interview? What came out of it for you?
I So there's a certain rhythm to the whole interview as you come full circle again to talking about the client. Do you have any closing comments as you look at this interview again, how you feel about your work here with Phil?	**T** I think it was useful for me to watch the tape. I think I got a deeper understanding about my work with the client and what was going on with Marty and I. Certainly what was going on with Marty and I, watching it now as opposed to being in it. Yeah, that's about it, I mean, it was useful. I guess I feel, now I feel a lot more relaxed than I did then.
S From a very personal point of view, I feel it was **a very warm kind of feeling, personally in the interaction with Phil.** He's very rewarding 'cause he's very forthcoming and open as I said before. It's been very helpful for me as a supervisor to watch the work and to make explicit to myself the motivation behind what I was doing. Where the interventions came from. And to get a sense of the relationships between what I do and what conceptually I believe the process to be as a way of continuing to refine my own work in the area. And this helps.	**I** Just in general or specifically in this context?
	T Well, I'd say both. In general, I think, I came in feeling more relaxed than I did for the supervision, but also, as I said before having talked about my anxiety and feeling I was working with you was a big point here.
I Well, I think that one of the things that is so apparent is the kind of thinking that goes behind each intervention that isn't obvious, in the immediate interview. As the interview unfolds that thinking becomes more recognizable as you're able to articulate it here. It's been a learning experience for me to get behind your words and understand what you were thinking and why you were doing certain things. Thank you.	**I** Well, as you look back on this interview, is there any point in which you would have liked the supervisor to do something differently, have Marty do something differently.
	T [laughs] **I'm laughing because it's my baloney. I guess, what I mean is, he said something about the little boy and I guess there was a part of me that wanted Marty to rescue me a little and just say, "Phil, you seem anxious, what's going on?" And sort of help me through that, wanting Daddy to take care of everything as opposed to my saying, "Wait a minute, Marty. I'm feeling pretty anxious right now. Let's talk about what's happening here 'cause this is driving me crazy."**

And being more of an adult about it and just tolerating and talking about whatever feelings get in the way of my doing that.

I Today, that's exactly what you did, very early on, which shifted the way you reflected on the supervision.

T Yeah, I probably could've even done it right at the beginning.

I Just get it over with.

I [laughing] One of the things that it seemed didn't happen in the interview, and that was something you had been asking for, was to talk about what went on between you and Marty in the immediacy of the supervision. How do you feel that might've changed the direction of the interview?

T Well, **I would've been less defended.** Just having said how I was feeling. Having Marty hear it. I think I would've felt more in contact with him. I think I start to feel like there's this thing around me, and I'm just scaring myself and I'm kind of self-contained and it doesn't feel very good. And having made contact, that would've dropped away some. And so the way it might've changed the interview was I would've been able to really let myself go into my memories of my experience with the client. I wouldn't have been so consumed with feeling threatened here. And it would've been "OK, I'm safe here; now I can think about the client."

For example, I think I could've thought about the client, and what went on and probably more easily said, "You know, Marty, I really didn't pay a lot of attention to the relationship we had," because I wouldn't have been as concerned about feeling bad about revealing that kind of shift once I had made contact with him.

I Yes. And that would've led to more collaboration between you and Marty.

T Right, we would've gone farther faster and deeper.

I At the end of the interview, you did appear to make that connection.

T Yeah.

I And it just might have happened more quickly, perhaps. You don't know that, but that would be something that you would like to try.

SAS Analysis

Supervisory relationship: contract and structure (involvement)

Trainee factor: learning needs

In the final moment of the interview, the supervisee feels able to disclose his own discomfiture in the interview and its parallel structure to the client's behavior in the counseling relationship.

The supervisor's reflection points out his clear expectations of his role as a supervisor that the meaning of the interaction be brought back to the counseling relationship and the relevancy to the supervisee's development as a therapist. An interesting closing note is the value he placed on the reflective experience in helping him articulate what he does and how to do it better.

As the supervisee ends his reflections, he connects his own behavior as the nice little boy to his behavior in the supervision interview, wanting the supervisor to rescue him and address his anxiety. In many ways, this insight confirms the supervisor's trust that the supervisee would work on his own emotional awareness and that the last intervention, "things to chew on," was, in fact, prophetic. By not rescuing him early on by uncovering his anxiety, perhaps the supervisor enhanced the opportunity for the supervisee's self-discovery and empowerment in the professional role. In the final moments, the supervisee created a connected meaning at all three levels of relationships: counseling, supervisory, and reflective. Perhaps this speaks of the powerful affect that processes, such as reflective process, might have in the training of therapists and supervisors.

It is my hope that these entwined interviews will stimulate thinking about the power of the process of supervision as a teaching and learning tool and about the value of reflecting on the experience of supervision to uncover the meaning and language beneath the words. Although I have provided an SAS analysis, as well as my running commentary in the reflective interviews themselves, I hope that these will be just a beginning to understanding. I encourage students of supervision to create their own analysis and meaning of this rich piece of work.

I am left with the importance of the supervisor's keen sensitivity to the relationship of supervision and to its intrinsic connection to the counseling relationship. All aspects of the supervisory relationship appeared vital to the supervisor's decision making. This process exposed his honoring of the privacy and individuality of the supervisee by pacing the uncovering of the supervisee's identification with the client. This was done not for his own need of knowing but for the supervisee's timing of the act of discovery. Although early on in the interview the supervisor suggests that the trainee attend to his feelings in the counseling relationship, the supervisee's response leads him to divert from this topic until he sees the supervisee ready to connect with these feelings. His patience for the pace of the interview, his respect for the contract of supervision, and his trust in the structure of the relationship itself all allow him to use his keen insight in a gentle and timely fashion. The supervisor does not push to understand the anxiety but, rather, lets it guide his pacing of dealing with the trainee's vulnerability and identification with the case.

In a simple phrase—"Nice little boy?"—the supervisor brings to the surface, although just barely, his insight into the trainee's dilemma. He leaves it hanging poignantly between them for the trainee to turn in his mind and to use for his own personal and professional awareness. He does not rescue him in a way that would collude with the supervisee's old pattern of being taken care of because of his fragility. The supervisor models a way of dealing with fragility without rescuing but by empowering, an approach that is obviously relevant to the work with the client.

Although in hindsight it might be suggested that the supervisor deal more directly with the trainee's anxiety, nonetheless, that anxiety was revealed without probing at the last moment of the interview. The supervisee so freely offers his analysis in the reflective interview, piecing together the multiple connections between the counseling relationship, the supervisory relationship, the reflective relationship, and his own personal struggle. It cannot be forgotten that the intervention of the supervision interview was "to chew on" it, and indeed the trainee does, applying his intellectual facility with practice to the power of his personal awareness. The SAS model merely offers a language and an approach to talk about these events. The meaning is in the practice itself and the participants' shared knowledge.

6

Supervising the Consultation Group

⟨❧⟩ The training of supervisors is linked to the understanding of the tasks of supervision. The trainer must ask, "What is the subject matter of my teaching and how will I explicate its character?" Therefore, the first step in understanding how to teach supervision is to identify those factors of supervision that are potentially influential to the process and outcome of supervision. The Systems Approach to Supervision (SAS) presents a framework and a language, gleaned from empirical and practice knowledge, that identifies the factors that may play a role in the supervisor's decision making.

Transcriptions of supervision interviews have been used in this book to define and illustrate the various factors of the model. This method may also be used when clinicians have recordings of their supervision work and the interaction itself becomes the subject of the case analysis (Kagan & Kagan, 1990). A broader examination of the supervision work is also valuable. The use of the "case method" approach focuses on the presentation of client histories, accompanied at times with examples of the supervision interaction, and followed by a conceptualization of the supervision situation and suggestions for interventions. This approach takes the learner beyond the immediacy and the more atomistic view of moment-to-moment interaction toward understanding the supervision situation historically and contextually.

Chapter 6 illustrates the use of the SAS model in teaching supervision within the context of a group consultation on supervision. The model can be used as a frame of reference for an individual practitioner to think through a dilemma, for case consultation, or for training in supervision.

Three Relational Contexts

Potentially, a multitude of relationships are directly or indirectly part of any discussion of training in supervision. Each supervisor may have several trainees and in turn each trainee may have several clients. Furthermore, in the group consultation, there is not only the relationship between each supervisor and the trainer but also the relationships between the various supervisor members. Clearly, not all of these relationships will be discussed explicitly in the group nor will the trainer know all of these relationships in detail. When supervisor members raise issues in the group, however, their perspective will be shaped by their observation and experience of these various relationships and contexts. The consultative group in supervision exists in a context of complexity fueled by the individual and collective energy of these relationships.

Any discussion of the teaching of supervision must involve a discussion of the practice of supervision and the practice of counseling. All three processes—teaching supervision, supervision practice, and counseling practice—are necessarily linked by their concurrence and the supervisors' and supervisees' roles in the group consultation on supervision and the counseling relationship, respectively. Because the distinctions between these three contexts of teaching and practicing are easily confused, for the sake of clarity, I have named them as follows: The *counseling relationship* refers to each or all of the counselor trainee's counselor-client dyads; the *supervisory relationship* refers to each or all of the supervisor's supervisor-trainee dyads; and the *consultative group* refers to the group of supervisors who meet with a trainer to discuss and learn about their practice of supervision. By understanding the links between these three relational contexts, the tasks and processes of teaching supervision in a group setting might be further illuminated (Holloway, 1994).

In the SAS model, the consultative group is depicted as an institutional factor because the trainer represents the agency, educational programs, and national ethics, standards, and policies. The consultative group plays a role in creating the organizational climate around the practice of supervision and the training program in general. The counseling relationship and the client are represented on the client factors wing of the model. The links between these contexts are created through the dual roles of the counselor-supervisee and the supervisor-group members. The processes that emerge from these encounters resonate with one another not only because of the crossover of individuals but also because of the various topics of discussion. The group consultation may deal with any of the roles or issues that emerge in these three interrelated contexts.

The beginning supervisor arrives in the consultative group immersed in each of these relational contexts. The parties seek guidance from the leader on issues that emerge from any of the three contexts. Central to the purpose of the group, however, are questions that relate to supervisory performance of each relationship. The supervisors face two enormous tasks: What should I teach? How should I create a relationship that facilitates the trainee's learning the teaching objectives? With these questions as a point of departure, the trainer can begin by providing a context for the supervisor's experience. Reference to the model may assist the supervisor in identifying the source or sources of the current dilemma, how these factors interrelate, and how the factors influence the three relational contexts.

A multileveled analysis penetrates each relationship and enhances the opportunity to recognize the context in which each issue emerges and how it influences the other contexts. Such an analysis should benefit the participants in devising an intervention that addresses the primary problem and that is targeted to the appropriate context or contexts. For example, a supervisor's issue of anxiety may be related to the fear of inadequacy among peers in the consultative group, or it may be related to a particular trainee's demands for direct instruction to break through a counseling impasse. In the first instance, the intervention might be carried out entirely in the consultative group by discussing issues of competition and collaboration within the peer group. The group process would be instrumental in the success of the intervention and in relieving the supervisor's anxiety. In the second instance, the group could help to identify the source of the problem in a specific supervisory relationship and devise an intervention strategy. The character of the counseling relationship might also be considered in devising this strategy. In each case, the leader would encourage group members to reflect on how the influence an intervention directed to any of the three contexts might affect work in any of the other.

Stories of Teaching in Supervision

Through my years of teaching supervision, I have collected tales of supervisors' struggles to become more effective in teaching the practice of counseling.

With each story, I have used the SAS model to demonstrate its use in a consultative process. Assume, in each of these tales, that the focus is on the teaching of supervision in either the consultative group or an individual consultation on supervision practice. Common themes have emerged across the years. With each theme, I have established the context, the players, the dilemma, and the way in which participants worked through the dilemma to find a workable hypotheses and intervention for the supervisor.

The SAS model is the framework for the case analysis and provides the common language for discussion. Each case study is accompanied by a three-part figure depicting the different factors as they relate to the case (Figure 6.1). The supervisor's original intervention and thinking is depicted in the Supervisor's Dilemma figure. The strategic analysis, including salient factors and critical discoveries that emerged from the discussion, is shown in the SAS Analysis figure. Finally, the Process Matrix of Supervision figure, indicating the original task and function of the supervisor and the suggested target for intervention, is depicted. The purpose of the diagrams is to emphasize the evolutionary change in focus throughout the process and to demonstrate the way in which the SAS model may be used graphically in case analysis.

Case 1: The Long Reach of the Director

The Supervisor's Dilemma. The supervisor brought to the consultation group two issues: (a) the supervisee was resistant to begin with clients; and (b) the supervisor was concerned about bringing too much of her own orientation into the process of supervision.

The Clinical Service Setting. The clinical setting was a university counseling center. The director had been in place for many years and was very supportive of the training program. There were five master's-level practicum students in training at the center. Although the center had been training students for a number of years, there was no clear set of guidelines to orient them or to guide supervisors.

The Supervisor. The supervisor had been a full-time staff counselor at the center for more than 5 years. Although she was currently taking a practicum in supervision, she had also been supervising at the center for a number of years.

The Trainee. The trainee was a 2nd-year master's student who was completing her final practicum requirement. She had extensive experience in working with the chronically mentally ill but had little exposure to a college-age population.

The Supervisor's Story

I felt it was my responsibility to orient Alexandra to the center. There was really no set orientation that the director had set up, and since I was ultimately responsible for her clinical behavior, I felt compelled to make all the rules and regulations clear to her. I ended up making up a packet of orientation materials largely out of my own personal position of how it should be done rather than based on some center policy. Then I felt really exposed; I really felt I had overstepped my authority, but I couldn't stop myself, even having recognized this. Usually, I'm a nice, follow-the-rules-and-do-a-good-job kind of person, but I surprised myself about how intent I was about laying down the rules of the supervision. On my first brief meeting with Alexandra, I gave her the packet and suggested that she spend a week familiarizing herself with the center and the staff. I really didn't spend as much time with her during this first session as I would have liked to, and I noticed that she seemed a little shy and anxious about being with me. I recognized her hesitancy, but I couldn't attend to it. It just lay before me ready to pick up and hold and find a way to melt it down, but I couldn't bring myself to do it. I just wanted her to understand the policies and the organization. In retrospect, I'm pretty confused about what I did in that meeting since I see myself as very relationship oriented. At any rate, off she went, and I went back to a desk of papers and a gnawing discomfiture with what I had just done.

After 2 weeks, Alexandra came back to me and reported that she had read through everything, understood the organization, had met the staff, and was not ready to see clients. I was not happy. I didn't want to deal with what I interpreted as her resistance. What would make her more ready? I agreed to have her sit in on an intake with me, and this seemed to allay her anxiety. And still we didn't talk about my growing impatience with her neediness or her source of anxiety. As circumstance would have it, at the last minute I had to cancel the intake because I was called out on an emergency. Alexandra was left without the observation and without supervision for another week. I heard from other staff that she wanted to change supervisors, although she wouldn't tell anyone why. All my plans of being the competent supervisor had fallen apart.

The consultative group was concerned. An experienced supervisor was really feeling out of control with her trainee and was not understanding how the relationship had progressed to this point. They were particularly surprised because they experienced the supervisor as warm and giving and very process oriented. What was getting in the way of establishing a facilitative relationship with this trainee?

They probed the supervisor factors: Was there something in the way that the trainee presented herself that really disturbed the supervisor? Were the supervisor's expectations about her role as supervisor that much different from the trainee's expectations? They probed trainee factors: Was the trainee that inexperienced that she lacked the skills and confidence to see clients? After all, it was her second practicum. Was her training for practicum inadequate? They probed institutional factors. Was this trainee just not suited to the clientele at the agency? Was there a climate in the center that might intimidate the trainee?

During the discussion, the supervisor began to realize that she liked the trainee, and she recognized the trainee's anxiety as a normal part of her inexperience with this clientele. The supervisor also saw that her efforts to do away with the trainee's anxiety by giving her more

166

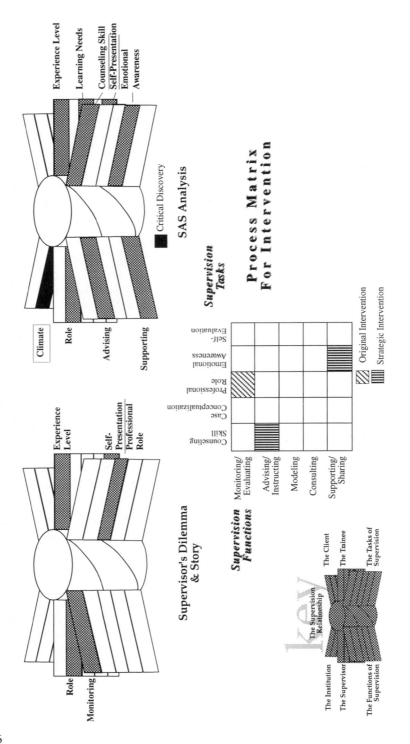

Figure 6.1. Case Study 1: SAS Analysis in Supervision Consultation

information or showing her how she worked were not really working. Essentially, there was no facilitative relationship in which she could understand more fully what was causing her as a supervisor to behave differently in this relationship. What were her expectations for her role as the supervisor?

In being asked this last question, the supervisor stopped and blurted out that there were no clear expectations from the center about her role as supervisor and she felt vulnerable and alone in devising a meaningful training experience. As much as she had worked in having the director establish a coherent set of principles around training and orientation, it had not happened, and she felt that she must carry the ball if it were to be done at all. She talked about a serious breach of ethics by a trainee at the center a few years previously. Although she wasn't the supervisor, she knew that there had not been adequate training or supervision for this trainee, and she blamed the center for not monitoring the trainee's work. In revealing this history, she began to realize that she was very angry with the director for not taking a leadership role in the training nor giving her an opportunity to formally have the responsibility of setting up a program that protected the center, the supervisors, and the trainees. Her anxiety around the training had only been exacerbated by the trainee's feelings of unpreparedness and anxiety. She tried to handle the trainee's anxiety in the way that she was handling her own, and she had forgotten about the establishment of a working relationship.

The SAS Analysis. In this example, the more obvious factor of trainee inexperience and anxiety obscured the underlying issue of the history of the training program in the center and the director's lack of attention to those issues that the supervisor thought were serious and potentially disastrous for the training. The supervisor's submerged anger toward the director and anxiety about the program only exacerbated the trainee's anxiety about seeing clients. If the consultation had focused only on the trainee's anxiety, the supervisor might not have discovered the influence of the training program's history on her work in supervision. Once she acknowledged her anger, she was able to focus on developing the supervisory relationship (see SAS analysis, Figure 6.1). She decided to focus on helping the trainee gain the skills and confidence needed to work with a new clientele. She decided that she was not able, at the time, to confront the director with her concerns but wanted to gain his approval for her outline for supervisory practice. Although this would not change the entire training program, at least she felt that it would enable her to work individually within a set of policies that the director had approved. She needed to feel protected in her work with trainees. (See Process Matrix, Figure 6.1.)

Case 2: Missing the Connection

The Supervisor's Dilemma. The supervisor was disturbed that she was not equally involved with both of her trainees and wondered if her differential supervisory treatment was a cultural phenomenon (Figure 6.2 shows the SAS analysis for the case study developed from this dilemma.

The Clinical Service Setting. The trainees were seeing their first clients in a practicum setting. They had been meeting with the supervisor for 2 months.

The Supervisor. The supervisor was a Latin American woman who had considerable clinical experience. She was very respected both within her agency and in the larger professional community. As an expert in multicultural counseling, she was often asked to be a consultant on race and ethnic relations in a variety of organizations.

The Trainee. The supervisor was working with two trainees. Lily was very dynamic and psychologically minded. She had no experience in counseling prior to coming into a master's program in counseling. Marge was at the same stage of her training program but had been working in a residential treatment center for a number of years. Both trainees were European Americans, but Marge, who was bilingual in Spanish and English, had lived in Latin cultures.

The Supervisor's Story

My supervision is so different with these two trainees. With Lily, I find myself filled with enthusiasm and anticipation for the process between us, whereas with Marge it is like pulling teeth. I am so directive. I experience myself asking one question after another and then telling her how I think about counseling. Yet with all of this work, I don't hear from her, not in a real sense. I hadn't expected this from Marge; although she is not Latin, she knows my language and has lived in a culture similar to mine. I had expected a greater affinity between us. There are times when we speak in Spanish and yet even then there is a barrier, a lack of feeling involved with her, whereas Lily seems to think the way I do about a relationship. What I worry about the most is the comparing that I am doing. I find myself wishing that Marge would be more like Lily. I don't know if she has good skills because I can't seem to get her involved in supervision. Maybe this is her way of dealing with relationships. You know sometimes I feel that I want to talk more about her family history to try to figure out why she won't connect with me. I am so disappointed because I really think that she has potential and there is so much more we could do.

The group was surprised at this contrast in these two trainees but more specifically in the lack of connection that the supervisor felt with Marge. They began to focus on Marge. What interpersonal or self-presentation

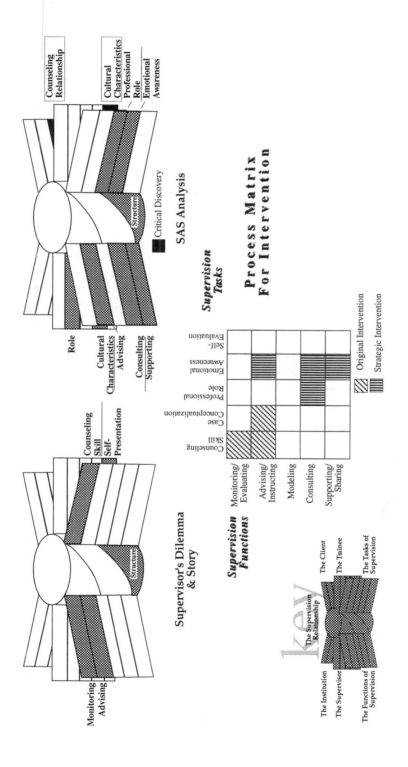

Figure 6.2. Case Study 2: SAS Analysis in Supervision Consultation

factors were getting in the way of her being in supervision? What were her learning needs? Maybe because she had been practicing, she wasn't feeling as needy for supervision. What, really, was her level of experience? Was she hiding her anxiety about not being as competent as her supervisor might think given her previous counseling experience? What was this family thing and how was it a part of supervision? Maybe it was OK not to be very engaged with the trainee; maybe that connection wasn't a necessary part of empowering the trainee. What were the supervisor factors here? Was the supervisor expecting too much of the relationship and of the linguistic or possible cultural connection? Maybe her expectations were too high? Finally, the group centered on the structure of the relationship as it related to the cross-cultural factors.

The SAS Analysis. The recognition that the relationship was the center of the difficulty led the consultation group to discuss the three factors of the relationship: the contract between the participants, the phase of the relationship, and the interpersonal structure. The supervisor had been careful in laying out her assumptions and worldview of supervision to the trainees. She had invited them to discuss any aspects of this with her and share their own thoughts and feelings about the cross-cultural aspects of their relationship in supervision. The structure of the relationship itself in each case had taken different forms, and the group first asked her to chart where she felt most comfortable in a supervisory relationship with regard to power and involvement. She felt that both culturally and professionally she valued mutual engagement and shared power, power that would be most characterized by using a consulting or supporting function with her trainees. In other words, she liked to minimize the distance between herself and her trainee while still maintaining the role and responsibility of the supervisor. When she characterized the relationship of each of her two trainees using power and involvement, she discovered that with Lily she was in a professional relationship that fit these ideals, whereas with Marge she felt forced to use functions such as advising and monitoring, resulting in a more controlling use of power or "power over" and with, at best, a neutral affiliation or involvement. She also realized that the more she tried to create situations where she would be more connected with Marge, the more Marge pulled away. Finally, in desperation she would start giving advice and that seemed to alleviate Marge's anxiety, but she herself felt greatly discouraged. She felt that as supervisor, she wasn't living up to her model and was being too authoritative. The consultative group wondered if the supervisor had expressed these feelings of being disconnected and of not knowing what Marge thought about the clinical issues that were facing her or how she experienced the supervisory relationship. The supervisor recognized that this type of intervention would in and of itself demand a greater connection with Marge because it dealt with the immediacy of the situation. (See SAS analysis, Figure 6.2.)

The supervisor found herself pulling away from Lily in an effort to equalize the situation between the two trainees. She was very reserved with both trainees and resented the fact that she didn't feel able to be herself. The supervisor was concerned about her expectations for supervision and began to question whether her expectations were realistic in the context of a Eurocentric view. At issue was whether it was appropriate for her to expect a more connected relationship in supervision. Could this trainee learn the necessary skills in a more distant relationship? The ramifications for the trainee of not making warm and substantial connections in the counseling relationship were of critical concern to her. The supervisor watched the development of the counseling relationship closely to see if a similar interpersonal structure would be established by the trainee with the client. With her clients, Marge was reserved but warm and inviting in her manner. The supervisor began to question once again the cross-cultural issues that have been operating with the trainee. Was she not connecting because she did not value the supervisor's expertise as a woman and a Latin American? Was she not switching to a referent base of power because she saw the supervisor as so different in attitude and values? The issues of culture, gender, and role were all possible factors in understanding the trainee's lack of involvement in supervision (see Process Matrix in Figure 6.2). The supervisor decided to discuss these issues with the trainee in the context of worldview. She started the conversation in a very general, almost academic, sense, but eventually the discussion began to focus on the personal experiences each of them had in developing their values and goals as professionals. Finally, the trainee revealed that she felt uncomfortable with the supervisor because she perceived her as very powerful and knowledgeable and she resented that power. Her experience in Latin cultures had not been entirely positive; although she was drawn to the openness between people, her contrasting reserve made her feel intimidated and unseen. In that situation, she left feeling unaccepted and resentful in spite of her host family's efforts to make her a part of the family. She acknowledged that being with her supervisor reminded her of this experience. She felt inadequate in forming a relationship with the supervisor and was afraid that the supervisor would also find her inadequate. Through this discussion, both trainee and supervisor began to form a relationship that was more meaningful, more connected, and more sensitively attuned to the differences between them.

Case 3: Just Teach Me How to Do It!

The Supervisors' Dilemma. Both supervisors came to me bewildered and confused. Their trainees were not accepting supervision. They were unwilling to talk about their own feelings and thoughts about the counseling relationship and about the supervisory relationship. What was the cause of their supervisees' resistance? The supervisors were deeply concerned about the supervisees' futures as counselors because they were unable to engage in the supervisory process.

The Clinical Service Setting. This was a small, nonprofit community agency that offered services to low-income people. All counseling sessions of trainees were audiotaped for supervision purposes.

The Supervisors. Both Rebecca and Georgine were European American women. They were friends, and both had clinical positions in a small community training center. They were advanced in their clinical skills and experience and were dedicated professionals. They were supervising beginning-level practicum students because of their commitment to training professionals and because of their enjoyment of the supervision process.

The Trainees. The trainees were both mature individuals who had entered the counseling profession from other fields. They were eager to learn how to do counseling and were very involved in their placement setting. One trainee was a European American male who had been a teacher for 5 years. The other trainee was a bicultural, European American and American Indian female who had worked extensively in community action organizations prior to returning to the university for counselor training.

The Supervisors' Stories

Rebecca: My supervisee is having difficulty establishing boundaries with her client, and it seems at times that the two of them are friends chatting on the street. I have explored with the trainee the difference between friendships and therapy and felt that although she had an intellectual understanding of this, she wasn't able to translate this into the practice of her role. The chatting, although somewhat diminished in the sessions, seems unpredictable, and I don't think she can recognize the boundaries between the two roles. So that is when I decided to begin a process of emotional exploration with her. I've worked really hard at bringing her into her own awareness and felt satisfied with her willingness to self-disclose about her personal feelings in reference to this client. In fact, I followed this up with two more supervisory sessions in which we probed the meaning of friendships in her culture and the need to feel accepted as a person and professional. I really enjoyed the complexity and connection between the professional boundaries and their connection with the cultural background of the counselor. I began to teach her about the importance of separation and the implications of dual relationships and ethics. She really became very tearful and then shut down. I didn't really understand what had happened, and then in the next and last session before today she came in very angry with me for intruding into her personal world and my lack of sensitivity to cultural background. She insisted that I stick to supervision and teach her the skills of the profession, not try to be her therapist. I was so shocked at the intensity of her reaction and even more shocked that she felt I was mixing up the boundaries.

Georgine: I really know what you are going through. My trainee seems completely incapable of exploring his own emotional response to his client. He's really trying to befriend his client and is actually giving her feedback on how he sees her as a woman. I think that he is trying to assure her that she is a nice person, someone that he would find attractive. I am so exasperated with him. He is unable or unwilling to get at what made it so necessary to reach across his professional boundaries like this. I have confronted him several times on this inappropriate behavior with the client. Last time I observed his counseling session with this client, I was totally undone. He seemed to be deliberately seductive with her. In the last supervision session, he told me in no uncertain terms to lay off him about exploring his feelings about the client and that what he really needed was to learn the skills of being a counselor. If he wanted therapy, he'd pay a counselor for it.

Both supervisors sat across from me for their joint consultation hour. Rebecca is a very thoughtful and still type of person. Her quiet intelligence is probably the first view one has of her. There is a persistence and tenacity in the way she takes hold of an idea and runs underground with it. She has a keen set of antennae that pick up the nuances of behaviors and their meaning. She looked pretty discouraged today, and running through her demeanor was something of a rage, at least what might be the glimpse of a rage for Rebecca. She started her tale at a higher pitch than usual, and I was immediately alerted to the intensity she held.

Georgine held a certain serenity about her. She has a great way of being quietly present, delivering searing confrontations with hardly a ripple in her composure and yet with a support and warmth that leaves a lingering feeling that you are cared about in spite of the fact that, clearly, there are things you need to change. They looked at me expectantly, knowing my predilection for complex interpersonal analysis; I could feel their suggestion that I begin an exploration of their feelings in their respective supervision relationships. I felt tugged by the seduction of their intensity and our history of untangling the webs of emotion and behavior in relationship. I knew just as surely that it must be different this time. They needed to be taught rather directly the boundaries of their roles and the meaning of the contract and development of the supervisory relationship, just as surely as their students needed to understand the boundaries of their roles as counselors. I needed to give to them what their students were asking—that is, an understanding, experientially, of the importance of skill acquisition in empowerment. As boring and interpersonally ignorant as it may seem to them in this moment, I must remind them of the purpose of their supervision contract and the level of experience of their trainees. I offered them the possibility that their trainees just did not know how to show warmth and genuineness within the framework of a counseling relationship. This was indeed a parallel process with the counseling and supervisory relationship that needed to be stopped at the consultative level. We needed to engage in a clear and careful analysis of their supervisory method.

And so, initially, we began a process of examining the skills that the trainees lacked and thought about supervisory approaches to teach these skills. We kept the focus on skills that might help facilitate the trainees in learning the role of counselor. I could tell that they were dubious and really wanted to divert our attention to their feelings about not being appreciated as supervisors after all their work with and attention to these fledgling counselors. I resisted and waited until we had dealt with the skills and teaching methods; and then we ventured into talk of relationship, culture, and gender and how these factors were influencing their involvement with their trainees. (See Supervisor's Dilemma and Story, Figure 6.3.)

The SAS Analysis. The supervisors had not misread the difficulty the counselors were having in the development of the counseling relationships, but they had chosen a counseling function to focus almost exclusively on the trainees' emotional awareness to address this issue. Initially, the counselors found themselves following this lead but then felt that they were being seduced into a counseling relationship and being denied the skills that they needed to act differently. The supervisors needed to return to their understanding of the supervisory contract. Had they maintained the boundaries of the supervisory relationship? They needed to examine the phase of relationship and the level of experience of the trainee. They were in fairly new relationships in which deep self-disclosure might have been seen as premature. Their persistent focus on the trainees' self-disclosure was overly intense. Although an appropriate venture initially, it soon became overly demanding and seemingly unrelated to the client's issues. These were beginning-level counselors, and they needed to learn a level of skill that could help them implement their intellectual understanding of the counselor role. They needed skills other than their friendship skills to create a facilitative and warm relationship. The supervisors' own preferences for interpersonal awareness and counseling-type interventions in supervision—that is, their expectation of the role of the supervisor being too narrowly defined—prevented them from acknowledging the need to provide skill training to these trainees. The importance of the gender and cultural differences between the supervisors and their trainees also played a role in their lack of sensitivity to the trainees' anger. The supervisors assumed that the trainees' use of relationship skills were based on some dysfunctional reason for needing to be friends with their clients. Although they were able to engage in a conversation with their trainees about cultural mores and tradition in professional relationships, in action they were defying those norms in their persistence for self-disclosure and more intimate conversation. The trainees felt that their behaviors with their clients were being interpreted in a way that maligned their intentions. Note that in Figure 6.3, the SAS analysis identifies the potential parallel processes across the three relationships: the trainees' counseling relationships (client factor wing), the supervisory relationships (relationship core), and the consultative relationship (institutional factor wing).

Eventually, the trainees were able to explain their intentions to their supervisors from a cultural and a gender perspective. The supervisors were able to specifically identify those behaviors of the trainees that were ineffective in the counseling context, and the trainees were able to suggest ways that they would be with the client that would ameliorate the situation but still feel genuine and culturally and gender congruent. Rebecca finally began a discussion of counseling approaches that were most effective with her trainee's own cultural groups and the differences in relational structure and role that would be expected in cultures other than European American. For both supervisors, understanding the meaning of their initial supervisory focus on personal awareness from both a cultural and a gender perspective was very important in finding a way to appropriately relate to their supervisees (see Process Matrix, Figure 6.3).

Case 4: The Infection Spreads

The Supervisor's Dilemma. The supervisor was very clear that she had made a mistake in her supervision. She had not seen the process in the group supervision and had intervened to produce what she labeled as disastrous results. What should she have done differently? How would others in the group have handled it? How was she going to get back to a working relationship with her trainee?

The Clinical Service Setting. The consultative group of beginning-level supervisors met weekly to discuss their work with their trainees. The trainees were seeing clients in a community mental health setting and were in their 2nd year of practice.

The Supervisor. This was a beginning-level female supervisor with limited clinical experience. She provided individual supervision and group supervision as a part of her clinic responsibilities.

The Trainee. This is a beginning-level counselor in his early 20s with relatively extensive experience in paraprofessional self-help groups. He is currently seeing several clients in a community mental health setting.

176

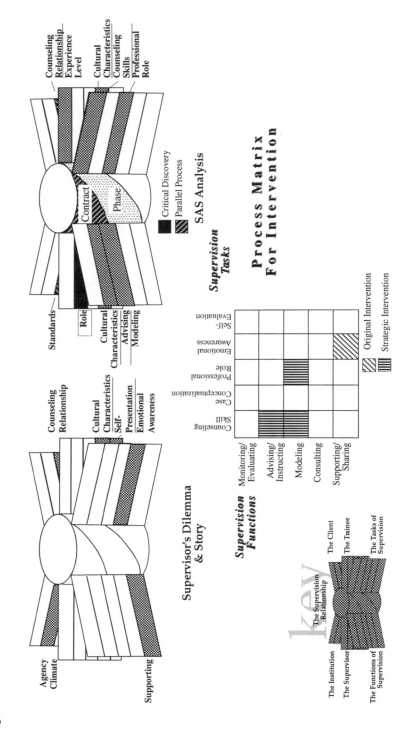

Figure 6.3. Case Study 3: SAS Analysis in Supervision Consultation

The Supervisor's Story

OK, group. The primary problem is with my supervisee in the group supervision. He really has me stymied. He absolutely wants my attention but then rejects it. The entire group is giving him an incredible amount of air time, but he is totally unresponsive. In fact, he has told them that he is angry with them for putting the focus on him. Yet in individual supervision, he is very talkative and always runs over the hour. I was very frustrated and angry with him last week. He ran over 45 minutes late and then asked for an extra supervision session that week. Last group meeting, Barbara [see "The Consultation" section below] and I decided we would confront him with the double messages that he was sending to the group. When I did it, I had this rotten feeling that the timing wasn't right. The group had been putting a lot of effort into helping another group member work through her countertransference with a client. I used the idea of countertransference to tell my trainee that I felt some of that was happening between him and I. The group seemed really confused but not Barbara's trainee. Generally, she's pretty reserved in the group discussion, but she really self-disclosed. She said that she felt that her supervision was really an open process and she could tell her supervisor if she had a problem with her. The rest of the group didn't seem to understand what was going on, so at that point I launched into an explanation of countertransference in supervision. I thought it might be interesting for them to understand that their supervisors were human and vulnerable to such transgressions. By the time I had finished, my trainee was livid. He got up and stomped out of the group. I just sat there immobilized, and Barbara took over. I don't know whether I should have run after him, discussed it in the group, or what. We just all went back to analyzing one of the case presentations.

I walked into the classroom, pleased to be there. I liked working with this group on my favorite topic of supervision. It was Susan's day. She was to consult and was busy handing out the brief synopsis of her "dilemma." Susan was a powerful and bright force in the classroom. She really had a way of bringing the focus to the underbelly of the supervision process. Susan had a close woman friend in the group, Barbara, and their connection was quite apparent to the group. Barbara was backup. She often supported Susan's exploration of the group process and on occasion offered a different contrasting view. Such excursions invariably brought a momentary sharpness to Susan's look, but it was quickly smoothed over as Barbara handed back the conversation to Susan's skillful guidance.

I listened to Susan's story of her difficulty with her trainee and how it was manifesting itself in the laboratory group. I wondered whether Barbara was aware that she would probably be a focus in this consultation. Glancing up from my reading, I saw the color rise in Barbara's face as she listened and her furtive look to Susan, who nodded supportively in her direction. "What next," I wondered. Although the group was making good progress in understanding the dilemma of Susan's supervisory relationship, there was no indication from Susan that any of their suggestions would be helpful. Barbara, meanwhile, was silent throughout this time. Then, one of the group members pointed out that the situation seemed to involve Barbara but that she had not participated in the discussion. This question seemed to allow Barbara to begin her story of difficulty with her trainee, and the group spent some time focusing on her issues in individual supervision. There had still been no attention given to the supervision group. The tension between Susan and Barbara seemed to be increasing as the attention was directed to Barbara. I made this process observation to the group. This began to uncover Susan's and Barbara's conflicts in coleading the group. Barbara experienced Susan as dominating the interaction, and Susan, for her part, felt that she was forced to do this because Barbara was so reticent about participating. The consultation group immediately recognized that this dynamic had also happened in the consultation group—Barbara receiving attention for being silent and Susan being given the floor for fear of confronting her and not knowing whether she would take the discussion to a deep personal level. The discussion then evolved into an understanding of how their trainees were acting out the coleaders' unspoken tension and frustration with each other. Finally, the group returned to the issues of Susan's trainee and how to intervene with his neediness, anger, and rejection in the individual supervision. (See Supervisor's Dilemma and Story, Figure 6.4.)

The SAS Analysis. The focus of the consultation was finally directed to the actual source of difficulty—the relationship between two members of the consultative group. Although their way of interacting with one another had infected both the laboratory group and their relationship with their trainees in individual supervision, the issue between them—vying for attention and approval from their peers and from me in the consultation team—was the source of their competition. The entire group worked at understanding how they bowed to Susan's power, often looking to her for the lead on an issue. Although not all had been aware of this dynamic previously, they had noticed Barbara's quietness and acquiescence to Susan. Others had felt put off by the relationship that they perceived between Barbara and Susan and tried to stay away from both of them. The intervention was directed toward the consultation group as a whole, and when the group was willing to deal directly with their interpersonal conflicts, they were able to move to problem solving regarding Barbara and Susan's supervisory group and their relationships with their trainees. The supervisors worked with their trainees by sharing with them their own difficulty in coleading and how they thought that might be affecting the supervisory relationships. They encouraged the trainees to self-evaluate their own collusion with this process. Both supervisors and supervisees collaborated in a process to stop this conflict and asked to begin once more to focus on the learning needs of the trainees. Figure 6.4 (SAS analysis)

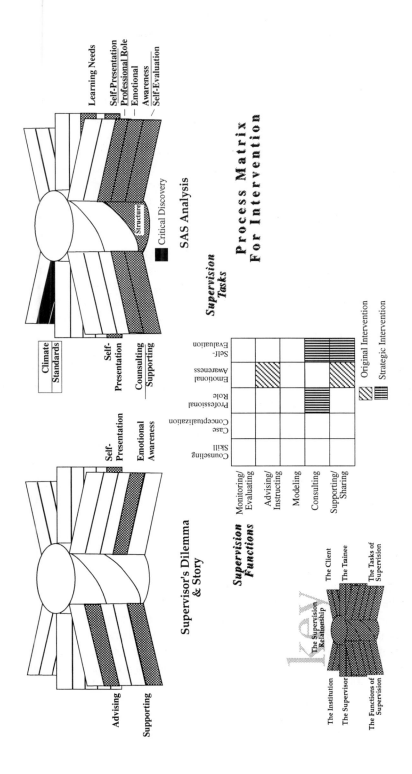

Figure 6.4. Case Study 4: SAS Analysis in Supervision Consultation

illustrates the infection of the problem from the consultation group (represented in the institutional factors of agency climate and agency standards) to the supervisory relationships. Although the consultation group dynamics were targeted to begin the change process, the process matrix (Figure 6.4) identifies the intervention suggested for Susan's individual supervisory relationship.

Concluding Remarks

This book is not a training manual of supervision; it does not contain a list of supervision techniques, and to some this will be disappointing. It is a book that asks practitioners and educators of supervision to reflect on what they do in supervision, to ask difficult questions about the meaning of their work, to uncover their own intuition and use a language that allows others to understand what they know. It is a book that attempts to make sense of the research and practice knowledge of supervision and synthesize it in a way that is immediately practical and relevant to asking these questions. These examples are only a glimpse of all that can happen in the layers of relationships that we create in supervision. The working through of the examples is an effort to reveal a way to apply a framework, the SAS model, to the real work of supervision. The model comes from the work and then gives back to the work a way to talk about it that goes beyond our scattered musings to a critical analysis of what we do and how it affects supervisees with whom we work and the clients with whom they work. It is the reflection of our work in these relational contexts that can lead to the articulation of a grounded and considered approach to supervision.

My teaching and consulting in supervision across the helping professions has indelibly influenced the conceptualization of the SAS model. The live work of doing supervision and teaching people to do supervision has convinced me that there is no "how to" and no "should be"; rather, there is a need for reflective supervisors with a language to express their insights and decision making. The SAS model has been a tool to offer supervisors to analyze their work, be deliberate in their teaching, and continually search for better ways to teach the person before them. It has also been my intention in this book to capture some of the live practice of supervision, connect it to empirical knowledge, and, perhaps, make research live for the practitioner.

In this book, I have written of my conceptualization of supervision and have translated this conceptualization into a model. I have offered some examples for definitional purposes in addition to illustrations of how to apply the model in different contexts. I have tried to be explicit and concrete about a very complex instructional method. In spite of my efforts to capture the SAS model for the printed page, however, the excitement of dialogue, clarification, and demonstration that come from learning in an interactive atmosphere cannot be captured. This might also be said of the nature of supervision. The best of supervision will appear in the creative moments of an accomplished supervisor with an engaged student. The belief that supervision does involve artistry as well as skill, however, cannot stop us from striving to establish a method to guide the efforts of supervisors to understand the principles of pedagogy, learn the skill of supervision, and apply creatively these methods with the individual learner. It is my hope that this book offers a method for dialogue about supervision that anchors the conversation in the knowledge of science and the intuition of practice.

APPENDIX

The Association for Counselor Education and Supervision Standards for Counselor Supervision

Core Areas of Knowledge and Competency

The proposed Standards include a description of eleven core areas of personal traits, knowledge and competencies that are characteristic of effective supervisors. The level of preparation and experience of the counselor, the particular work setting of the supervisor and counselor and client variables will influence the relative emphasis of each competency in practice.

These core areas and their related competencies have been consistently identified in supervision research and, in addition, have been judged to have face validity as determined by supervisor practitioners, based on both select and widespread peer review.

1. Professional counseling supervisors are effective counselors whose knowledge and competencies have been acquired through training, education, and supervised employment experience. The counseling supervisor:

    1.1 demonstrates knowledge of various counseling theories, systems, and their related methods;

    1.2 demonstrates knowledge of his/her personal philosophical, theoretical and methodological approach to counseling;

    1.3 demonstrates knowledge of his/her assumptions about human behavior; and

NOTE: These standards were authored by the ACES Supervision Interest Network and were adopted by the American Association for Counseling and Development in 1989. © ACA. Reprinted with permission. No further reproduction authorized without written permission of the American Counseling Association.

1.4 demonstrates skill in the application of counseling theory and methods (individual, group, or marital and family and specialized areas such as substance abuse, career-life, rehabilitation) that are appropriate for the supervisory setting.

2. Professional counseling supervisors demonstrate *personal traits and characteristics* that are consistent with the role. The counseling supervisor:

   2.1 is committed to updating his/her own counseling and supervisory skills;

   2.2 is sensitive to individual differences;

   2.3 recognizes his/her own limits through self-evaluation and feedback from others;

   2.4 is encouraging, optimistic and motivational;

   2.5 possesses a sense of humor;

   2.6 is comfortable with the authority inherent in the role of supervisor;

   2.7 demonstrates a commitment to the role of supervisor;

   2.8 can identify his/her own strengths and weaknesses as a supervisor;

   2.9 can describe his/her own pattern in interpersonal relationships.

3. Professional counseling supervisors are knowledgeable regarding *ethical, legal and regulatory aspects* of the profession, and are skilled in apply this knowledge. The counseling supervisor:

   3.1 communicates to the counselor a knowledge of professional codes of ethics (e.g., AACD, APA);

   3.2 demonstrates and enforces ethical and professional standards;

   3.3 communicates to the counselor an understanding of legal and regulatory documents and their impact on the profession (e.g., certification, licensure, duty to warn, parents' rights to children's records, third party payment, etc.);

   3.4 provides current information regarding professional standards (NCC, CCMHC, CRC, CCC, licensure, certification, etc.);

   3.5 can communicate a knowledge of counselor rights and appeal procedures specific to the work setting; and

   3.6 communicates to the counselor a knowledge of ethical considerations that pertain to the supervisory process, including dual relationships, due process, evaluation, informed consent, confidentiality, and vicarious liability.

4. Professional counseling supervisors demonstrate conceptual knowledge of the *personal and professional nature of the supervisory relationship* and are skilled in applying this knowledge. The counseling supervisor:

   4.1 demonstrates knowledge of individual differences with respect to gender, race, ethnicity, culture and age and understands the importance of these characteristics in supervisory relationships;

   4.2 is sensitive to the counselor's personal and professional needs;

   4.3 expects counselors to own the consequences of their actions;

   4.4 is sensitive to the evaluative nature of supervision and effectively responds to the counselor's anxiety relative to performance evaluation;

      4.5 conducts self-evaluations, as appropriate, as a means of modeling professional growth;

      4.6 provides facilitative conditions (empathy, concreteness, respect, congruence, genuineness, and immediacy);

      4.7 establishes a mutually trusting relationship with the counselor;

      4.8 provides an appropriate balance of challenge and support; and

      4.9 elicits counselor thoughts and feelings during counseling or consultation sessions, and responds in a manner that enhances the supervision process.

5. Professional counseling supervisors demonstrate conceptual knowledge of *supervision methods and techniques,* and are skilled in using this knowledge to promote counselor development. The counseling supervisor:

      5.1 states the purposes of supervision and explains the procedures to be used;

      5.2 negotiates mutual decisions regarding the needed direction of learning experiences for the counselor;

      5.3 engages in appropriate supervisory interventions, including role-play, role reversal, live supervision, modeling, interpersonal process recall, microtraining, suggestions and advice, reviewing audio and video tapes, etc.;

      5.4 can perform the supervisor's functions in the role of teacher, counselor, or consultant as appropriate;

      5.5 elicits new alternatives from counselor for identifying solutions, techniques, responses to clients;

      5.6 integrates knowledge of supervision with his/her style of interpersonal relations;

      5.7 clarifies his/her role in supervision;

      5.8 uses media aids (print material, electronic recording) to enhance learning; and

      5.9 interacts with the counselor in a manner that facilitates the counselor's selfexploration and problem solving.

6. Professional counseling supervisors demonstrate conceptual knowledge of the *counselor developmental process* and are skilled in applying this knowledge. The counseling supervisor:

      6.1 understands the developmental nature of supervision;

      6.2 demonstrates knowledge of various theoretical methods of supervision;

      6.3 understands the counselor's roles and functions in particular work settings;

      6.4 can identify the learning needs of the counselor;

      6.5 adjusts conference content based on the counselor's personal traits, conceptual development, training, and experience; and

      6.6 uses supervisory methods appropriate to the counselor's level of conceptual development, training, and experience.

7. Professional counseling supervisors demonstrate knowledge and competency in *case conceptualization and management.* [The counseling supervisor:]

7.1   recognizes that a primary goal of supervision is helping the client of the counselor;

7.2   understands the roles of other professionals (e.g., psychologists, physicians, social workers) and assists with the referral process, when appropriate;

7.3   elicits counselor perceptions of counseling dynamics;

7.4   assists the counselor in selecting and executing data collection procedures;

7.5   assists the counselor in analyzing and interpreting data objectively;

7.6   assists the counselor in planning effective client goals and objectives;

7.7   assists the counselor in using observation and assessment in preparation of client goals and objectives;

7.8   assists the counselor in synthesizing client psychological and behavioral characteristics into an integrated conceptualization;

7.9   assists the counselor in assigning priorities to counseling goals and objectives;

7.10 assists the counselor in providing rationale for counseling procedures; and

7.11 assists the counselor in adjusting steps in the progression toward a goal based on ongoing assessment and evaluation.

8. Professional counseling supervisors demonstrates [*sic*] knowledge and competency in client *assessment and evaluation*. The counseling supervisor:

8.1   monitors the use of tests and test interpretations;

8.2   assists the counselor in providing rationale for assessment procedures;

8.3   assists the counselor in communicating assessment procedures and rationales;

8.4   assists the counselor in the description, measurement, and documentation of client and counselor change; and

8.5   assists the counselor in integrating findings and observations to make appropriate recommendations.

9. Professional counseling supervisors demonstrate knowledge and competency in *oral and written reporting and recording*. The counseling supervisor:

9.1   understands the meaning of accountability and the supervisor's responsibility in promoting it;

9.2   assists the counselor in effectively documenting supervisory and counseling related interactions;

9.3   assists the counselor in establishing and following policies and procedures to protect the confidentiality of client and supervisory records;

9.4   assists the counselor in identifying appropriate information to be included in a verbal or written report;

9.5   assists the counselor in presenting information in a logical, concise, and sequential manner; and

9.6   assists the counselor in adapting verbal and written reports to the work environment and communication situation.

10. Professional counseling supervisors demonstrates [*sic*] knowledge and competency in the *evaluation of counseling performance*. The counseling supervisor:

    10.1 can interact with the counselor from the perspective of evaluator;

    10.2 can identify the counselor's professional and personal strengths, as well as weaknesses;

    10.3 provides specific feedback about such performance as conceptualization, use of methods and techniques, relationship skills, and assessment;

    10.4 determines the extent to which the counselor has developed and applied his/her own personal theory of counseling;

    10.5 develops evaluation procedures and instruments to determine program and counselor goal attainment;

    10.6 assists the counselor in the description and measurement of his/her progress and achievement; and

    10.7 can evaluate counseling skills for purposes of grade assignment, completion of internship requirements, professional advancement, and so on.

11. Professional counseling supervisors are knowledgeable regarding *research in counseling and counselor supervision* and consistently incorporate this knowledge into the supervision process. The counseling supervisor:

    11.1 facilitates and monitors research to determine the effectiveness of programs, services and techniques;

    11.2 reads, interprets, and applies counseling and supervisory research;

    11.3 can formulate counseling or supervisory research questions;

    11.4 reports results of counseling or supervisory research and disseminates as appropriate (e.g., inservice, conference, publications); and

    11.5 facilitates an integration of research findings in individual case management.

The Education and Training of Supervisors

Counseling supervision is a distinct field of preparation and practice. Knowledge and competencies necessary for effective performance are acquired through a sequence of training and experience which ordinarily includes the following:

1. Graduate training in counseling;

2. Successful supervised employment as a professional counselor;

3. Certification as a National Certified Counselor, Certified Clinical Mental Health Counselor, Certified Rehabilitation Counselor, or Certified Career Counselor;

4. Certification by a state department of education or licensure by a state as a professional counselor;

5. Graduate training in counseling supervision including didactic courses, seminars, laboratory courses, and supervision practica;
6. Continuing educational experiences specific to supervision theory and practice (e.g., conferences, workshops, self-study); and
7. Research activities related to supervision theory and practice.

The supervisor's primary functions are to teach the inexperienced counselor and to foster their professional development, to serve as consultants to experienced counselors, and to assist at all levels in the provision of effective counseling services. These responsibilities require personal and professional maturity accompanied by a broad perspective on counseling that is gained by extensive, supervised counseling experience. Therefore, training for supervision generally occurs during advanced graduate study or continuing professional development. This is not to say, however, that supervisor training in the pre-service stage is without merit. The presentation of basic methods and procedures may enhance students' performance as counselors, enrich their participation in the supervision process, and provide a framework for late study.

August 1988

References

Abbey, D. S., Hunt, D. E., & Weiser, J. C. (1985). Variations on a theme by Kolb: A new perspective for understanding counseling and supervision. *The Counseling Psychologist, 13,* 477-501.

Accreditation Committee. (1986). *Accreditation handbook.* Washington, DC: American Psychological Association.

Alexander, P. A., & Judy, J. E. (1988). The interaction of domain-specific and strategic knowledge in academic performance. *Review of Educational Research, 58,* 375-404.

Altman, I., & Taylor, D. A. (1973). *Social penetration: The development of interpersonal relationships.* New York: Holt, Rinehart & Winston.

Altucher, N. (1967). Constructive use of the supervisory relationship. *Journal of Counseling Psychology, 14,* 165-170.

American Counseling Association. (1981). *American Counseling Association ethical guidelines.* Alexandria, VA: Author.

American Psychological Association. (1992). *American Psychological Association ethical guidelines for practice.* Washington, DC: Author.

Ashby, J. D., Ford, D. H., Guerney, B. G., & Guerney, L. (1957). Effects on clients of a reflective and leading type of psychotherapy. *Psychological Monographs, 7,* 1-32.

Atkinson, D. R., Morten, G., & Sue, D. W. (1989). *Counseling American minorities: A cross-cultural perspective* (3rd ed.). Dubuque, IA: William C. Brown.

Barak, S. A., & LaCrosse, M. (1975). Multidimensional perceptions of counselor behavior. *Journal of Counseling Psychology, 22,* 471-476.

Barrett-Lennard, G. T. (1962). Dimensions of perceived therapist response as causal factors in therapeutic change. *Psychological Monographs: General and Applied, 76*(43, Whole No. 562).

Bartell, P. A., & Rubin, L. J. (1990). Dangerous liaisons: Sexual intimacies in supervision. *Professional Psychology: Research and Practice, 21*(6), 442-450.

Bartlett, W. E. (1983). A multidimensional framework for the analysis of supervision of counseling. *The Counseling Psychologist, 11*(1), 9-18.

Baumeister, R. F. (1982). A self-presentational view of social phenomena. *Psychological Bulletin, 91*, 3-26.

Berger, C. E., & Calabrese, A. M. (1975). Some explorations in initial interaction and beyond: Toward a developmental theory of interpersonal communication. *Human Communication Research, 1*, 99-112.

Bergin, A. E., & Garfield, S. L. (1986). *Handbook of psychotherapy and behavior change.* New York: John Wiley.

Bernard, J. M. (1979). Supervisor training: A discrimination model. *Counselor Education and Supervision, 19*, 60-68.

Bernard, J. M., & Goodyear, R. K. (1992). *Fundamentals of clinical supervision* (pp. 307-344). Boston: Allyn & Bacon.

Beutler, L. E., & McNabb, C. E. (1981). Self-evaluation for the psychotherapist. In C. E. Walker (Ed.), *Clinical practice of psychology* (pp. 397-439). New York: Pergamon.

Borders, L. D. (1989). Developmental cognitions of first practicum supervisees. *Journal of Counseling Psychology, 36*, 163-169.

Borders, L. D., & Fong, M. L. (1989). Ego development and counseling ability during training. *Counselor Education and Supervision, 29*, 71-83.

Borders, L. D., Fong, M. L., & Cron, E. A. (1988). In-session cognitions of a counseling student: A case study. *Counselor Education and Supervision, 28*, 59-70.

Borders, L. D., Fong, M. L., & Neimeyer, G. J. (1986). Counseling students' level of ego development and perceptions of clients. *Counselor Education and Supervision, 26*, 37-49.

Boyd, J. (1978). *Counselor supervision: Approaches, preparation, practices.* Muncie, IN: Accelerated Development.

Bradley, L. J. (1989). *Counselor supervision: Principles, process, practice.* Muncie, IN: Accelerated Development.

Burns, C. I. (1994). Declarative knowledge differences in expert and novice counselors. *Dissertations Abstracts International, A54*(08), 2891. (University Microfilms No. 9402010)

Byrne, D. (1971). *The attraction paradigm.* New York: Academic Press.

Carey, J. C., Williams, K. S., & Wells, M. (1988). Relationships between dimensions of supervisors' influence and counselor trainees' performance. *Counselor Education and Supervision, 28*, 130-139.

Carifio, M. S., & Hess, A. K. (1987). Who is the ideal supervisor? *Professional Psychology: Research and Practice, 3*, 244-250.

Carkhuff, R. R., & Berenson, B. G. (1967). *Beyond counseling and therapy.* New York: Holt, Rinehart & Winston.

Carroll, M. (1995). *Counseling supervision: Theory, skills, and practice.* Unpublished manuscript, Roehampton Institute, London.

Chenault, J. (1968). A proposed model for a humanistic counselor education program. *Counselor Education and Supervision, 8*, 4-7.

Cherniss, C. (1980). *Staff burnout: Job stress in the human services.* New York: Russell Sage.

Chi, M. T. H. (1985). Interactive roles of knowledge and strategies in the development of organized sorting and recall. In S. F. Chipman, J. W. Segal, & R. Glaser (Eds.), *Thinking and learning skills* (Vol. 2, pp. 457-484). Hillsdale, NJ: Lawrence Erlbaum.

Chickering, A. W. (1969). *Education and identity.* San Francisco: Jossey-Bass.

Cole, M., Kolko, D., & Craddick, R. (1981). The quality and process of the internship experience. *Professional Psychology, 12*, 377-384.

Coleman, H. L. K., Wampold, B. E., & Casali, S. L. (1994). Ethnic minorities' ratings of ethnically similar and European American counselors: A meta-analysis. *Journal of Counseling Psychology, 42*, 247-294.

Cook, D. A., & Helms, J. E. (1988). Visible racial/ethnic group supervisees' satisfaction with cross-cultural supervision as predicted by relationship characteristics. *Journal of Counseling Psychology, 35*, 268-274.

Cormier L. S., & Hackney, H. (1993). *The professional counselor: A process guide to helping.* Boston: Allyn & Bacon.

Cummings, A. L., Hallberg, E. T., Martin, J., Slemon, A. G., & Hiebert, B. A. (1990). Implications of counselor conceptualizations for counselor education. *Counselor Education and Supervision, 30,* 120-134.

Demos, G. G., & Zuwaylif, F. (1962). Counselor attitudes in relation to the theoretical positions of their supervisors. *Counselor Education and Supervision, 2,* 280-285.

DePaulo, B. M. (1992). Nonverbal behavior and self-presentation. *Psychological Bulletin, 111,* 203-243.

Dodds, J. B. (1986). Supervision of psychology trainees in field placements. *Professional Psychology: Research and Practice, 17,* 296-300.

Dodenhoff, J. T. (1981). Interpersonal attraction and direct-indirect supervisor influence as predictors of counselor trainee effectiveness. *Journal of Counseling Psychology, 28,* 47-52.

Doehrman, M. J. (1976). Parallel processes in supervision and psychotherapy. *Bulletin of the Menninger Clinic, 40*(1), 1-104.

Dunlap, D., & Goldman, P. (1991). Rethinking power in schools. *Educational Administration Quarterly, 27,* 5-29.

Dye, H. A., & Borders, L. D. (1990). Counseling supervisors: Standards for preparation and practice. *Journal of Counseling and Development, 69,* 27-32.

Efstation, J. F., Patton, M. J., & Kardash, C. M. (1990). Measuring the working alliance in counselor supervision. *Journal of Counseling Psychology, 37,* 322-329.

Egan, G. (1982). *The skilled helper* (2nd ed.). Monterey, CA: Brooks/Cole.

Ekstein, R. (1964). Supervision of psychotherapy. Is it teaching? Is it administration? Or is it therapy? *Psychotherapy: Theory, Research and Practice, 1,* 137-138.

Ekstein, R., & Wallerstein, R. S. (1958). *The teaching and learning of psychotherapy.* New York: Basic Books.

Ellis, M. V., & Dell, D. M. (1986). Dimensionality of supervisor roles: Supervisors' perceptions of supervision. *Journal of Counseling Psychology, 33,* 282-291.

Ellis, M. V., Dell, D. M., & Good, G. E. (1988). Counselor trainees' perceptions of supervisor roles: Two studies testing the dimensionality of supervision. *Journal of Counseling Psychology, 35,* 315-324.

Ericson, P. M., & Rogers, L. E. (1973). New procedures for analyzing relational communication. *Family Process, 12,* 245-267.

Flavell, J. H. (1981). Cognitive thinking. In W. P. Dickson (Ed.), *Children's oral communication skills* (pp. 35-60). New York: Academic Press.

Follett, M. P. (1951). *Creative experience.* New York: Peter Smith. (Original work published 1924)

Fredenberger, J. J. (1977). Burn-out: The organizational menace. *Training and Development Journal, 31*(7), 26-27.

French, J. R. P., Jr., & Raven, B. H. (1960). The bases of social power. In D. Cartwright & A. Zander (Eds.), *Group dynamics: Research and theory* (2nd ed., pp. 607-623). New York: Peterson.

Friedlander, M. L. (1984). *Hill counselor verbal response category system—revised* (Tests in microfiche; Test collection, No. 012397, Set I). Princeton, NJ: Educational Testing Service.

Friedlander, M. L., Keller, K. E., Peca-Baker, T. A., & Olk, M. E. (1986). Effects of role conflict on counselor trainees' self-statements, anxiety level, and performance. *Journal of Counseling Psychology, 33,* 1-5.

Friedlander, M. L., & Schwartz, G. S. (1985). Toward a theory of strategic self-presentation in counseling and psychotherapy. *Journal of Counseling Psychology, 32,* 483-501.

Friedlander, M. L., Siegel, S. M., & Brenock, K. (1989). Parallel processes in counseling and supervision: A case study. *Journal of Counseling Psychology, 36,* 149-157.

Friedlander, M. L., & Snyder, J. (1983). Trainees' expectations for the supervisory process: Testing a developmental model. *Counselor Education and Supervision, 22*, 342-348.

Friedlander, M. L., & Ward, L. G. (1984). Development and validation of the supervisory styles inventory. *Journal of Counseling Psychology, 4*, 541-557.

Friedlander, M. L., Ward, L. G., & Ferrin, H. (1984, August). *A behavioral analytic model for evaluating counselor training programs.* Paper presented at the annual meeting of the American Psychological Association, Toronto, Canada.

Friedler, F. (1950). A comparison of therapeutic relationships in psychoanalytic, nondirective, and Adlerian therapy. *Journal of Consulting Psychology, 14*, 436-445.

Garfield, S. L. (1994). Research on client variables in psychotherapy. In A. E. Bergin & S. L. Garfield (Eds.), *Handbook of psychotherapy and behavior change* (4th ed., pp. 190-228). New York: John Wiley.

Garner, R. (1987). *Metacognition and reading comprehension.* Norwood, NJ: Ablex.

Gendlin, E. (1962). *Experiencing and the creation of meaning.* New York: Free Press.

Glaser, R. (1984). Education and thinking: The role of knowledge. *American Psychologist, 39*, 93-104.

Goldberg, D. A. (1985). Process, notes, audio, and videotape: Modes of presentation in psychotherapy. *The Clinical Supervisor, 3*(3), 3-13.

Goodyear, R. K. (Producer). (1982). *Psychotherapy supervision by major theorists* [Videotape series]. Manhattan: Kansas State University, Instructional Media Center.

Goodyear, R. K. (1990). Gender configurations in supervisory dyads: Their relation to supervisee influence strategies and to skill evaluation of the supervisee. *The Clinical Supervisor, 8*(3), 67-79.

Goodyear, R. K., Abadie, P. D., & Efros, F. (1984). Supervisory theory into practice: Differential perception of supervision by Ekstein, Ellis, Polster, and Rogers. *Journal of Counseling Psychology, 31*, 228-237.

Goodyear, R. K., & Bradley, F. (1983). Theories of counselor supervision: Points of convergence and divergence. *The Counseling Psychologist, 11*, 59-68.

Goodyear, R. K., & Robyak, J. E. (1982). Supervisors' theory and experience in supervisory focus. *Psychological Reports, 51*, 978.

Greenberg, L. S., & Pinsof W. M. (Eds.). (1986). *The psychotherapeutic process: A research handbook.* New York: Guilford.

Guest, P. D., & Beutler, L. E. (1988). Impact of psychotherapy supervision on therapist orientation and values. *Journal of Consulting and Clinical Psychology, 56*, 653-658.

Gutierrez, F. J. (1982). Working with minority counselor education students. *Counselor Education and Supervision, 21*, 218-226.

Gysbers, N. C., & Johnston, J. A. (1965). Expectations of a practicum supervisor's role. *Counselor Education and Supervision, 2*, 68-75.

Hansen, J. C. (1965). Trainees' expectations of supervision in the counseling program. *Counselor Education and Supervision, 2*, 75-80.

Hansen, J. C., & Barker, E. N. (1964). Experiencing and the supervisory relationship. *Journal of Counseling Psychology, 11*, 107-111.

Hansen, J. C., Pound, R., & Petro, C. (1976). Review of research on practicum supervision. *Counselor Education and Supervision, 16*, 107-116.

Hansen, J. C., Robins, T. H., & Grimes, J. (1982). Review of research on practicum supervision. *Counselor Education and Supervision, 2*, 68-75.

Harrar, W. R., Vandecreek, L., & Knapp, S. (1990). Ethical and legal aspects of clinical supervision. *Professional Psychology: Research and Practice, 21*(1), 37-41.

Harvey, O. J., Hunt, D. E., & Schroder, H. M. (1961). *Conceptual systems and personality organization.* New York: John Wiley.

Hector, M. A. (1977, March). *Competency-based counselor supervision.* Paper presented at the annual convention of the American Personnel and Guidance Association, Dallas, TX.

Helms, J. E. (1984). Toward a theoretical explanation of the effect of race on counseling: A black and white model. *The Counseling Psychologist, 12*(4), 153-165.

Heppner, P. P., & Handley, P. G. (1982). The relationship between supervisory expertness, attractiveness, or trustworthiness. *Counselor Education and Supervision, 8,* 23-31.

Heppner, P. P., & Roehlke, H. J. (1984). Differences among supervisees at different levels of training: Implications for a developmental model of supervision. *Journal of Counseling Psychology, 31,* 76-90.

Hess, A. K. (Ed.). (1980). *Psychotherapy supervision: Theory, research and practice.* New York: John Wiley.

Hess, A. K., & Hess, K. A. (1987). Psychotherapy supervision: A survey of internship training practices. In R. Dana & W. T. May (Eds.), *Internship training in professional psychology* (pp. 328-340). Washington, DC: Hemisphere.

Hester, L. R., Weitz, L. H., & Anchor, K. N. (1976). Supervisor attraction as a function of level of supervisor skillfulness and supervisees' perceived similarity. *Journal of Counseling Psychology, 23,* 254-258.

Hill, C. E., Charles, D., & Reed, K. G. (1981). A longitudinal analysis of changes in counseling skills during doctoral training in counseling psychology. *Journal of Counseling Psychology, 28,* 428-436.

Hillerbrand, E., & Clairborn, C. D. (1990). Examining reasoning skill differences between expert and novice counselors. *Journal of Counseling and Development, 68,* 684-691.

Hinde, R. A. (1979). *Towards understanding relationships.* New York: Academic Press.

Hirsch, P. A., & Stone, G. L. (1983). Cognitive strategies and the client conceptualization process. *Journal of Counseling Psychology, 30,* 566-572.

Holloway, E. L. (1982). Interactional structure of the supervision interview. *Journal of Counseling Psychology, 29,* 309-317.

Holloway, E. L. (1984). Outcome evaluation in supervision research. *The Counseling Psychologist, 12*(4), 167-174.

Holloway, E. L. (1987). Developmental models of supervision: Is it development? *Professional Psychology: Research and Practice, 18,* 209-216.

Holloway, E. L. (1988). Models of counselor development or training models for supervision: Rejoinder to Stoltenberg and Delworth. *Professional Psychology: Research and Practice, 19,* 138-140.

Holloway, E. L. (1992a, July). *A bridge of knowing: The scholar-practitioner of supervision.* Keynote address presented at the International Conference on Supervision, Roehampton Institute, London.

Holloway, E. L. (1992b). Supervision: A way of teaching and learning. In S. D. Brown & R. W. Lent (Eds.), *Handbook of counseling psychology* (pp. 177-214). New York: John Wiley.

Holloway, E. L. (1994). Overseeing the overseer: Contextualizing training in supervision. *Journal of Counseling and Development, 72,* 526-530.

Holloway, E. L., & Acker, M. (1988, May). *Engagement and power in clinical supervision.* Workshop presented at the Oregon Association of Counselor Education and Supervision, Corvallis, OR.

Holloway, E. L., Freund, R. D., Gardner, S. L., Nelson, M. L., & Walker, B. E. (1989). Relation of power and involvement to theoretical orientation in supervision: An analysis of discourse. *Journal of Counseling Psychology, 36,* 88-102.

Holloway, E. L., & Neufeldt, F. A. (in press). Supervision: Contributors to treatment efficacy. *Journal of Consulting and Clinical Psychology.*

Holloway, E. L., & Poulin, K. (1995). Discourse in supervision. In J. Siegfried (Ed.), *Therapeutic and everyday discourse as behavior change: Towards a micro-analysis in psychotherapy process research* (pp. 245-273). New York: Ablex.

Holloway, E. L., & Roehlke, H. J. (1987). Internship: The applied training of a counseling psychologist. *The Counseling Psychologist, 2,* 205-260.

Holloway, E. L., & Wampold, B. E. (1983). Patterns of verbal behavior and judgments of satisfaction in the supervision interview. *Journal of Counseling Psychology, 30,* 227-234.

Holloway, E. L., & Wampold, B. E. (1986). Relation between conceptual level and counseling-related tasks: A meta-analysis. *Journal of Counseling Psychology, 33,* 310-319.

Holloway, E. L., & Wolleat, P. L. (1980). Relationship of counselor conceptual level to clinical hypothesis formation. *Journal of Counseling Psychology, 27,* 539-545.

Holloway, E. L., & Wolleat, P. L. (1981). Style differences of beginning supervisors: An interactional analysis. *Journal of Counseling Psychology, 28,* 373-376.

Holloway, E. L., & Wolleat, P. L. (1994). Supervision: The pragmatics of empowerment. *Journal of Educational and Psychological Consultation, 5*(1), 23-43.

Hosford, R. E., & Barmann, B. (1983). A social learning approach to counselor supervision. *The Counseling Psychologist, 11*(1), 51-58.

Hunt, D. E., & Sullivan, E. V. (1974). *Between psychology and education.* Hinsdale, IL: Dryden.

Inskipp, F., & Proctor, B. (1989). *Skills for supervising and being supervised* (Principle of Counseling audiotape series). East Sussex, UK: Alexia.

Ivey, A. E. (1993). *Instructors manual for counseling and psychotherapy: A multicultural perspective.* Boston: Allyn & Bacon.

Jabukowski-Spector, P., Dustin, R., & George, R. L. (1971). Toward developing a behavioral counselor education model. *Counselor Education and Supervision, 10,* 242-250.

Jackson, S. E., Schwab, R. L., & Schuler, R. S. (1986). Toward an understanding of the burnout phenomenon. *Journal of Applied Psychology, 71*(4), 630-640.

Jones, E. E., & Pittman, T. S. (1982). Toward a general theory of strategic self-presentation. In J. Suls (Ed.), *Psychological perspectives on the self* (Vol. 1, pp. 237-262). Hillsdale, NJ: Lawrence Erlbaum.

Kadushin, A. (1985). *Supervision in social work* (2nd ed.). New York: Columbia University Press.

Kagan, N. L., & Kagan, H. (1990). IPR—Validated model for the 1990s and beyond. *The Counseling Psychologist, 18,* 436-440.

Kennard, B. D., Stewart, S. M., & Gluck, M. R. (1987). The supervision relationship: Variables contributing to positive versus negative experiences. *Professional Psychology: Research and Practice, 18,* 172-175.

Kolb, D. A. (1984). *Experiential learning.* Englewood Cliffs, NJ: Prentice Hall.

Lambert, M. J. (1974). Supervisory and counseling process: A comparative study. *Counselor Education and Supervision, 14,* 54-60.

Lambert, M. J. (1980). Research and the supervisory process. In A. K. Hess (Ed.), *Psychotherapy supervision: Theory, research and practice* (pp. 423-452). New York: John Wiley.

Lambert, M. J., & Werthemier, M. (1988). Is diagnostic ability related to relevant training and experience? *Professional Psychology: Research and Practice, 19*(1), 50-52.

Leary, T. (1957). *Interpersonal diagnosis of personality: A theory and a methodology for personality evaluation.* New York: Ronald Press.

Lemons, S., & Lanning, W. E. (1979). Value system similarity and the supervisory relationship. *Counselor Education and Supervision, 19,* 13-19.

Littrell, J. M., Lee-Borden, N., & Lorenz, J. (1979). A developmental framework for counseling supervision. *Counselor Education and Supervision, 19,* 129-136.

Loevinger, J. (1976). *Ego development: Conceptions and theories.* San Francisco: Jossey-Bass.

Loganbill, C., Hardy, E., & Delworth, U. (1982). Supervision: A conceptual model. *The Counseling Psychologist, 10*(1), 3-42.

Marikis, D. A., Russell, R. K., & Dell, D. M. (1985). Effects of supervisor experience level on planning and in-session supervisor verbal behavior. *Journal of Counseling Psychology, 32,* 410-416.

Martin, J. S., Goodyear, R. K., & Newton, F. B. (1987). Clinical supervision: An intensive case study. *Professional Psychology: Research and Practice, 18,* 225-235.

Martin, J. S., Slemon, A. G., Hiebert, B., Hallberg, E. T., & Cummings, A. L. (1989). Conceptualizations of novice and experienced counselors. *Journal of Counseling Psychology, 36,* 395-400.

McNeil, B. W., Stoltenberg, C. D., & Pierce, R. A. (1985). Supervisees' perceptions of their development: A test of the counselor complexity model. *Journal of Counseling Psychology, 32,* 630-633.

McRoy, R. G., Freeman, E. M., Logan, S. L., & Blackmon, B. (1986). Cross-cultural field supervision: Implications for social work education. *Journal of Social Work Education, 22,* 50-56.

Menne, J. M. (1975). A comprehensive set of counselor competencies. *Journal of Counseling Psychology, 22,* 547-553.

Miars, R. D., Tracey, T. J., Ray, P. B., Cornfeld, J. L., O'Farrell, M., & Gelson, C. J. (1983). Variation in supervision process across trainee experience levels. *Journal of Counseling Psychology, 30,* 403-412.

Miller, F. E., & Rogers, L. E. (1987). Relational dimensions of interpersonal dynamics. In M. E. Roloff & G. R. Miller (Eds.), *Interpersonal processes: New directions in communication research* (pp. 117-139). Newbury Park, CA: Sage.

Miller, G. R. (1976). *Explorations in interpersonal communication.* Beverly Hills, CA: Sage.

Morton, T., Alexander, C., & Altman, I. (1976). Communication and relationship definition. In G. Miller (Ed.), *Explorations in interpersonal communication* (pp. 105-125). Beverly Hills, CA: Sage.

Mueller, W. J., & Kell, B. L. (1972). *Coping with conflict: Supervising counselors and psychotherapists.* Englewood Cliffs, NJ: Prentice Hall.

Murphy, G. L., & Wright, J. C. (1984). Changes in conceptual structure with expertise: Differences between real-world experts and novices. *Journal of Experimental Psychology: Learning, Memory, and Cognition, 10,* 144-155.

Myrick, R. D., & Kelly, F. D. (1971). A scale for evaluating practicum students in counseling and supervision. *Counselor Education and Supervision, 10,* 330-336.

Najavits, L. M., & Strupp, H. H. (1994). Differences in the effectiveness of psychodynamic therapists: A process-outcome study. *Psychotherapy, 32,* 114-123.

National Association of Social Workers. (1980). *National Association of Social Workers published guidelines.* Washington, DC: Author.

National Association of Social Workers. (1980). *Standards for the private practice of clinical social work.* Washington, DC: Author.

Nelson, M. L. (1993). A current perspective on gender differences: Implications for research in counseling. *Journal of Counseling Psychology, 40,* 200-209.

Nelson, M. L., & Holloway, E. L. (1990). Relation of gender to power and involvement in supervision. *Journal of Counseling Psychology, 37,* 473-481.

Orlinsky, D. E., Grawe, K., & Parks, B. K. (1994). Process and outcome in psychotherapy—Nocheinmal. In A. E. Bergin & S. L. Garfield (Eds.), *Handbook of psychotherapy and behavior change* (4th ed., pp. 270-378). New York: John Wiley.

Parham, T. A. (1989). Cycles of psychological nigrescence. *The Counseling Psychologist, 32,* 431-440.

Patterson, C. H. (1983). A client-centered approach to supervision. *The Counseling Psychologist, 11*(1), 21-26.

Pedersen, P. (Ed.). (1985). *Handbook of cross-cultural counseling and therapy.* Westport, CT: Greenwood.

Penman, R. (1980). *Communication processes and relationships.* London: Academic Press.

Perry, W. G., Jr. (1970). *Forms of intellectual and ethical development in the college.* New York: Holt, Rinehart & Winston.

Polanyi, M. (1967). *The tacit dimension.* New York: Anchor.

Poole, M. S., Folger, J. P., & Hewes, D. E. (1987). Analyzing interpersonal interaction. In M. E. Roloff & G. R. Miller (Eds.), *Interpersonal processes: New directions in communication research* (pp. 221-256). Newbury Park, CA: Sage.

Pope, K. S., Levenson, H., & Schover, L. R. (1979). Sexual intimacy in psychology training: Results and implications of a national survey. *American Psychologist, 34,* 682-689.

Pope-Davis, D. B., Reynolds, A. L., & Vasquez, L. A. (1992). *Multicultural counseling: Issues of ethnic diversity* [Videotape series]. Iowa City: University of Iowa, AVC Marketing.

Poulin, K. L. (1994). Towards a grounded pedagogy of practice: A dimensional analysis of counseling supervision. *Dissertation Abstracts International, B54*(09), 4931. (University Microfilms No. 9505214)

Putney, M. W., Worthington, E. L., Jr., & McCullough, M. E. (1992). Effects of supervisor and supervisee theoretical orientation and supervisor-supervisee matching on interns' perceptions of supervision. *Journal of Counseling Psychology, 39*(2), 258-265.

Rabinowitz, F. E., Heppner, P. P., & Roehlke, H. J. (1986). Descriptive study of process and outcome variables of supervision over time. *Journal of Counseling Psychology, 33,* 292-300.

Rappaport, J. (1986). In praise of paradox: A social policy of empowerment over prevention. In E. Seidman & J. Rappaport (Eds.), *Redefining social problems* (pp. 141-160). New York: Plenum.

Reising, G. N., & Daniels, M. H. (1983). A study of Hogan's model of counselor development and supervision. *Journal of Counseling Psychology, 30,* 235-244.

Rickards, L. D. (1984). Verbal interaction and supervisor perception in counselor supervision. *Journal of Counseling Psychology, 31,* 262-265.

Rinas, J., & Clyne-Jackson, S. (1988). *Professional conduct and legal concerns in mental health practice.* Norwalk, CT: Appleton & Lange.

Robyak, J. E., Goodyear, R. K., & Prange, M. (1987). Effects of supervisors' sex, focus, and experience on preferences for interpersonal power bases. *Counselor Education and Supervision, 26,* 299-309.

Robyak, J. E., Goodyear, R. K., Prange, M. E., & Donham, G. (1986). Effects of gender, supervision, and presenting problems on practicum students' preference for interpersonal power bases. *Journal of Counseling Psychology, 33,* 159-163.

Rokeach, M. (1967). *Value survey.* Sunnyvale, CA: Halgeen Tests.

Rounsaville, B. J., Chevron, E. S., & Weissman, M. M. (1984). Specification of techniques in interpersonal psychotherapy. In J. B. W. Williams & R. L. Spitzer (Eds.), *Psychotherapy research: Where are we and where should we go?* (pp. 160-172). New York: Guilford.

Rounsaville, B. J., O'Malley, S. S., Foley, S., & Weissman, M. M. (1988). Role of manual-guided training in the conduct and efficacy of interpersonal psychotherapy for depression. *Journal of Consulting and Clinical Psychology, 56,* 681-688.

Russell, R. K., Crimmings, A. M., & Lent, R. W. (1984). Counselor training and supervision: Theory and research. In S. Brown & R. Lent (Eds.), *The handbook of counseling psychology* (pp. 625-681). New York: John Wiley.

Schatzman, L. (1991). Dimensional analysis: Notes on an alternative approach to the grounding of theory in qualitative research. In D. R. Maines (Ed.), *Social organization and social process* (pp. 303-314). New York: Aldine.

Schlenker, B. R. (1984). Identities, identifications, and relationships. In V. Dorlega (Ed.), *Communication, intimacy, and close relationships* (pp. 71-104). San Diego, CA: Academic Press.

Schlenker, B. R., & Leary, M. R. (1982). Social anxiety and self-presentation: A conceptualization and model. *Psychological Bulletin, 92,* 641-669.

Schon, D. A. (1983). *Educating the reflective practitioner.* San Francisco: Jossey-Bass.

Sergiovanni, T. J. (1983). *Supervision: A perspective* (3rd ed.). New York: McGraw-Hill.

Solomon, B. (1983). Power: The troublesome factor in cross-cultural supervision. *Smith College Journal School for Social Work, 10,* 27-32.

Stein, J. (Ed.). (1975). *Random House college dictionary* (rev. ed.). New York: Random House.

Steinhelber, J., Patterson, V., Cliffe, K., & LeGoullon, M. (1984). An investigation of some relationships between psychotherapy supervision and patient change. *Journal of Clinical Psychology, 40,* 1346-1353.

Stenack, R. J., & Dye, H. A. (1982). Behavioral description of counseling supervision roles. *Counselor Education and Supervision, 21,* 295-304.

Stoltenberg, C. (1981). Approaching supervision from a developmental perspective: The counselor complexity model. *Journal of Counseling Psychology, 28,* 59-65.

Stoltenberg, C. D., & Delworth, U. (1987). *Supervising counselors and therapists.* San Francisco: Jossey-Bass.

Stoltenberg, C. D., & Delworth, U. (1988). Developmental models of supervision: It is development. A response to Holloway. *Professional Psychology: Research and Practice, 19,* 134-137.

Stoltenberg, C. D., Pierce, R. A., & McNeil, B. W. (1987). Effects of experience on counselor trainees' needs. *The Clinical Supervisor, 5*(5), 23-32.

Stone, G. L. (1980). Effects of experience on supervisor planning. *Journal of Counseling Psychology, 27,* 84-88.

Strong, S. R. (1968). Counseling: An interpersonal influence process. *Journal of Counseling Psychology, 15,* 215-224.

Strong, S. R., Hill, H. I., & Nelson, B. N. (1988). *Interpersonal communication rating scale* (rev.). Unpublished manuscript, Virginia Commonwealth University, Richmond.

Strong, S. R., & Matross, R. P. (1973). Change process in counseling and psychotherapy. *Journal of Counseling Psychology, 20,* 125-132.

Strozier, A. L., Kivlighan, D. M., & Thoresen, R. W. (1993). Supervisor intentions, supervisee reactions, and helpfulness: A case study of the process of supervision. *Psychotherapy: Theory, Research and Practice, 24,* 13-19.

Struff, H. H., Butler, S. F., & Rosser, C. L. (1988). Training in psychodynamic therapy. *Journal of Consulting and Clinical Psychology 56,* 689-695.

Sue, D. W., & Sue, D. (1990). *Counseling the culturally different: Theory and practice* (2nd ed.). New York: John Wiley.

Sugarman, L. (1985). Kolb's model of experiential learning: Touchstone for trainers, students, counselors, and clients. *Journal of Counseling and Development, 64,* 264-268.

Sundland, D. M. (1977). Theoretical orientations of psychotherapists. In A. S. Gurman & A. M. Razin (Eds.), *Effective psychotherapy: A handbook of research* (pp. 189-222). New York: Pergamon.

Sundland, D. M., & Feinberg, L. B. (1972). The relationship of interpersonal attraction, experience, and supervisors's level of functioning in dyadic counseling supervision. *Counselor Education and Supervision, 12,* 187-193.

Supervision Interest Network, Association for Counselor Education and Supervision. (1993). ACES ethical guidelines for counseling supervisors. *ACES Spectrum, 53*(4), 5-8.

Swain, D. (1981). *Behaviorally anchored rating scale for recipients of psychotherapy supervision: Instrument construction.* Unpublished master's thesis, Auburn University.

Tannenbaum, S. I., Green, V. J., & Glickman, A. S. (1989). The ethical reasoning process in an organizational consulting situation. *Professional Psychology, Research and Practice, 20,* 229-235.

Teyber, E. (1988). *Interpersonal process in psychotherapy: A guide for clinical training.* Chicago: Dorsey.

Tracey, T. J., Ellickson, J. L., & Sherry, P. (1989). Reactance in relation to different supervisory environments and counselor development. *Journal of Counseling Psychology, 36,* 336-344.

Tracey, T. J., Hays, D. A., Malone, J., & Herman, B. (1988). Changes in counselor response as a function of experience. *Journal of Counseling Psychology, 35,* 119-126.

Truax, C. B., & Carkhuff, R. R. (1967). *Toward effective counseling and psychotherapy: Training and practice.* Chicago: Aldine.

Tyler, F. B., Brome, D. R., & Williams, J. E. (1991). *Ethnic validity, ecology, and psychotherapy: A psychosocial competence model.* New York: Plenum.

Walsh, J. F. (1994). One-way between subjects and design: Simulated data and analysis using SAS. *Teaching of Psychology, 21,* 53-55.

Wampler, L. D., & Strupp, H. H. (1976). Personal therapy for students in clinical psychology: A matter of faith? *Professional Psychology, 6,* 195-201.

Ward, L. G., Friedlander, M. L., Schoen, L. G., & Klein, J. C. (1985). Strategic self-presentation in supervision. *Journal of Counseling Psychology, 32,* 111-118.

Wedeking, D. F., & Scott, T. B. (1976). A study of the relationship between supervisor and trainee behaviors in counseling practicum. *Counselor Education and Supervision, 15,* 259-266.

Wessler, R. L., & Ellis, A. (1983). Supervision in counseling: Rational-emotive therapy. *The Counseling Psychologist, 11*(1), 43-50.

Whiston, S. C., & Emerson, S. (1989). Ethical implications for supervisors in counseling of trainees. *Counselor Education and Supervision, 28,* 318-325.

Wiley, M. O., & Ray, P. B. (1986). Counseling supervision by developmental level. *Journal of Counseling Psychology, 33,* 439-445.

Winter, M., & Holloway, E. L. (1991). Effects of trainee experience, conceptual level, and supervisor approach on selection of audiotaped counseling passages. *The Clinical Supervisor, 9*(2), 87-104.

Wolleat, P. L. (1974). What the counselor needs to know: Dimensions of counselor behavior. In G. Farwell, N. R. Gamsky, & P. Mathieu-Coughlan (Eds.), *The counselor's handbook* (pp. 123-131). New York: Intext Educational.

Worthington, E. L., Jr. (1984a). Empirical investigation of supervision of counselors as they gain experience. *Journal of Counseling Psychology, 31,* 63-75.

Worthington, E. L., Jr. (1984b). Use of trait labels in counseling supervision by experienced and inexperienced supervisors. *Professional Psychology: Research and Practice, 15,* 457-461.

Worthington, E. L. (1987). Changes in supervision as counselors and supervisors gain experience: A review. *Professional Psychology: Research and Practice, 18,* 189-208.

Worthington, E. L., & Roehlke, H. J. (1979). Effective supervision as perceived by beginning counselors-in-training. *Journal of Counseling Psychology, 26,* 64-73.

Worthington, E. L., Jr., & Stern, A. (1985). The effects of supervisor and supervisee degree level and gender on the supervisory relationship. *Journal of Counseling Psychology, 32*(3), 252-262.

Zuniga, M. E. (1987). Mexican-American clinical training: A pilot project. *Journal of Social Work Education, 23*(3), 11-20.

Author Index

Subject Index

Words of Supervision

For
Our words shape the space between us.
They fall from us to be heard as they are meant.
The journey, across the abyss of our separateness, is filled
With the shadows of history and talks past.
Now meaning becomes the property of the other.
To shape, to form, to turn over in the mind,
And then, to let words fall away.
Thus continues a cycle of intention, of meaning, of purpose,
Blanketing time, layer on layer, clouding the transparency
Of the soul.
The soul, perhaps to be delivered full and vulnerable on
The next turn, the next word.
In supervision we talk. We move one phrase upon another
To create a language of understanding and
Weave a relationship of history.
The warp of our talk is the relationship.
It girds itself against the errors of our words,
The misspokens, the not spokens,
The misunderstandings of our history.
The weft moves back and forth between us. You feel the
Rhythm of the shaft work itself around a warp of Relationship, changing
tension as it moves, creating a
Pattern of woven goods that reflect the color of our Intentions and the
design of our meaning.

About the Author

Elizabeth L. Holloway is Professor in the Department of Counseling Psychology and Director of the Educational and Psychological Training Center at the University of Wisconsin—Madison. She has a long career in the research, teaching, and practice of clinical supervision. She is a Fellow of Division 17 Counseling Psychology of the American Psychological Association and holds a Diplomate in Counseling Psychology of the American Board of Professional Psychology. She has been a leader in professional training issues both nationally and internationally, evidenced by her writings, research awards, and keynote addresses on supervision and professional training in many parts of the world.

This book focuses on her model for the training and practice of supervision. It has evolved from her experience in working with practicing supervisors and educators in the United States, Great Britain, Europe, and Asia. She has tried to capture for the printed page the dynamic thinking and work that has unfolded at these workshops. She says, "My greatest personal challenge in creating this book was to bridge the knowledge of researchers and practitioners while making it accessible to both groups. Building bridges has always been an integral part of my professional and personal life."

The SAS Model

*A Systems Approach
to Clinical Supervision*

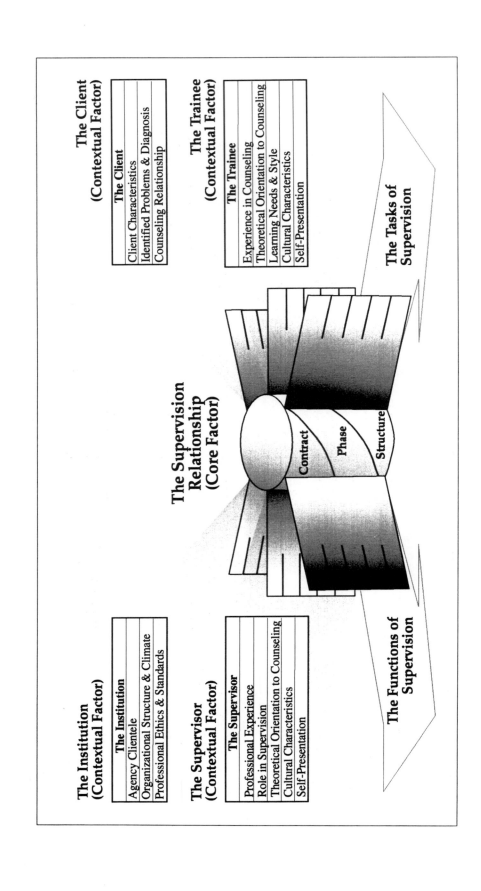

The Institution
(Contextual Factor)

The Institution

Agency Clientele
Organizational Structure & Climate
Professional Ethics & Standards

The Supervisor
(Contextual Factor)

The Supervisor

Professional Experience
Role in Supervision
Theoretical Orientation to Counseling
Cultural Characteristics
Self-Presentation

The Supervision
Relationship
(Core Factor)

Contract

Phase

Structure

The Client
(Contextual Factor)

The Client

Client Characteristics
Identified Problems & Diagnosis
Counseling Relationship

The Trainee
(Contextual Factor)

The Trainee

Experience in Counseling
Theoretical Orientation to Counseling
Learning Needs & Style
Cultural Characteristics
Self-Presentation

The Tasks of
Supervision

The Functions of
Supervision

Process Matrix

Supervision Tasks

Supervision Tasks
Counseling Skill
Case Conceptualization
Professional Role
Emotional Awareness
Self-Evaluation

Supervision Functions

Supervision Functions
Monitoring/Evaluating
Advising/Instructing
Modeling
Consulting
Supporting/Sharing

Supervision Tasks

Supervision Functions	Counseling Skill	Case Conceptualization	Professional Role	Emotional Awareness	Self-Evaluation
Monitoring/Evaluating					
Advising/Instructing					
Modeling					
Consulting					
Supporting/Sharing					